KU-275-175

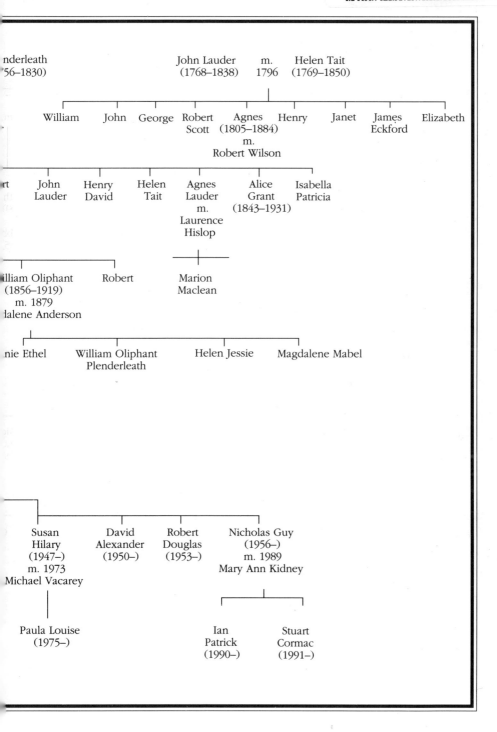

nderleath
56–1830)

John Lauder   m.   Helen Tait
(1768–1838)   1796   (1769–1850)

William   John   George   Robert   Agnes   Henry   Janet   James   Elizabeth
                              Scott   (1805–1884)   Eckford
                                          m.
                                    Robert Wilson

rt   John   Henry   Helen   Agnes   Alice   Isabella
      Lauder   David   Tait   Lauder   Grant   Patricia
                                        m.   (1843–1931)
                                        Laurence
                                        Hislop

illiam Oliphant   Robert   Marion
(1856–1919)   Maclean
  m. 1879
lalene Anderson

nie Ethel   William Oliphant   Helen Jessie   Magdalene Mabel
               Plenderleath

Susan   David   Robert   Nicholas Guy
Hilary   Alexander   Douglas   (1956–)
(1947–)   (1950–)   (1953–)   m. 1989
m. 1973   Mary Ann Kidney
Michael Vacarey

Paula Louise   Ian   Stuart
(1975–)   Patrick   Cormac
                                          (1990–)   (1991–)

Tak' Tent o' Time

Memories
of a
Post-Edwardian

Edinburgh Childhood

Elaine Mary Wilson

Elaine Mary Wilson

PLENDERLEATH
PUBLISHING

First published in Great Britain in 1992 by
Plenderleath Publishing, 90 Morningside Drive, Edinburgh EH10 5NT

Copyright © 1991 Elaine Mary Wilson

ISBN 1 874086 00 1

The Author asserts the moral right to be identified as the author of
this work.

The photograph of 'Mackay and Chisholm', Princes Street is included
by courtesy of Edinburgh City Libraries.

Cover design and original illustrations (except page 105) by Harriet Wylie.

No part of this publication may be reproduced or transmitted in any form or
by any means without permission in writing from the publisher except by a
reviewer who wishes to quote brief passages in connection with a review
written for insertion in a magazine, newspaper or broadcast.

Typesetting by Marshall Hart, Edinburgh.

Printed and bound in Great Britain by Billings & Sons Ltd, Worcester.

TO

(with due acknowledgement to Dodie Smith)
MY 'Dear Octopus'
Past and Present
Macdougalls, Aulds, Tytlers, Stewarts, Chisholms, Wyses
Plenderleaths, Gibbs, Wilsons, Lauders and Ainslies

and up and down, in and out the branches of their Family Trees

and
to Edgar
whose gift of an Amstrad and conversion
of the coal-hole to workroom to house it made it all easier

and
to
Rosemary who made it possible

ACKNOWLEDGEMENTS

With special thanks

to

Shona Cowie who knows how to track down elusive ancestors

and to

my sisters Marjorie Annie and Moira Edith

who responded helpfully to all requests for information,

as did various Glasgow cousins,

Alison Waterston who knows about the Monks of St Giles,

my nephew David who knows about trains,

Anne Walker who found Violet Neish

who searched for and found a negative showing in location

the now vanished sundial of the title,

Harriet Wylie for her illustrations

and Catherine Hart for setting the manuscript out.

CONTENTS

Continues

Introduction

TAK TENT O'TIME
ERE TIME BE TINT

AT THE START of our marriage my husband and I lived in Newtonmore in a house up a hill road from which we had a wide view stretching over the Spey valley to the Grampians. There was also, from a landing window and framed by pine trees, a smaller and to me especially pleasing glimpse of the further away and higher peaks of the Cairngorms, even to the corrie where snow might still be lying in June and from which it scarcely seemed to melt before it relaid itself. Pointing this view out to a usually perceptive friend I was amazed to hear her brush it aside and say merely, "What a pity these people have that ugly shed in their garden." My eyes on Coire Mairead I had never seen the shed.

I am aware that in this story some may feel I have cleared away too many sheds but in truth, apart from the transient passions and feelings of injustice which beset all young children, my early childhood was very happy.

Apart from the knowledge that every life is important, why, one may understandably ask, write at all about an ostensibly uninteresting one? Over ten years ago in Florence my sister Marjorie, my daughter Penelope and I were sitting in happy tourist anonymity on the steps of a church, slices of pizza and glasses of Chianti in our hands. I was recounting a vivid dream of the previous night involving a girl with a poppy-wreathed hat, "Why in the world" said I, "should I dream of Lena Anderson?"

"I don't know," said Marjorie, "who was she anyway?"

Her question made me suddenly realise that not only were there years of family life and background of which my children were ignorant but that to much of it too, my younger sisters were strangers. "Write down all you remember," said Marjorie "and you can have that old postcard of Inverleith Pond to keep." This was noble of her indeed, being as she is a keen collector of paper ephemera, especially of postcards, and although Inverleith Pond is part of all our memories she was particularly acquaint with it.

So—after many a summer—here I come. Not, I hope, giving the impression like too many a sundial that I mark only the sunny hours but in the spirit of one glimpsed on the gable of a building in Glasgow, to—

'Tak' tent o' Time ere Time be tint.'

CHAPTER ONE

The Further and Further Away Walk

THOUGH it is sixty years ago and more I can hear yet the despairing venom in my little brother's voice when he, in the summer of 1918, happily playing with his bricks and wooden toys—train, tank and field ambulance with Red Cross painted on its canvas top—was bidden put them away and get ready for a walk—

"Not," he would wail, "the furver and furver away walk."

Too often it was.

What to his four-and-a-half-year-old legs was possibly a torment was nothing to my experienced seven-year-old ones and less than nothing to those of unrevealed age of my mother, who, unsupported, or with hazel walking stick, or leaning on the current baby's pram, was a walkaholic pleased at finding her addiction passed on to me with another, the inability to resist the temptation of a strange and beckoning byway. In her journal for 1916 when an unexplored detour on a Hawick walk turned out to be a very long road home ('it was very pretty') she also noted 'It is a blessing Elaine is such a good walker' adding 'her tongue goes on unceasingly all the time'. I welcome this tribute to me. Too often the comments scattering her early journals refer to me as 'difficult' or 'very domineering' whereas Ian is repeatedly described as 'a dear wee soul'.

She made the walks interesting for us by telling the names of trees and birds and ferns and flowers—the scabious, knapweed, bluebells, bedstraws, campions, gentians and comfreys—which lent a multicoloured wealth to the verges of the quiet sweet-smelling traffic- and pesticide-free roads of Scotland during the summers of the 1914-1918 war.

Preparations for the 'dear wee soul's' winter walks were trying. He stood, magnificently inert, while his attendant, mother or maid, stuffed his limbs into gaiters, gloves, shoes and coat (blue, with a narrow black velvet collar), buttoned it up and added his round black felt hat with elastic under the chin. In summer it was easier, a change of shoes and a straw hat if the day were sunny.

His jaundiced description of our usual walk as being further and further away was not strictly accurate in that we often made a circular tour of it from and back to our rented villa in the Renfrewshire village of Bishopton. There was a tree at the halfway mark where sometimes we would turn and retrace our steps but as often we continued and then, his mind having as yet apparently no concept of a circle, he lamented every step of the journey until surprised by the welcome sight of home.

Bishopton is today almost a dormitory suburb but then it was real country where I, a town child, was thrilled to be sent on occasional evenings, jug in hand, with Mary the maid to a neighbouring farm for extra milk. Mary and I both enjoyed these outings with their mild freedom and the, for me, slight hint of danger, for to reach the farm we had to go on the 'main' road, which my mother invested with peril.

"Mind the motors!" she would call to us and we did—all three or four of them chuntering past where now a busy carriageway from Glasgow sustains a steady flash of traffic.

I do remember that the extra milk was often for the production of curds and whey, a delicacy which held a love-hate fascination for me. It looked so white and pure and its taste, if insipid, was not too unpleasant—Little Miss Muffet enjoyed it—but its texture and the way it slithered about my mouth I found revolting. However, thoughts of penance to come in no way detracted from the immediate joys of the evening excursion.

Sometimes the start of the further and further away walk was prelude to a diversion down a side road to a strip of sand on the Clyde

2

at Erskine Ferry. Then we went armed with spades and pails and biscuits and fruit. Straightening ourselves up from building castles and harbours and dams we would gaze over the Clyde to dredgers keeping the channel deep enough for ocean-going ships and marvel at the thought that a little upstream of us, 'within living memory', men had been able to wade from one shore to the other before the canny burghers of Glasgow got busy digging out the river bed so that trade could flow to the doors of their warehouses along the bonny Broomielaw and other wharfs. 'Within living memory' was scarcely applicable to us as it was during the last quarter of the eighteenth century that the river between Dumbuck and Glasgow had been narrowed, making the current flow faster thereby helping the dredgers to scour out its bed. Though I could not imagine my great-uncles and their business friends wanting to spend time paddling across from Renfrewshire to the northern shore and back, I firmly believed they could have done so. Perhaps 'within living memory' referred to what they had been told by their great-uncles. I also believed that the initial digging had been done by the merchants themselves and to this day can scarcely look at the upper reaches of the Clyde below Glasgow without getting a picture of top-hatted, soberly-suited, elderly gentlemen, probably bearded like my Uncle John, diligently, with wooden spades like mine, digging out their river. My image is no way less impressive than the reality of navvies and dredgers and machines and as convincingly symbolic of the determination of the businessmen of the West of Scotland.

Further down the river on the opposite shore was the great rock of Dumbarton, ancient stronghold of the people of Strathclyde, from whose castle Mary Stewart as a little girl of five had sailed away to become for a brief spell Queen not only of the Scots but also of France. We did not rate Dumbarton too highly. 'Once the capital of Scotland'? Rather presumptuous we thought. Everyone knew our Edinburgh was capital of Scotland.

Across the water too was Cardross where Robert the Bruce had died, perhaps of leprosy, and where my mother's artist Uncle Jack Stewart had lived and her brothers David and Willie and cousin

3

Charlie. They were but of academic interest to us for we had but rarely met our uncles and the others not at all, but Robert the Bruce was another matter. I knew of Bannockburn, of the misleading fires lit on the Carrick coast and of the cave on Rathlin, while the Bruce's spider was the hero of an unending saga spun by my mother to alleviate the trials of unpopular rituals such as going to bed and hair-washing.

One day on the shore at Erskine Ferry we saw a piece of living history mingle with the past when we had our first sight of camouflaged ships. As, at a distance of under half a mile, they were to us neither invisible, nor visible as waves, but were quite clearly ships painted with zebra stripes, we formed a poor opinion of German common sense and decided that besides being bad, our enemy must also be stupid.

If the further and further away walk undiluted by an excursion to the shore was anathema to my brother, the diversion was not unalloyed bliss for me. He could not read but I could, and there, nailed to a tree at the point where the shore road debouched from the inland one, was a notice which announced starkly, 'Private. Trespassers will be prosecuted.'

A law-abiding child, I would pull at my mother's sleeve and point it out to her, but she with callous abandon would just march on, pushing our baby sister before her, telling me not to be silly and that it did not matter.

Did not matter indeed!

I followed as unobtrusively as possible, expecting irate game-keepers and landowners, perhaps even policemen, to erupt from the quiet wood and arrest us, baby, pram and all. I enjoyed the shore but on our homeward way only breathed easily again when we were past that baleful notice on the tree. Fear must have etched a deep mark on my mind for I can still see, clear as day, that corner with grassy verge leading to grey, lichened, dry-stane dyke, some stones fallen on the ground and beyond them the fateful tree. No more than did my brother realise that the furtherest away circle leads somewhere back to its beginnings, did I that the notice applied to the wood and

4

not to the road alongside. Perhaps the hint of danger added just that piquancy to the expeditions which has made them live on so clearly in my memory.

Miraculously, despite comprehensive roadworks and the despoliations of the years, that strip of sand by Erskine Ferry on the quiet Clyde is still there to be glimpsed when I pass over it on Erskine Bridge, though sometimes I scarcely see it as my eyes mist at remembrance of things past and of that little brother who has finally gone along the further and further away walk to some unknown return.

CHAPTER TWO

First Beginnings

MY OWN JOURNEY along the further and further away walk started in what seems now, historically more than chronologically speaking, a very long time ago. Despite changes, I feel still the same essential me. It is the scenery along the way that has changed beyond belief. As a school-girl I sat for hours on the ledge of the cupboard whose upper part was a glass-fronted bookcase with a medley of books. From it I read boys' adventure yarns—my history is still re-inforced with memories of G. H. Henty's *Wulf the Saxon, Knights of the White Cross* and the exploits of Nat and other British lads in Haiti, the Rockies and the Punjab, as is my view of the wider world also coloured by the experiences of R. M. Ballantyne's heroes and of W. H. Kingston's three midshipmen as they worked their way in various stations up the ranks of the Navy to admiral. There were Band of Hope inspired tales in which neglected waifs expired in the streets outside public-houses or, more happily, persuaded their drink-sodden parents to take the pledge, and a today-unreadable volume about the Scottish Convenanters. There was also a book about the clans and tartans of Scotland. From it I gained the information that of all the clans without the prefix Mac, ours was the only one whose chief could claim the right to the prefix The before his name. As the old saying had it, there was The Devil, The Pope and The Chisholm. This, despite the company, seemed special. So one talks of The Flood, The Conquest and The Restoration and so to me, no matter what conflicts have raged before or since, that of 1914-1918, the war to end all wars, will always be The War.

I was born a little before it. Having advanced so far along the way, I could regret that my journey did not start a year earlier for then I could have claimed—without fear of much increased decrepitude—Edwardian birth with all that age's panache of elegance—parasols, wide-brimmed stately hats and subtle hint of delicious fastness and vice. As it is, I am a Georgian—not perhaps of the best period—but of the pedestrian one of George the Fifth. "Scots or Scottish, but never Scotch", we were told in Composition classes, "Scotch is a drink", a remark not very enlightening to the well-brought-up daughters of mainly teetotal Presbyterian Edinburgh citizens. But Georgian, like Scotch, has many labels. To me, one equates with fine silver—which is appropriate as the baby born on Thursday 2nd February 1911 was the first child of a partner in the Princes Street firm of Mackay and Chisholm, Goldsmiths and Silversmiths to H.M. the Queen.

Though born not far from grace—two doors from a church, on the Feast of Candlemas and, judging from my mother's journal, a wanted child—I cannot feel my entry into the world gave her much immediate pleasure. Childbirth was too often a rough ride at the beginning of this century and for her I fear it was so. She would have had in her mind too the knowledge that her own mother had died, if not in childbirth yet of a complication of pregnancy 'peritonitis and haemorrhage', a fact which to her credit she never told me when I was rather casually having our family up and down Highland glens. Also her doctor was one of those unsympathic types, plain-spoken to the point of brusqueness, who survived in my own experience to the middle of the century but who are now thankfully becoming extinct. He was moreover her in-law's much thought-of family doctor, connected by some ramification of kinship or church, so there was no escaping him. I antagonised him by mismanaging my moment of advent. My mother records the event—

'It was one of the coldest nights of the winter with frost and fog. Owing to the frost-bound roads the doctor's horse and cab could scarcely go at anything beyond a walking pace. Consequently Elaine made her appearance almost before he did.'

7

As the monthly nurse, Nurse Cunningham, was both efficient and caring, this could classed as a Good Thing. Family tradition has it that when he arrived, stamping his feet and swinging his arms and very angry as he had been forced to walk the last half-mile, he delivered his customary meed of sympathy to the effect that there was a long time to wait yet and the patient would be worse before she was better. He was wrong. I was born almost immediately at 2.25 am. Admittedly, the earliest hours of the twenty-four on the coldest night of the year cannot have been a pleasant time to be tramping the streets of Edinburgh but my mother—and probably the horse—must have suffered more than he did. The horse would have had to slither down the entire slope of Edinburgh's cobbled New Town streets before reaching the levels of Inverleith Row. It was a recurrent childhood horror in winter to hear the grinding of brakes and the uncontrolled clatter of hooves on stone as unfortunate horses came to grief on those treacherous hills. I hope this one survived to go on more pleasant jaunts.

One might have thought I had done enough to jeopardise my welcome but I had arrived nameless, quite evidently not the Ian Stewart expected. My father fancied Constance but for some never-to-us-at-least explained reason this was considered risible. Could she have been an old flame? My mother would have liked Barbara, me too, had I been able to discuss the matter, after the aunt who had brought her up and who in memory as in life has always been one of my favourite people. Aunt Barbara, however, had forbidden this, she at least must have envisaged the possible delayed arrival of Ian Stewart. All Barbaras on the distaff side of the family were unlucky. She was unlucky. Hearing this in later years I wondered how. She had a choice of homes, Ardenlee in Glasgow and first Hazelcliffe, then Dunira, on the Isle of Bute, with Uncle John and Uncle Harry and Mary in the kitchen, a dog and cat, not to mention one of the earliest cars, a yacht and a fishing-boat. What more could she need? I know now that when, after years of ill-health, her mother died in 1874 she, as daughter at home, was left to house-keep for her father and brothers though there was a seemingly short and probably not

8

happy interregnum of second wife. Before her father died in 1899, she suffered the grief of seeing her two youngest brothers die as young men and a sister-in-law and baby niece also, as did in sad circumstances, a bare month later, her own sister. In 1909 another brother died, yet never to me did she appear remotely unhappy or frustrated but always, discounting the typically pithy Scottish tang to her tongue, seemed to be enjoying her life, 'Werena' ma hert licht I wad dee.'

I think she was naturally young in spirit, and hope she eventually felt she had led a fulfilled life. In an entry in her journal for 1920 my mother confirms this impression of mine. Before Christmas she gave a children's party for about thirty-three guests—with a conjuror!

'Aunt B. came from Glasgow for the party and enjoyed it immensely. She stayed for about a week afterwards. For an old lady of her years (they must be pretty considerable) [actually seventy-two] she is most active and sprightly and young in her manner. It is strange and pathetic how the spirit in so many cases keeps youthful while the body ages so quickly. Is it an omen of the spirit's immortality—or indestructibility? Something that has persisted or will persist through many changes of abode.'

If my love counts for anything, Aunt Barbara was many times blessed. As in her lifetime more than one Barbara did die young, perhaps to love I should also add gratitude that my walk did not peter out into a premature dead-end.

I was in due course fitted out with a name which complimented my two grandmothers, the still very present strong-minded Agnes Helen and the shadowy unknown Mary Jane. My mother, through whose being ran a streak of often ill-considered sentiment, predictably turned the Helen to Elaine—Elaine was not commonplace or ordinary—nor was it then, I only ever knew one other until the present post nineteen-forties spate of them. We were often to suffer from her dislike of the ordinary. While my fortunate friends had their hair tied back, or even sported pig-tails which she despised and I coveted, and my lucky cousin had hers, to I may say her disgust, dragged back to expose her forehead and ears, my locks were flowing free to conceal those very features. Out shopping with our mothers, I would meet class-mates in their plain navy nap school coats but I was not 'looking ordinary' in my brick-coloured one with shoulder cape and velvet collar. My summer dresses were not shop-produced prints of unexciting pattern such as 'everybody' wore but were artistic hanging garments, perhaps of oriental chintz made with considerable dedication by my deluded mother, though I must confess to being much attached to my 'banana' dress of brown, orange and yellow vertical stripes. When I see photographs of Augustus John's family as children, I am irresistibly reminded of us and wonder afresh at the metamorphosis of a son to an admiral. Perhaps early conditioning gave him an affinity with cocked hat and braid. Uncommon or not, I did not as a child dislike my name, Elaine Mary, nor was I discountenanced by jests about the fair, the lovable, the lily-maid, spared I suspect to the swarms of today's Elaines to whom *The Idylls of the King* is probably as nearly sealed a book as unfortunately is the Bible. Nonetheless, today I would happily settle for plain Ellen or Mary unadorned.

CHAPTER THREE

Talk of Many Things

I FEEL I SHOULD be able to remember something of the first two years of my life when so much was learned and every experience was new but of course I cannot and so must go back to the new mother's journal. 'She was not a big baby but was considered a very pretty one.' I like the modesty of 'was considered', by whom, one wonders, the neighbours, pram-peepers or just the proud parents? I would have been the first to concur in this judgement for I can see myself, not many years later, prinking in front of the mirror in my parents' bedroom and thinking how terrible it must be to be a *plain* child. Sad (and bad) for one's ego that such innocent self-regard fades, or is ruthlessly stamped out.

'She was certainly a very wide-awake one [baby] and never wasted much time in sleep.' Nor, according to my father, did I let him waste much time either as he spent many of the watches of the night walking up and down, jiggling me in his pyjama-clad arms to the tune, with rhythm exaggerated, of 'Lord a-aa lit-tle band and low-ly'. Accented thus, it makes an excellent lullaby, especially when the jiggling of crib or baby is fairly robust, much more effective than many another better-known, and one which instinctively years later I found myself humming over my own children. 'Her first journey was to Glasgow in April, where she also had and enjoyed her first motor-ride, in Mrs Anderson's motor,' a case of the child being mother to the woman, 'motor-rides' being still one of my great pleasures.

'She was put into short clothes there,' a landmark then though not now in this age of the baby-gro. 'Was at North Berwick in June when she refused to allow herself to be wheeled on the sands.' Do most children have a fear of the insecurity of a beach? Our first daughter indeed with cries of "Big bath!" rushed headlong over the sands at Fairlie and into the sea with all her clothes on (and that in the middle of a long journey) but our third, much of an age, beholding the beach at Ballywalter, staunchly refused to set foot on it but determinedly bent her legs with red boot appendages up under her as we struggled to support her not inconsiderable weight.

'Had another and longer motor-run.' These occasions are worthy of recall for although now most babies make their first journey home by car or ambulance in a matter of days or hours, at this time very few people owned cars. My family never had one until my brother and I grew up and lashed out eight pounds on an elderly vehicle. Its registration letters were V C which we took as a good omen and indeed it dared and did most things.

'Her first tooth was cut at Lundin Links in September and she took her first step all alone at North Berwick in July 1912. She began to walk with assistance in June at Pitlochry.' Certainly I got about. Sometimes I almost feel I can remember some of it, though this is probably due to the fact that as I was the first child far more snapshots were taken of me than of my brother or either of my sisters so the backgrounds of my experiences are recognisable to me. Thanks to a rather mildewed photograph album I know what I looked like at various ages of weeks, in my pram or in the arms of a still debilitated mother or grim-faced Aunt Barbara both of whose expressions could have stemmed from inexperience or determination not to crush the superabundance of lawn and broderie anglaise hanging from my well-nourished form. In common with most mothers of those days, mine considered the more adipose the infant, the bonnier and healthier. Judged by this standard, I look to have been entirely satisfactory but was to be outshone years later by sisters Marjorie and Moira. Regarding Marjorie, my mother first comments suspiciously on a new-fangled idea of feeding a baby undiluted cow's milk but added that it seemed to be a good idea as baby certainly put on more weight than either of her other two children had done. On the eleventh of August 1918, she writes enthusiastically, 'we weighed baby today.' (If you had no suitable scales you made an excited journey to the chemist.) 'She is 17 1/2 lbs or rather more which is simply splendid for her age, only five months on the first of this month. I wished I had known about the whole milk system for the others. I am sure it would have made them much fatter at the same age.' She makes us sound like poultry being fattened up for the Christmas market.

My baby clothes were kept for later members of the family so I know what I wore. Working from the skin outwards, there was first the flannel binder. Bound round the abdomen, the end secured by needle and thread, this was worn until the navel healed. I remember a sister's nurse assembling the bathtime paraphernalia, the blue rimmed white enamel bath on its stand, the cork bathmat, the soap, the powder (Johnson's then as often now), the bath thermometer (in wooden casing it floated), the warm towels and aprons, the cotton-wool, the jar of boracic ointment and something other, boracic lotion perhaps, in a saucer for eyes and ears. Then there was the slightly warmed chamber-pot (enamel), the clothes over the clothes-horse, the screen between the fire and the door and finally, before collecting the reason for all this activity, the nurse had to remember to thread her needle, biting the end of the thread off in her teeth. If all this sounds intimidating, it was homely, unlike the demonstration of the bath given to their baby brother of a few days as a treat for his two slightly older sisters, my grandchildren, by a large, imposing visiting maternity nurse, all hung about with safety-pins and scissors. Looking down on them from her navy-blue height over a well-developed bosom and rolling her sleeves above the elbow she said,

"Now! —Who can bring me some old newspapers?"

Wide-eyed, they stared back at her, envisaging who knows what pictures of a baby-brother 'take-away'.

Under the aegis of my mother's monthly nurses, baby's bath was quite a performance. Older members of the family were welcome as audience but definitely discouraged from entering or leaving when the curtain was, as it were, up.

"Well—if you must Go—go, but open the door gently and shut it at once. Don't let in The Draught."
Return from the necessary journey triggered off a reverse panic.

Once the bath was over, baby dried and powdered and sewn into its binder, and the needle put away in a safe place, the cross-over vest was added. Over the (triangularly folded) towelling nappy was wrapped a flannel pilch, a not-very-adequate piece of extra protection like a waist petticoat. Here I am confused, though convinced that a barracoat came next, a long sleeveless flannel garment, with herring-boned tucks and scalloped hem. In summer this would have been made of lawn. Socks and soft shoes were optimistically added to waving feet and then, over a petticoat itself a work of art, came the beautiful culmination of the wardrobe, the gown, of lawn or cotton. This bore further wonders of embroidery, broderie anglaise, insertion, pintucking and lace. Tapes and ribbons or material waist-bands might fasten this garment but often there were tiny buttons to inveigle through minute button-holes or more possibly button loops. Baby habits being the same then as now and plastic pants not invented, there must have been many a time when all this finery was donned to be almost immediately discarded. Hours of washing and ironing must have been involved in the keeping dry and respectable even one baby. Small wonder that the humblest middle-class homes aspired to a maidservant as one might today to a tumble-drier. Cousin Minnie, erstwhile one of the earliest Norland Nurses, possibly spoke truly enough for a sizeable proportion of mothers of the first decades of the century though her pronouncement made to me in 1944 hardly seemed realistic,

"There is no doubt—a baby is one woman's work."
We were, according to temperature, topped by a matinée jacket of wool or some lighter material then securely bound by one of my grandmother's Shetland shawls. She knitted a procession of them, garter stitch in the centre I think, with lacy outside panels. When she had finished the knitting, her youngest daughter took over and

14

spreading a sheet on the floor laid the shawl on it and carefully pinned the points into perfect shape. Later on in our lives these shawls kept us warm as we sat up in bed in usually rather icy bedrooms, victims of colds or sickness, or more happily we snuggled into them as we stepped in short-sleeved taffeta dresses into shared taxis taking us to winter parties. Finally the few that became shrunk and matted ended their days adorning our dolls and teddies. My grandmother wore a chatelaine round her waist with a gadget of silver for holding her ball of wool. I suspect Lewis Carroll may have had a grandmother like mine for in her knitting activities she did resemble the Looking-glass Sheep.

My mother made a story for me of how one of those large shawls had come to her rescue. It was on the general's (domestic not military) afternoon off that I, with a baby's instinctive feel for doing the wrong thing at the right time, decided to test out my new mother.

I yelled.

And yelled.

My ignorant and distracted mother, having tried everything from burping to feeding to Gripe Water to Dinneford's Fluid Magnesia, decided an open nappy pin must be lurking about my person and to my unabated roars divested me of all—gown, barra, vest, pilch, nappy, the lot. Then from the kitchen clanged the tongue of the swinging bell attached to the bell-pull at the gate. Panicked at thought of a strange supercilious lady caller, probably childless or the mother of an impeccable family, all she could think to do was wrap me firmly in my shawl and go with me to the door, hoping I would not drip through the interstices.

"And who was it?" A year or so later I would unfailingly ask though I knew the answer. Disappointingly, only a message boy, soon despatched.

Most annoyingly I can remember nothing of a much more dramatic event when as an older baby I was parked halfway down the garden in my high pram. By vigorous rocking I upset it and was rescued by our next-door neighbour who leapt the palings then, sweeping me up in his arms, marched in at the back door and presented me to my

15

astonished mother. In my later mind's eye I see this scene as a reversal of Ford Madox Brown's wronged mother with her 'Take your son, Sir' amending it perhaps to 'Madam, your child.' This neighbour, Mr Rose, was, when I was conscious of knowing him, a tall sober black-garbed and black-haired man with a high colour. His wife was the same, but female. A Mr and Mrs Noah. He may have been a banker. I am willing to concede that other people may have seen them differently. I cannot conceive how he got so expeditiously and safely from their garden to ours for the paling was of iron spikes. A hero indeed. I cannot recall having much to do with them. They were childless, older I fancy than my parents, and kept a more flowery garden with flourishing sweet peas. Obviously they were just as neighbours should be, unobtrusive but there in case of need.

The neighbours on the other side were a family of two sons and daughter who all eventually went off to South Africa—or so my memory tells me. I hope they did, for it is part of their legend but my mother's journal has just told me they moved to Comely Bank— a nearby district. Perhaps a halfway stop. The daughter, at around twelve, was a typically shapeless early twentieth-century schoolgirl, her figure less the result of nature than of the current abominable gym-tunic with box-pleats and coloured girdle accentuating the adolescent wearer's lack of waist. She was patient with my five-year-old self and I admired both her and her gym-tunic and have always thought kindly of Dorothy. Two pleasant if colourless sisters lived nearby too—one a widow, one unmarried. They both dressed in grey with touches of black or violet and I never could tell the one from the other without long scrutiny. I stood on the pavement, my eyes rivetted to their faces waiting for the moment when one would laugh or open wide and reveal a gold-filled back molar which gave me my bearings and I knew a Miss from a Missis.

Of all the neighbours, the family in the house beyond Dorothy was of most importance to me, at least the son was. I can remember only once seeing Cecil's father. His mother was a blonde, perhaps a little highly coloured. Possibly she was merely more fashionable than my mother and her friends which would not have been difficult as many of them were older and already had large families and wore 'suitable' clothes. My mother tended to the artistic and affected to despise fashion although her journal shows this not to be true of her youth. Her later attitude may have been a rationalisation dictated by economics. As I have no clear picture of Cecil's mother at all, not even as children usually have of like or dislike, only of a pleasant maid, I think she must have been socially inclined and literally 'not at home' on the few occasions I visited their house. If I rarely visited Cecil's house, he as rarely visited mine, and this, to quote the Walrus, was odd because we liked each other. When I ran in and said, "Cecil says can I go and play with him?" I was conscious always, with the excuses, of an atmosphere, not voiced but none the less tinged with disapproval, which was very inhibiting. It cannot have been entirely due to the fact that a kindly maid sometimes referred to him as 'your little sweetheart' (talk of sweethearts was common).

Perhaps it was just part and parcel of my mother's absurd possessiveness—she hated any of us straying beyond the home. When I was a schoolgirl she often turned down Saturday afternoon invitations from my grandmother to go and play with my cousin on the grounds that "Elaine likes staying at home to help Willie in the garden" an attitude I doubt if my father had ever noticed. For years too I used to wonder why my cousin only once chose me as her companion on weekend visits to Dundee with our grandmother and aunt to our doctor uncle's home but always took another classmate. Years later my aunt told me they had invited me till they tired—I being presumably still dead set on weeding! With Cecil, the atmosphere eventually so got through to me that when he called his invitation across the intervening garden I retired out of sight behind our wash-house to re-appear after a suitable interval and shout back "She says I can't come".

Despite these obstacles, our friendship flourished like that of pen-friends, probably to the entertainment of the Kennedys who must have been involuntary (if not voluntary) recipients of our confidences and opinions. I remember discussing our underwear and exhibiting our semmits which seems an innocent enough diversion—surely not

17

connected with a visiting ban? We vied with each other in our exchanges. I remember dramatically retailing a story, entirely I am sure apocryphal as are so many wartime rumours, that I had heard Mary exclaiming over with a friend in the kitchen. I spent a great deal of my time there, often under the table, kitchen conversations being so much more racy than those of my mother and baby brother in the parlour. This tale concerned a German Zeppelin come to commit some 'frightfulness' over the British Isles. Seeing a trainful of people it made to attack it but the train had a resourceful driver who very sensibly drove into a tunnel. After some time he ventured out only to find the Zeppelin waiting for him so he cunningly reversed and emerged from the other end. "And do you know what?" I shouted over the Kennedy grass... but you will have guessed the rest. Cecil and I were quite overcome with anguish for the unfortunate passengers shuttling to and fro through the dark with no prospect of escape and tortured ourselves with thoughts of the calamitous outcome had a second train crashed into the fugitive in the tunnel.

I have a last picture of Cecil in alien surroundings. My mother and I having one day walked further than usual from Penicuik emerged on the Edinburgh to Carlops hill-road and were resting by a dyke when along came an open motor. Travelling as it was at the sedate pace of the second decade of the century, we had time to recognise eachother and Cecil's father stopped his car. His mother and mine exchanged greetings but, inhibited as children often were in those days by the presence of their parents, Cecil and I just stared.

CHAPTER FOUR

Departures and Arrivals

AN EARLY memory I can date with certainty is of the day my brother arrived to annex the name that had been awaiting him two years, nine months and eighteen days. I am sure however that some of my memories pre-date this if only because he was not around to complicate travel. There is the hazy memory of staying in a strange large building where I and my nurse Chrissie had meals with other children and adults, including men, where there was an atmosphere of jollity and—oddly—kippers. I have been told this was Dunblane Hydropathic where the nurses and their charges shared a small dining-room with the guests' chauffeurs. Kipper no doubt figured on the breakfast bill of fare. There was also a very long staircase down which I made my careful and assisted way. My mother has told me I was greatly admired, as would be any not unattractive two-year-old, but indeed until we grew and held opinions which crossed hers she did genuinely tend to think her children beautiful and clever. I entered the archives of memorable family sayings by giving the brush-off on these stairs to a gushing lady with the words, probably not unconnected with the chauffeurs, "I like gentles." I had forgotten the words but I do remember being annoyed with a silly woman who for no reason laughed at something I had said.

While still without Ian, my mother and I were able to make frequent trips 'through to Glasgow' to visit Aunt Barbara and the uncles. Despite having to 'take the car' (cable tram) up to Princes Street to either the Caley or Waverley station—we usually favoured the Caley, I think the other line might have been slower—these excursions seem in retrospect to have been made with greater comfort and despatch before 1914 than at any time since. Honesty compels me to admit that occasionally our tickets were bought for us by my father or by the firm's messenger out on his errands. Even when that chore was not spared us, it all seemed easier, no frustration of long queues at understaffed ticket offices or of shut gates at platforms with megaphone blaring above, "Your" (so far non-visible) "train is being cleaned for you!"

Apart from the soot indigenous to steam railways, our train would be standing clean and ready for us and ready moreover long before its advertised time of departure so that even anxious travellers like our family could board it twenty or so minutes early.

First and Third railway classes existed which implied there were three. Where was second? This exercised my mind for years. I knew one—two—three. Why did railways count one—three? Apparently when in the 1830s main-line traffic built up to any considerable amount there were indeed at least three classes. In 1875 the Midland reduced these to two but not apparently having my prowess in counting labelled them First and Third. Scottish lines followed their lead in 1893 but it was not until 1956 that British Rail made the change from First/Third to First/Second.

In the compartments, mirrors and photographs of places of beauty or interest were framed above the seats. As a child I must sometimes have travelled First for I remember large, for me too large, seats from which my legs stuck out uncomfortably and very ornate antimacassars. Not that these last were ever of much benefit to us children—initially we did not reach up to them and in no matter what class we travelled we were enjoined to not lay back our heads. (You never knew whose had been there before.)

Sometimes we booked a compartment for longer journeys, Edinburgh to Oban perhaps. Then we took sandwiches and milk and thermoses and could spread ourselves out all over the seats. When we did not reserve a compartment we took pleasure in the dodge, no doubt as old as the railway age, of stationing the youngest, dirtiest and most girny children by the windows to scare away all but besotted child-lovers. Travelling on those bygone trains with—or even without—children was not all bliss. Above all else loomed the worry as to whether it would be a corridor train. Putting aside the question of germs in a train lavatory, it was infinitely better to have one than not, even if you were jerked about as the train fled through twisting glens and you vainly tried to follow maternal instructions to not touch the seat. This sanitary preoccupation made the reserved compartment good sense. A potty for small children could be concealed among the hand luggage. I seem to remember amazing acts of legerdemain when my father successfully emptied it as the camber of the track tilted the train to one side. This was presumably through a lowered window, even my father would scarcely have opened a door to exercise this manoeuvre though that was not entirely beyond the bounds of possibility, he quite enjoyed a challenge and he could be besides a distinct trial to us on journeys. He kept on vanishing.

"There's time yet… I'll go for a paper," and off he would go past the ticket-collector and out of sight into the main part of the station. On return he would announce he was just going to check the luggage in the van and disappear in the opposite direction. Never did he step into the carriage until the very last minute, verified by careful scrutiny of his gold breast-pocket watch on its chain, to mingled and anguished cries of "Daddie! Willie! We're moving! Get in!"

Now I can almost sympathise. He merely wished to be disassociated till the last possible moment from the motley assemblage in his charge—a worried wife, a maid, an aggrieved and vocal cat in a basket, picnic hamper, teddies, comics, coats and anything up to four children one of whom at least was in a panic until he joined us. But all this searching the platform up and down interfered with one of the pleasures of sitting at Waverley waiting for the guard's whistle— the reading of the various advertisements fastened to the walls on shining enamel plates. My favourite was the blue and white

'They come as a boon and a blessing to men,
The Pickwick, the Owl and the Waverley Pen.'

If the train were not a corridor one, it might thoughtfully make an

21

extended stop at a junction and children would be hustled out to the waiting-rooms. This was another torment. Was it safer to go and risk being left behind or not to go and be borne off leaving one's family stranded? Dog owners who had descended for very similar reasons could at least keep an eye on the train as they paraded their leashed companions. On the Oban line, Crianlarich was the child and dog comfort station. I think the engine had a drink too and passengers could get tea, in china cups—with saucers. There was no need to gulp the tea. The cups could be put off at any of the next stations. Some lucky people picked up lunch or tea baskets. We envied them. It was duller to bring our own although the contents were probably more to our taste. One hot summer day a near calamity proved a boon. The sandwiches had gone dry and the paste ones were hard and curling at the edges and the milk for our drink had leaked into the basket. It had however oozed all over the tomato sandwiches turning them moist and thirst-quenching, the best indeed I have ever tasted.

Our father needless to say, always descended at Crianlarich, "Just time for a pipe". He meant a lit one. For most of his life, except when dealing with customers, his pipe, lit or unlit, travelled with him in his mouth. It was as much part of him as was his gold watch with which he had mystified us all in our time when we found as young children that when he held it we could blow it open. This trick was on par with another when he immersed the sponge in our bath then brought it out in his hand—dry.

Journeys to and from Glasgow were short. On arrival at Queen Street or Central, with glimpse of the Clyde, we took a cab or were met by a car (motor this time) and driven off to Ardenlee, 59 St Andrew's Drive, Pollockshields. I have clear memories of going on these visits to afternoon tea-parties with my mother and enjoying unaccustomed rich cakes and shortbread and biscuits. Well-to-do Glasgow people were not ostentatious with their wealth but took it for granted and enjoyed the benefits it could bring them, (they were also generous in promoting charities and the cultural arts) and I noticed and appreciated the comfortable armchairs and sofas and cushions into which one could burrow, so different from those in the more austere Edinburgh drawing-rooms. I had happy afternoons at the house of an older person, Mrs Anderson (but not Lena), a friend of Aunt Barbara's. Under her piano, on a most affluent carpet and among screens, I played at being the Little Bear, one of my favourite alter egos, or Tyro, Mrs Anderson's Skye terrier to whom I was greatly attached. The luxuriant flowing locks over my eyes suited me to this part. I could be lured out now and then to accept a chocolate ("Take two!") from a decorative box of Glasgow size and richness.

We used to make too a regular visit to a much older lady, again one of Aunt Barbara's acquaintances, but this was more of a duty call. I think my mother was a little in awe of our hostess and I would never have had the temerity to be even a very little bear under the piano. There was a large family and it was a wealthy household but even so the daughters were carefully trained at home in all aspects of domestic management, not so much one imagines for the remote possibility of their becoming wives in humble homes as so that they could supervise every detail of their servants' work even to the manufacture of the family supply of soap. As far as I know they all 'married well' and I am sure ordered tablets and bars of commercial soap from their grocers. When I was older, my mother told me of another chore they had to undertake—hemming their own washable sanitary towels. On afternoon calls one might come on them industriously stitching these necessities of life. If a gentleman called they folded them away in their workbaskets under a linen towel. The end products sound rather more classy than the roughly folded remnants of nappies or household linen that I and many of my friends were fobbed off with in our early menstruating days before we discovered from magazine advertisements that there were alternative possibilities.

The Aulds' houses were a compromise between the typical Glasgow and Edinburgh styles. Perhaps because after their father's death in 1899 their homes had been set up by the brothers and sister in a ratio of three to one, they were not, though evidence of wealth was abundant, as overtly luxurious or tastefully decorated as those of many of their friends. Aunt Barbara was not a house-proud type and they spent their money on what they really valued, occasional foreign travel for the brothers and adequate help to enable them to sustain a pleasant life-style. They could also indulge individual hobbies. Uncle John and Uncle Harry kept pigeons, Uncle Harry had always a yacht and in his later life Uncle John collected barometers and clocks. When in their last home, Logie Aston in Bridge of Allan, the hour struck, it struck from all over the house at spaced intervals of seconds in an agreeable dislocation of bells and chimes.

On one early visit to Ardenlee, I shared a bed with sagging mattress with my mother. Despite the mattress, creature comfort was not wanting for the room was warmed by a coal-fire in whose light flickering on the walls I drifted happily into sleep. I awoke hours later to an appalling sense of suffocation. I had slid further and further down the bed but my mother joining me had, as the fire died down, pulled the blankets further and further up against the cold. Frantically I struggled up through layers of fluff to awake my mother and vow I would never sleep with her again. Could this have triggered off a years' long obsession with a fear of being buried alive, reinforced by an horrific tale of Edgar Allan Poe whose works I later immersed myself in one spring in the library of Melrose Hydropathic?

Happier bedroom memories are of the late summer of 1913. My parents had 'taken rooms' in North Berwick, a favourite holiday place with Edinburgh families. There were two golf-links, a swimming-pool built into the cold harbour rocks, tennis courts and the sheltered West and rather less sheltered East Bays for playing and bathing. At one time there was also what I referred to as The Red Gomplet, a paddle steamer called after a Scott novel of somewhat similar title which did pleasure cruises across the firth to Kirkcaldy. We went once only. The waters of the Forth appeared to be less tractable than those of the Clyde and even my salt-water-loving mother never felt inclined to venture again. A chief attraction of North Berwick was that it lay only about twenty-five miles from Edinburgh and there was an excellent service of trains enabling husbands and fathers to travel daily to their pursuits in the capital leaving their wives and children to enjoy the sands—and whiles thole an East coast haar. I slept in a low bed in my parents' room. That in itself dates the year. In 1914 there would have been a cot with baby occupant. I wakened early in the mornings—there was an east-facing window high in the wall opposite me—and to avoid disturbing my father and mother lay playing quietly with two celluloid dolls of about four inches in height. Their features and clothes were painted on. My favourite was a sailor. I ran my fingers up and down the ridges on his sides where the moulds had joined and over raised marks on his back. 'Made in Japan' they said—the first words I suppose I ever read. I liked the feel of the marks but not their presence. They subtracted from my sailor's reality. I, after all, did not have 'Made in Scotland' stamped on me.

The first treat of the day was when my father went to shave and I followed him for a dab of sweet-smelling soapy lather from his shaving-brush on the end of my nose.

"There you are, Tuppence," he always said.

I thought my father wonderful and tried to stay awake until he came home in the evening. Then he would lift me out of bed and carry me over to the high window and hold me up to see a light flashing off and on.

"Look!" he would say, "The May!"

He gazed. Was he seeing something of the romance of life beyond 59 Princes Street? It was rumoured that as a young man he had wanted to make the army his career but family duty and possibly lack of finance had ruled that out. He occasionally spoke of a desire to visit Egypt but sadly never did that either. I gazed too, entranced by the wonder of the light and of his tone.

"The May!" I breathed.

I had no idea what the May was, only knew that in an arbitrary fashion it shone for me when I was in my father's arms and never did during the day, for I had looked. My first encounter with other-worldly mystery, my earliest hint of Shangri-La or Tir-nan-og, it remains so, still unvisited. I look for it every night journey on the Edinburgh-King's Cross East Coast run, flashing on the sea's edge between Fife and Lothian.

On the evening of the twentieth of November 1913 I was lying in another small bed, sheltered from any possible draught from the open door by a tall Victorian scrap-screen which if still extant must be worth several hundreds of pounds. Kings, queens, flowers, birds, animals, children, natives of faraway places, palaces, castles and angels bedecked it. Again a fire was burning in the grate, this time in the nursery on the third floor of my Chisholm grandparents' home at 7 Claremont Crescent, Edinburgh. A second door led through into a large bedroom where slept my Aunt Annie (my father's elder sister), my slightly older cousin Ralph and baby cousin Kathleen. My grandparents at this time must have changed for dinner for when my aunt slipped in to see me I thought she was looking very lovely in a gauzy greenish-grey gown. Had I known the word I might have described her appearance as ethereal—and like some ethereal beings she bore a message.

"Dear little Elaine," she said—she was sentimental as well as kind—"do you know what you have at home?" Bemused, I stared at her in the fire-light.

"You have a dear little baby brother."

What nonsense I thought. I had no baby brother. Yet I was faintly disturbed. I had been taken for no discernible reason from my own home to that of my grandparents and tucked up in a strange bed. Odd doings were afoot. I put a bold face on it,

"I have not," I said, "that's my teddy-bear."

CHAPTER FIVE

Unto Us a Son

AUNT ANNIE had not been misinformed. When I returned home there indeed was Ian Stewart, flaxen-haired and blue-eyed.

Home, 39 Inverleith Gardens, was on the north side of Edinburgh, almost opposite the south end of Granton Road, a two-storey house, last but one in the terrace. Number 40 belonged to the athletic Mr Rose and beyond that was St James's United Free, now Inverleith Church of Scotland. Next came a large manse and two other big houses in their own grounds fronting on to the Ferry Road. Down the side of the last house ran the Cinder Path leading south between playing fields and a nursery garden to Arboretum Road, Inverleith Park, 'the Botanics' (The Royal Botanic Garden) and finally the Water of Leith and Stockbridge. On our front gate was a bronze-coloured name-plate with Strathearn beaten out on it in decorative lettering. It was at the Strathearn Hydropathic Hotel in Crieff that my parents first met. (They pursued their courting in Miss Cranstoun's now historic tea-rooms in Glasgow.)

Opposite the house, across what is now a busy bus route but then was a quiet road on which one could probably have sat down without seriously disturbing the traffic (not even the cable cars came as far), was Webster's, a livery stable. This with its horses, gaitered men, cabs and piles of steaming straw and unusual smell was an interesting place to visit—but in adult company as it was rather frightening. Who knew but when one of the champing monsters in its stall might not step back on you? With the degeneration of the years Webster's turned into a garage, useful, though it seemed a desecration to park our third-, fourth-, or fifth-hand first cars there.

Before viewing the interior of Number 39, access had to be gained, a thing not readily made easy by the famous Edinburgh contraption, the underground cable from porch to gate which activated a latch. There was a key-hole but no handle on the gate. A would-be caller had first to ring (pull-out not push-in the bell). The house-holder could then take a quick peek and if reassured that neither beggar, canvasser nor unwanted acquaintance stood there, advance into the porch and pull up the handle. Though similar if more sophisticated devices are now standard throughout the country, they seemed at that time to be unique to Edinburgh and were the object of much derision as betokening the supposed unfriendliness of the capital. Glasgow folk in particular, preening themselves on their city's reputation for hospitality, professed to find them very odd.

Our porch had an inner and an outer door. The inner door had in its upper panels lozenges of coloured glass which came to life in the sunlight. Inside, to the right, the stairs went up, two steps to a broader one, then a turn to the left and straight up to the last half-dozen which curved to the landing. The inside treads at the curve were very narrow, so I went up back foot joining the front on every step, right hand on wall-paper (never mind the oily stain), at the broad side against the wall. I remember the tapsalteerie sensation of falling down and also an occasion when a laden tray parted company with its bearer and crashed to the hall with considerable mess but surprisingly little damage.

Underneath the stairs was an 'underneath the stairs cupboard' in which lived everything that normally lives in such places, waterproofs, boots, pram and golf-clubs. To the left at the front of the house was the dining-room not often disturbed by us children as during the war years when our father was away we mostly lived and played and ate in the parlour, a pleasant south-facing room at the back of the house. Sharing a wall with the kitchen it was always warm and had too a fire-place of its own set corner-wise in the angle of a back and side wall. Here was the Ottoman, a green padded chest which held

28

blankets, old coats, rugs, discarded clothes and anything of a textile nature which ingenuity could store nowhere else—a treasure trove in later years for dressing-up. There was an uncomfortable creaking and scratchy basket-chair, upright chairs and a strong steady table good for drawing at and crayoning and painting. We had our meals off it too when it was covered by a farm-pictured nursery table-cloth, of Dutch design I think, with ducks parading over it. (As older children a meal we really enjoyed was the first in a rented summer lodging, when before our goods were unpacked— we 'took our own linen'—we ate off newspapers.) There were pleasant pictures on the parlour walls, mostly post-cards. Sargent's 'Carnation, Lily, Lily, Rose', with the delicate lilies and softly shining Japanese lanterns especially charmed me while several of Jessie Wilcox Smith's—'The Green Door', 'The Lily-Pond' and 'Among the Poppies' in particular, stirred my imagination. I felt like Alice with her Looking-glass. What was on the far side of the Green Door?

There was however one picture I most definitely did not like. It was of a Japanese lady. Japanoiserie had been fashionable since Whistler and my mother, who was a slight but quite talented artist, obviously felt its appeal. Perhaps her very black hair inclined her to a liking for Japanese beauties. One of our shopping treats was a visit to Henderson's Bazaar and Chintz shop in George Street, a marvellous repository of incense-scented products of the East—a forerunner of the many loosely styled 'ethnic' shops of today. This one plump, smiling, Japanese person however I could not like. Her eyes unsettled me, they were to me not almond-shaped but squinting, though what really made me feel uncomfortable was that her carefully dressed hair was skewered to the top of her head by what looked to me uncommonly like wooden knitting needles. She has left me still feeling a little uneasy with Japanese art.

Buphba's House and the *Invincible* were in the parlour. Buphba, a straw-stuffed fox-terrier with an alert air had been my inseparable companion from the time I was a few months old. He is a real period piece who would pass no toy-safety check today with his button eyes and metal strengthening inside his paws. His house was between four and five feet high, a three-flatted edifice of plain unvarnished wood which held our toys and early books. Most of the time its higgledy-piggledy contents lay open for all to see but if the room had to be made tidy (looking) a green-and-white striped curtain could be pulled down in front. One morning my mother sent the two of us into the kitchen telling us she was making a surprise and would call when it was ready. When we rushed in we found the middle shelf transformed into an open-plan dolls' apartment furnished with furniture she had made. Some time later my Aunt Edith who could have made a career for herself as cabinet-maker, upholsterer or dress-maker had her lot not so fallen as to make her the unmarried stay-at-home daughter, produced a two-storey dolls' house with stairs which gave the dolls more living space and which, despite being made—a wartime expediency—out of green-grocers' crates, stands today as strong as ever, exhibiting on its walls paper I recognise from our bedrooms and bathroom of Inverleith.

The *Invincible* was a magnificent red and blue wooden rocking-boat. There has always been some misunderstanding connected with it in my mind. When the parlour door was opened one Christmas morning to display our presents I naturally assumed it was for me. Had I not sailed on Uncle Harry's yacht? Not to mention being the older. Then it seemed that it was Ian's. The disappointment was severe, in practice the ownership scarcely mattered, what really irked me was the stupidity—which I was more than once to deplore!—of my parents in the matter of presents. Could they not see that I, bounding madly over the parlour floor, would make much better use of the *Invincible* than Ian, rocking placidly in the stern seat, ever would?

Now a recently discovered Journal of my mother's for 1915 exonerates my parents from any discrimination, exhibits my mother in an understanding and generous light and welcomely, if belatedly, resolves my nagging unease. It had been a difficult time, the war news was gloomy, the past November had been the coldest for fifty years, my father was having chickenpox in Army lodgings in Hamilton and my mother shingles in Edinburgh. On the 14th of

December she was recovered enough for a slight celebration.

> 'Today I got a cab and took Mary and the children up to Jenner's to see the toy bazaar. It is wonderful how the supply of toys keeps up tho' the German-made things are no longer to be had... I was very extravagant I'm afraid in the children's present. Elaine had set her heart on a wooden boat on rockers which cost—the smaller size—25/6. I never dreamt of giving so much for a toy but I explained carefully that it was to be between her and Ian so it won't come to much more than two separate toys.'

I can only conclude that my mother so overdid her careful explanation, in the cause of nursery peace, that I became confused. For all I know my brother may have been equally confused and thought the boat was mine! But shared or not—and the smaller size—it was probably one of the most rewarding presents we ever had. Singly or together, rocking madly up and down we could make it bound all over the parlour floor. My mother records me too chatting away with Kilunken as I ferried him about, he sitting at his invisible ease on the stern seat.

I am glad my misgivings as to the ownership of the *Invincible* have been resolved because in those early years my parents did sometimes seem to have a blind spot about presents. They often gave me books for which I am everlastingly grateful. Besides having annuals, interesting nature books, and Beatrix Potter, by the time I was seven I had *Alice in Wonderland, A Child's Garden of Verses, Peter Pan* and Amy le Fevre's *Child's Life of Jesus* stimulating my thoughts and from all of which I could make apt quotations. Other presents I appreciated were stencils and similar art sets including several do-it-yourself Alice pictures which had to be pieced together like a jig-saw from coloured adhesive sheets. But these and books apart, they did sometimes seem to need guidance. In the days before small bicycles and Fairy cycles, tricycles were coveted. None ever came my way though Ian was given a magnificent one with rubber tyres. I did indeed get much pleasure from a scooter—and did not grudge my little brother being given one at the same time despite its being two years before it was his due!

31

Everyone got pleasure from the scooters which arrived on Christmas morning 1918.

> 'Santa is supposed to have scored heavily against Mummy this time because the chief of his gifts to them were "scooters" which I had always declared they would never be permitted to have. We heard squeals of excitement when they saw Mary bringing in their stockings and "scooters". Mary says E's first remark was "I wonder what Mummy will say because she doesn't like "scooters". When they were dressed they rushed into our room in great excitement especially Elaine. "Mummy, we've got something that I think you'll be very angry about when you see them." Then they both produced their scooters in great glee.'

The trouble, I suppose, was that as a general rule they gave us what they, but not I, thought suitable, partly, I suspect from odd comments in my Mother's Journals, to stir Ian into activity—there was never any need to stir me—but mostly, I suspect, because in the early years of the century boys were seen as Little Men and girls as Little Women. No one had ever heard of sex-stereotyping nor would they have greatly cared if they had.

We must have been rather contra-suggestible children as, despite gifts like a beautiful doll's bed, sheets, blankets, covers and pillows hand-stitched by my mother, I spent most of my later childhood steeped in my father's G. H. Hentys, W. H. Kingstons, and R. M. Ballantynes and my younger aunt's bound copies of *The Captain*, (she must have been just such an other) and fervently wishing I had been born a boy (Andrew). One of my friends had the same dream and on many a Saturday afternoon we dropped over the wall from her garden into a spinney belonging to a nursery-garden and there Jack and Andrew explored and encountered (and overcame) dangers in the Rockies, on the high seas and the frozen wastes of Russia. I never quite gave up the hope that a miracle would occur and I would grow up to be a boy, according to more than one autobiography a common hope among girls of that time. Freud was way off-centre with his theory of penis envy. Few little girls of today need to wish they had been born boys but at the beginning of the century it was just plainly obvious that opportunities and freedom were there for the male and not for the female. There were some bold exceptions but for the most part teaching, typing or nursing were the occupations waiting to ensnare us.

On the other hand, despite tricycle (and half the *Invincible*) at four and a half Ian's one object in life was to be a girl. When a visitor took him to be one—he was wearing a pinafore over his tunic and ribbon tied fillet-wise round his hair—my mother assured her nothing could please him better. 'He will scarcely allow anyone to call him by his own name but as he every day almost gives himself a different name it is rather difficult to remember them at times. He was Ruth for quite a long time, also Elsie and May.' I scored because I discovered I could get him to do anything by threatening to call him a boy! Saying his prayers at night he would end with the petition,

"Make me a good girl."
Squinting through his fingers at his mother who was pretending not to hear, he would repeat,

"I SAID—make me a good GIRL!"

CHAPTER SIX

Hot Buttered Toast

BEHIND the Strathearn dining-room was a well of a room, intended as maid's bedroom. Mary mostly slept with us, only occasionally in this little dungeon. I rather fancied it because it was snug and private and different, with room only for bed, dressing-table and chair. An interior window gave light from the hall but as the walls reached up to the roof a storey above, air was obtained from a skylight controlled by a long rope over a pulley. Next came the kitchen with window over the sink looking out south into the garden. There was a scrubbed wooden table, a dresser with wooden salt-box and the hub of the house, a black-leaded and silver-shining coal range. Lighting the range was the first act of the day, kindling having been left ready the night before for without its benevolent roar there would be only luke-warm water coming from the taps and no hot breakfast. I think Mary and Martha were both that prized asset 'good risers'—not much chance of being otherwise so long as they slept with us—though I remember them groaning as they rolled out of bed to face a new day, but in our next house the sounds of early morning traffic and the clang of the first tram-cars often came through my mother's voice as she hung over the banisters exhorting Ina, Peggy or Bridget to bestir herself, though here there was not the same urgency as we had a gas cooker too.

Once well away, the range was magnificent, red coals glowing through the bars, kettle steaming, porridge simmering, the tea-pot warming. In the afternoon it might heat the flat-irons and at tea-time with luck I was allowed to sit on the elaborate silvered fender toasting first one cheek and when that became uncomfortably hot the other, while I held the toasting-fork to an especially raked-out glow to produce toast for hot buttered toast, toast of a quality no grill or electric toaster has ever equalled.

The only pictures on the kitchen walls were calendars from local tradesmen— 'With the compliments of John Scott, Grocer and Provision Merchant'. I took it very kindly of John Scott and the Butcher and Greengrocer to send us these tokens of goodwill not realising there were other families whose custom was valued as much as ours. Favourite subjects were kittens and collies, picturesque Old English cottages and massively hooved Clydesdales with haloes of gulls breasting the slopes of ploughed fields. The kitchen scarcely needed pictures for on the mantelpiece and shelves were tea-caddies and curved biscuit-tins with paintings of Mrs Siddons and of Gainsborough and Reynolds ladies with trailing feathers in their hats. There was also a Hans Hals cavalier taking his ease with out-stretched legs and smoking a long pipe. On the wall opposite the range, below the line of jangling front-door and room bells, were three silver ashet covers—like the three bears, one big, one middle-sized and one tiny—which shone in the light of the fire.

We often had our meals with Mary in the kitchen, sometimes a special tea when her mother came to visit her bringing with her Kathleen, her youngest daughter. She was a little older than I was and we were both too shy to speak. I do not know what she may ever have been told about me but hope she regarded me with an awe equal to that in which I held her. For a start she had beautiful, long, *straight* hair reaching well below her waist. She could sit on it, I was told. Of course she was far too shy to demonstrate, so I took this on trust as I did the other fact I had been told about her—she could not step on a bus without being sick! This struck me as the height of sensitivity, though a mite inconvenient—she lived some fifteen miles from Edinburgh in Gorebridge. I admired her for being able to indulge this whimsy. What did she do? Did the bus wait for her— or did she have to wait by the roadside till the next bus came along

35

when the performance was presumably repeated? But there, these were spacious unregimented days and she and her mother probably travelled by train as innumerable branch railway lines wandered then all over Lowland Scotland.

Gorebridge was a mining village though for some reason I do not think Mary's father was a miner—a baker perhaps? Mary and her older sister Ella must have 'gone into service' very young for when in 1917 her eldest brother became a war casualty he was only nineteen and Mary had been with us two or three years. I remember a highland girl telling me that when she first went off to work in the 'big house' she was fourteen and she and the other maids much of an age spent their afternoons playing hide-and-seek amongst the rhubarb in the vegetable garden. Ella may have been the more ambitious, for she I think ranked purely as a childrens' nurse, though she did not seem as sympathetic and patient as Mary who appeared content to be a 'general'.

Mary was a pleasant-looking plumpish person with light brown curling hair. She wore rimless glasses and had a mouthful of the whitest most china-looking teeth I have ever seen. This enhanced her charms in our eyes. It was not everyone who could put back in and out their own teeth. She must have been very even-tempered for she never objected to our interest in this aspect of her appearance although to our disappointment she would not demonstrate her expertise as often as we could have wished. She was naturally 'good with children' never, I suppose, having stopped to ask herself what one did to become so. With my mother she shared in the care of the house and of us. She often took us for our afternoon walk (a fetish of the times in search of fresh air), often arranging to meet Ella similarly employed with her two charges, both boys. We never fraternised, the younger, like Ian, was still pram-bound and the older nervy and unsociable. Being an inveterate little pitcher I gathered that he, although older than I, still wet his bed. "And *she* said," a downward glance at me, "mumble… mumble… mumble… mumble", "So I just said, 'well, …mumble …mumble." Not I judged a happy home for Ella nor indeed the unfortunate lad. I used to see him, although I never knew him, in later years at my brother's school and hoped life was treating him better. His shame was safe with me.

Ella's next family again consisted of two boys. The one in the pram became mildly important in the musical world and the elder, a year or so older than I, as a book-seller. As a small boy he was a terrible show-off. I expect he hated having to go for walks with two nannies, two babies and a girl. He rarely spoke to me but once sufficiently unbent at the East Gate of Warriston Cemetery to expound to me the meaning of richocheting, choosing to demonstrate by hurling gravel hard against a wall so that it stotted back and hit me. He then made off at speed on his superior scooter (spoked wheels and a brake). Another time he ran it at my legs.

At this time I used to irritate my mother and Mary on our walks with my jackdaw propensities. As I remember, I was sorry for any discarded object—pencil, hair-ribbon, buckle, and would pick them up and stuff them in my pocket. I could have been seen as an embryo collector or premature environmentalist. Sadly, my guardians were neither prescient nor sympathetic and just said it was a nasty dirty habit and to throw the things away.

Specialist shops today are filled with playthings designed to encourage muscle, eye and brain co-ordination and to subtly educate. Fun they undoubtedly are for child and adult but I am at times Philistine enough to query their value in terms of possible initiative and imagination loss. Children are superb improvisers ready to put their possessions to all manner of uses unintended by their creators, even something as simple as tying string to the handles of two dolls' tea-cups thereby transforming them into a field communication system. With us, real activities with Mary or Martha of necessity took the place of these specialised aids. When Mary scoured the steps I added my piece of decoration to the white scrolls round the edges, and when she did her baking I did mine, mixing and rolling the flour for scones and cutting it out with various sizes of cutter from thimbles to tumblers to cocoa tins on a large wooden pastry board like a tray with three raised sides. Almost better were the days when she said,

"Now, I must clean my silver."

On silver-cleaning days we saw that the range was drawing up nicely and the kettle balanced where it kept just off the boil in preparation for the later pot of tea (sterilised milk for me—ugh!) then laid out newspapers on the table before making an expedition all over the house to collect the family's store of silver. There were entrée and cake dishes, a rose bowl and christening mugs, tea-pot with cream jug and sugar bowl and tongs, besides gravy boats and sundry smaller objects, napkin rings and a condiment set whose cleaning involved carefully decanting the pepper. There were two crystal scent-jars with silver hinged lids, very difficult to clean, and my mother's dressing table set, brush, comb and mirror, perhaps the very one Uncle John had surprised her with on her twenty-first birthday. For a jewellers' family we had not very much. My mother said friends had avoided silver for wedding presents thinking there would be more than enough from my father's connections. In this they were mistaken but, as the family of a Goldsmith and Silversmith, we did know how to clean what we had. Not for us todays' tins of hard paste with scrappy pieces of sponge. We mixed our own pink liquid paste in an array of saucers and laid out cloths and soft bristled brushes and what I knew of as 'shammies'. There were worse ways of spending a winter's afternoon than in the warm kitchen, gossiping with Mary and busily rubbing away at her silver, with the firelight glinting on our handiwork—and the promise of hot-buttered toast to come.

CHAPTER SEVEN

Washday Bacchantes

IF SILVER-CLEANING afternoons were homely, cosy treats, washdays were treats too—of a completely different nature. Besides the kitchen, they involved the washhouse beyond with double sinks, mangle and copper. More importantly, they involved Mrs Marshall. Stout, with a hearty laugh and a rollicking way with her, gusts from an alien more robust existence blew from her into our quiet home. My wonder now is that a house demoralised by the activities of washday and her presence was able to rock back on an even keel before the next Monday came round.

My great-grandmother and grandparents were pillars of Dublin Street Baptist Church and supporters of its Home Mission centred in the Mission Hall at Canonmills, then a district of mixed housing with some very poor streets. My father, uncles and aunts ran various Sunday School and Bible Classes and my father led a flourishing Boys' Brigade company, the Forty-sixth. I have in my possession a slim blue volume, a *History of Dublin Street Baptist Church Edinburgh 1858-1958* written by Annie Mary Baines and presumably published about the latter year which gives an account of the conception of the Forty-sixth.

In September 1894 a daring proposal had been made to start a drilling class for boys, and permission to use the hall for this purpose on alternate Fridays, after the Band of Hope, was granted 'tentatively'. Three months later, however, the Deacons were dismayed to find that the drilling class was being called a 'Boys' Brigade'. At that time dummy rifles formed part of The Boys' Brigade equipment, and the Deacons considered that this savoured too much of militarism. A deputation was appointed to go into the matter, and by January 1895 the embryo Boys' Brigade was dead. Nearly nine years later, on 24th November 1903, Mr W. G. Chisholm applied for permission to form a Company of the Boys' Brigade, and this time permission was granted without opposition. The Forty-sixth was born.

My younger aunt, Edith, was involved with the Girls' Guildry. It was not all prayers and hymn-singing at the Mission. There were concerts, 'swarees' (soirées), the Brigade Annual Camp and sterner items like debates. My mother before her marriage had enjoyed running a small Bible Class for girls in Sherbrooke United Free Church of Scotland, Glasgow but took little part in the Dublin Street activities beyond occasionally playing the hymns for her husband's classes. She took, in general, a cooler view, noting once in her journal,

> 'Willie is to take part in a debate tonight at the Boys' Club on Tariff Reform and Free Trade. Willie is a keen Tariff Reformer. Mr Sharp his opponent is an equally keen Free Trader... It is supposed to be got up for the benefit of the boys of the club, but I'm afraid they won't do much of the debating. It should be very hot.'

The hall had a call to fame in earlier days as we can read on a plaque (designed by Tom Curr, son of Mackay and Chisholm's cashier)—

1850 1894
In this hall
Robert
Louis
Stevenson
First went
To school
circa 1857.

Father and son were both Dublin Street members and the son was the resurrector of the Brigade after the 1914-1918 war.

Mrs Marshall was caretaker of the Mission Hall from 1893 until her death in 1943 and was much appreciated as was attested by a Memorial put up to her there by the Boys' Brigade. I do not expect

40

her remuneration as caretaker was a living wage and I imagine work as a washerwoman was found for her among the women members of the church. As far as my mother was concerned, she was one of the services arranged for her by her mother-in-law as was her first servant, the eventually valued, but initially intimidating, Jessie Wallace who ruled her inexperienced young employers with an iron, albeit benevolent, rod. My mother always remembered the day she and her husband came back from a country walk bearing armfuls of spring blossom to fill the vases. Horrified, Jessie flung them out and refused to have them in the house. They were blackthorn, unlucky indoors (and in the button-hole), another superstition to add to my mother's wealth of them which I have inherited. When I knew Mrs Marshall she was the mother of young adults and lived with them and 'Mershall' for so she referred to him, at Canonmills in a rather depressing street. I got the impression that he was in some way unsatisfactory but this may have been due to the free and racy way she expressed herself. After all, at four, I had not much experience of life.

I revelled in the activity and urgency of washday. The range was stoked up higher and higher and dampers adjusted, the kettle gurgled and spat in readiness for innumerable cups of tea and steam billowed through from the washhouse with Mrs Marshall's laugh. She regaled Mary and any other listeners with tales which, judging by their riotous reception, it was maybe as well I did not understand. She was a realist and I am sure were she able to read this would take no offence when I say she was at this time no Miss Scotland nor even Miss Canonmills. Pale, lacking many teeth and shapeless, her voluminous skirt was surmounted by a sacking apron and on her head she wore a man's cap back-to-front from which escaped strands of steam-dampened hair. As she slapped and banged and rubbed the linen, she would break into songs in which I fervently joined, World War One lyrics perhaps, 'Keep the Home Fire Burning' or 'Tipperary' or a Moody and Sankey or other revivalist hymn, our favourite being 'Shall we gather at the river?' How we enjoyed the triumphant fortissimo of the chorus—

41

'YES! We'll gather at the river … that flows by the throne of God.'

'Shall we gather at the river,
Where bright angel feet have trod,
With its crystal tide for ever,
Flowing by the throne of God?'

CHORUS: 'YES! WE'LL GATHER AT THE RIVER,

The beautiful, the beautiful river,
Gather with the saints at the river,
That flows by the throne of God…

'Ere we reach the shining river,
Lay we every burden down;
Grace our spirits will deliver,
And provide a robe and crown.

Chorus: 'YES! ……………………………………………'

Mrs Marshall also expressed great admiration for my cleverness which made pleasant and unaccustomed hearing. Those with whom I shared day to day intimacy were unaccountably less impressed. "You're so sharp you'll cut yourself one day!" if a mark of attention was scarcely to be reckoned a compliment. One accomplishment of mine she refused to applaud. At this time I was earnestly practising whistling tunes in emulation of my father. "Eh! lassie" she would turn from the sink throwing up her hands, "a crawing hen and a whistling lass is no canny."

The rites of the second half of washday after the time-saving dinner of yesterday's bake-meats served up cold had been consumed, never went with the same abandon. All hands were growing tired and not so patient with a little girl who earlier had been allowed to help, even though she nearly mangled her fingers with the sheets. With luck, and sun, and a fair wind perhaps, the ironing was started. The two black fire-irons were standing ready on the trivet, faces towards the red-hot bars, the dinner-plates cleared from the table and a blanket and ironing-sheet spread there instead with the black fretted iron-holder. Tablecloths, clothes, bolster covers, pillow slips, towels, napkins were all collected, sprinkled with water, rolled and left ready in accordance with their kind until the irons were at the correct

42

temperature. Tested on a corner of the sheet or an old rag they sometimes left a singe mark when there would be a delicious warm smell in the air. Adepts held the irons up, close to their already glowing cheeks, to check their heat. The uninhibited spat on them and judged by the sizzle.

After being ironed, the linen was hung up to air on either the overhead pulley or a triple-sided clothes-horse placed near the fire, rather impeding passage. Helping to fold sheets was a good ploy but that more often took place on Tuesdays. Then Mary and I stood a sheet's length away from each other, each holding two corners. We halved and quartered the width of the sheet giving a good tug between each operation to straighten out wrinkles. Then I walked up to Mary, gave her my two corners, picked up the slack and walked backwards with it before we folded it again. The good tug following on every manoeuvre was in my opinion the best part of this exercise as should Mary's attention be momentarily distracted I could pull her end from her hands. As this meant the clean sheet landing on the floor it was a not very well-received joke, no more popular than the game in the garden when the wind was strong and my brother and I chased in and out among the drying sheets as they flapped and billowed like great white sails.

Too soon, it was time for Mrs Marshall to go home but first came the last and most relaxed cup of the day. When she had drunk this one, Mary carefully drained the dregs from her cup then putting it upside down on its saucer, turned it round three times before passing it across, unscanned, to Mrs Marshall with the request to "see what's in my cup". I leaned over her arm as she turned the cup in her hand.

"There's a looked-for letter ...and" (fishing out a long leaf) "a stranger... aye..." (testing its hardness) "it's a man, but he'll no be here the day..." She put the leaf on the back of one hand and struck it with the back of the fingers of the other, "Tuesday, Wednesday, Thursday, Friday," (the leaf fell off) "aye, Friday it'll be. And money-bags... I see money-bags... eh... but they're a long way off... but it will come... the money will come".

Mary would take the cup back and peer into it as if to confirm its foretelling—it was not unlucky to look in your own cup once it had been read—then her eye would catch the clock and from dreams of romance and prosperity her mind switched to the immediacy of supper. Rising reluctantly from the fire she gave voice to her invariable stop to present fun against which we recognised she admitted no appeal......

"Here! Come on! This'll no pay."

CHAPTER EIGHT

Blest be the Bed

UP STRATHEARN'S abrupt stairs were two double bedrooms, one single, the bathroom and the drawingroom. I feel myself plodding up one evening at the age of three, my mother ahead.

"Do you know what day this is?" she asked. "This is Christmas Eve. Tomorrow will be Christmas!"

Immediately I went into one of my quite conscious and remarkably pseudo acts—a favourite gambit of mine at this time.

"Don't tell me!" I said. "Don't tell me! I can't believe it!"
Of course I had no reason to doubt her but some remembrance of exaggerated adult expression fuelled my response.

The front bedroom was small and north-looking and not in regular use. The other two at the back of the house looked south to one of the world's most perfect views, over nursery gardens and the trees of Inverleith Park and the Botanic Garden to houses and spires of the New Town and higher to the skyline of Edinburgh. We had it all, from Arthur's Seat and the Calton Hill, along the ridge of the old town to the Castle and further west to St Mary's Cathedral with beyond it the Pentland Hills. I can still find it in me to pity a child not brought up with that vista daily to hand. A sense of the romance not only of Edinburgh but of place, was well established in me before I left that house at the age of eight, a sense heightened by the sounds which throughout my childhood floated through the clear northern air, of bells, surely more numerous then than now, and when the wind was in the right quarter, of distant bugles, from the Castle or some other military establishment no doubt, but to me they could have been the horns of Elfland.

My parents' bedroom was at the head of the stairs. As for much of this time my father was absent on war service it was for the most part my mother's from which she periodically exiled herself to the cold single bedroom when either of us had to be isolated, as children then were for even mild infectious diseases. I had chickenpox very comfortably there in the spring of 1918. Illnesses dragged on and on in those days, especially so in the case of chickenpox which was judged contagious until the very last scab fell off—and I was covered with spots. It cannot have been as much fun for my mother as she was eight months pregnant and very desirous of keeping Ian free of infection (she failed), and of getting me out of her room so that it could be scoured and disinfected for her confinement.

One of the keenest pleasures in life I am sure is the enjoyment of a mild childhood disease. Relaxed, with no responsibilities of life or lessons, nor with as yet any intimations of mortality, you are plied with food and drink and books and comics, even new toys or jigsaws. In the morning after washing and doing your teeth—all in basins in bed with a thick towel laid over the covers— you then sat shakily wrapped in a quilt while your bed was made smooth and crumb-free. After climbing back you pulled the bedclothes right up to your chin while the room was aired—windows open top and bottom—the carpet swept and the dusting done. Once the germs had all gone out and the windows were shut you sat up and breathed in the presumably healthier and certainly colder air.

As I sat, happily cocooned in my spotty retreat, downstairs and around life went on. Door and telephone bells rang, doors opened and shut, my little brother's voice could be heard, remote from me and any chance of squabbles. Only once was this peace shattered and that when I was much older in Wardie Road. Suddenly there was a most tremendous clatter and jangle and crash followed by a howl from our maid who was of a hit or miss, slapdash (not to mention porridge-burning) proclivity. Infectious or no, I left my bed and peeped over the banisters to find that while washing the hall she had somehow wedged her brush under the grandmother clock and brought it to the tiled floor. The lamenting author of this mishap was not at all hurt and I had time only for a word of commiseration before my mother, returning from shopping and entering on this scene of flood, spilt pendulums and woe added her outcry and I slipped back into bed. Usually household sounds were muted, changing from sweeping to the tinkle of dishes and then pleasant smells ascended the stairs in the van of dinner. After dinner came a slight comatose period, even a snooze, though this during chickenpox was taken with ears half-alerted for the door-bell for nearly every day my grandmother came to visit me. It occurs to me now that she may have been at least as much interested in the welfare of her pregnant daughter-in-law but naturally I thought her attentions were all for me, especially as she always brought my favourite sponge-cakes with her for my tea. These were of the kind still sold in packets for the making of trifle but of a vastly superior species, larger and crisper without and softer within. We had them as a follow-on from toast or muffins in the firelit dusk of the February day, for during illness there was a coal-fire in the bedroom. Another pleasure was to have a wash-down before it, cramped into the baby-bath on the hearth-rug. Sometimes this happened twice a day since with the imminent arrival of the monthly nurse and, as transpired, sister Marjorie, my mother was getting rather frantic in her efforts to rid me of my scabs and return me unblemished to where I belonged. It was thought water might loosen them but I was covered, even into my hair, so there was no quick expulsion from my Paradise.

During this illness I became able to read confidently. Some time previously I had gone with my mother to an educational publishers, McDougall's I suppose, in Craig's pleasant, now ravished by developer, eighteenth century St James's Square, where we possessed ourselves of a reading primer. About country children and animals, it was mostly in words of one syllable. In longer words hyphens separated the com-pon-ent parts. Being a class of one, I went through it quickly so it is not engraven on my mind as must be some of those Beacon and similar Readers which bogged down Education Authorities during the Second World War. Shortages of money and paper meant a class being thrown on the varying resources of individual teachers and it could be stuck with the same book for an entire year. Staff-rooms could chant them.

'Sing Mother sing.
Can Mother sing?
Mother can sing.
Sing to Pat Mother.
Sing to Mother Pat.
Sing Mother sing.'

So besides being a time of enjoyment, my chickenpox was also a time of achievement. Going to bed a moderate reader I emerged able to take in my stride the weekly *Rainbow* with Mrs Bruin and her Boys and Bluebell the little fairy school-girl besides annuals galore and books like Agnes Grozier Herbertson's *House of Bricks*. In this Freddie, like me, was ill in bed and like me built with bricks. The difference between us was that Freddie was visited by the Bee-man, a marvellous character who, with his dog, took up residence in Freddie's brick house.

All memories of childhood illness are not as happy as this. Whooping-cough was a nightmare. Three of us had it at the same time. We spent our days in the big upstairs nursery in Wardie Road all coughing and whooping at much the same time thus necessitating concerted rushes to be sick in a basin in the corner. If our mother or mother's help was in a mood for diversion she had it listening to our whoops which were all different. Ian provided another. He refused to be cheered by any of his favourite foods, especially he laid an injunction for the duration on poached eggs, feeling they were too good to be wasted in perpetual sicking-up. We eventually went to Melrose Hydropathic to recuperate where we were looked on a little askance as one of us, though guaranteed infection-free, retained an impressive whoop. From much earlier, I have dark confused memories of awakening to agonising earache which my parents tried to assuage with warm oil or to frightening attacks of what I suppose was a form of croup. As my mother propped me up against the pillows and tried to calm me she would call,

"Willie! you had better bring the Ipecac!"

I never knew whether or not to welcome the arrival of my pyjama-clad father with this remedy for I hated it although I recognised that it would bring me relief. It was liquid, its full name being the grand if misleading Ipecacuahana Wine and I was given some drops, probably in a wine-glass, the medicinal being the only use such things had in our home. Sure enough, in a short time I could cough away the obstruction, possibly be sick, but I could breathe again and soon, my chest perhaps rubbed with eucalyptus or camphorated oil and with the comfort of a freshly filled stone 'pig' and a reassuring night-light, I would drop off again into peaceful sleep.

Another time I dreaded the approach of my father was when he came bearing his favourite panacea whose name I was never sure of—a switched or, as I sometimes decided, Swiss egg. It was less of a cure than a source of nourishment—and did nothing to endear the Swiss to me—being a nursery variant of the restorative raw egg in brandy. I think it was in sweetened slightly warmed sterilised milk and I found it revolting, quite unlike his out-of-character other standby which he gave us when we were older and had a cold coming on. After a hot bath, or more likely hot mustard foot-bath in front of a fire, we would settle in bed with hot stone pig to await a hot toddy to ward off chills. This sweetened hot milk was more than palatable containing as it did the teetotaller's typical over-generous ration of (medicinal) whisky. By morning the cold had usually been routed.

In my normal state of health in our Inverleith Gardens home I slept in the room next to my mother's with Mary and, after Marjorie was born, Ian too. After being put to bed at a really ridiculously early hour I used to slip out of bed to gaze on the beautiful view over Edinburgh and spy on more fortunate mortals still up. Little wonder I felt a rapport with the small Robert Louis Stevenson—

> 'And does it not seem hard to you,
> When all the sky is clear and blue,
> And I should like so much to play,
> To have to go to bed by day?'

Sometimes, no way nearly ready for sleep, I read (bad for the eyes), or rose and engaged in other activities, pleasant by their surreptitiousness. In smallish houses they were usually quickly detected as when in a rented villa I enlisted my brother as fellow criminal and led him off to the bathroom where I thoroughly soaped the bath. He did not participate but was a very satisfactory audience as I slid up and down. I have always hated, whether lying or sitting, doing so looking at a blank wall so when in bed in Strathearn, because of the position of the window, I lay on my left side. Someone, it must have been a temporary maid, refused to let me do this on the grounds that I would squash my heart. Off she would go having bedded me down on my right side but lurk outside the door waiting for the creak as I turned when she would bound back in and turn me over again. It showed, I suppose, a gratifying desire for my welfare but started my waking nightmares when, as I lay facing the wall, eyes shut or open, there was a perpetual movement up it of giant black evil figures. Possibly I originated them myself by screwing up my eyes but I was unable to control them and became for a time quite terrified.

In the winter of 1919 the household was smitten with the Spanish Influenza, first my mother, then Mary, then Ian. Mary's turned to pneumonia so she was left to single occupancy of our room and Ian and I were put in beds moved into the drawing-room, a pleasing novelty. Ian was scarcely ill and Marjorie was caged in her drop-side beside us because there was nothing else to do with her. She was at an irritating stage for real invalids, walking round and round the cot shaking the bars, dropping down with a bump and bouncing up again.

I well remember the day I took to my bed. My mother, Mary and Ian had all gone down in their varying degrees at much the same time but I was determinedly up, though beginning to feel as ill as I did not know one could, much worse than chickenpox. I was refusing to admit it and angrily brushing aside all suggestions that I go to bed. I was with my father and doctor Uncle Ernie in the parlour when my father, who must have been fairly distraught in the midst of his ailing

50

household, showed a guile I did not know he possessed. Half rising
to his feet, but probably not knocking out his pipe, he said,

"Well—what about coming out for a bit on your scooter?"

That did it. Well did I know that I had no strength to step on the
scooter, let alone push it. I capitulated and joined the party in the
drawingroom. It was possibly the next day that our Aunt Edith
arrived to take over the house but she was scarcely with us before
the influenza took her over and she retired home to bed. Then a
Dublin Street connection, daughter of the firm's cashier, came down
but almost immediately had to retreat to see to casualties in the family
home. Finally a nurse was secured, two actually, the first succumbed
before she reached us. Whether her replacement was a good or bad
nurse I do not know. Certainly she was not agreeable. She tried to
reduce our chaotic sickroom to the tucked-in tidiness nurses like, but
as she had no way with children, nor I should imagine much time
to have a way, with little success. To my pride I had been second
worst in the house but by now both Ian and I were well enough to
welcome the absence of adult supervision and certainly to resent any
from an uncongenial stranger. As far as possible we untidily pursued
our individual avocations, he with bricks and models and I following
the extraordinary lives and habits of the Children of Israel as
described in the small-print, gilt-edged pages of a Victorian Bible
once the property of my deceased Great Uncle Robert given me by
Aunt Barbara, while Marjorie continued her athletic career round her
dropside. We had other, better grounds for disliking this nurse
because she dosed us, almost every day it seemed, with that
nauseous panacea of the early twentieth century, Castor Oil. Castor
Oil is bad enough in any guise but she chose, ineffectively, to attempt
to mask its taste with orange juice—after wartime shortages what a
waste of oranges. She spoilt oranges for me, I was into my teens
before I willingly ate another, as for years they brought back to me
an undercurrent of oily nastiness.

During all this time my father remained well, going when free of
us, to his business as usual. I believe he confessed to almost, for one
day, having a faint suspicion of a cold. I remember my grandmother

51

visiting us at the beginning of the household's collapse and telling us we must all gargle with and sniff up our noses a dilution of water and a patent medicine very popular at the time, though I believe it later fell into disrepute, called I think Yadil. I fancy my mother had been using it for I remember its strong garlic smell. My father however did not like strong smells like garlic or even cheese and said he was having nothing to do with it. I thought it very bold of him to speak back to and disobey my grandmother but on the other hand not at all the thing for my grandmother to speak to my father as she did.

"But Willie!" she said, "You must do it. It's most important."

To my shocked admiration my father went further and vulgarly said it seemed to be at least an economic measure as after having sniffed up you could spit out into a bowl and use it over and over again. He said he would stick to the pipe which was scarcely ever, lit or unlit, out of his mouth. Rarely did it belie his trust. The only virus to best it was that of chickenpox which he had to endure in Hamilton Barracks. Perhaps the Officers' Mess did not favour pipes.

CHAPTER NINE

Drawingroom Occasions

THE DRAWING ROOM was the scene for my mother's At Home days when she sat, hat on head, awaiting visitors on third Tuesdays, her Day. Aunt Barbara's was second Wednesdays as had been my mother's when she was Miss Stewart of Ardenlee. Then the room with the piano with candle-holders and painted flowers, the heavy black screen with decoration of silvery branches, and the tea-table covered with white lace-bordered cloth on which were set out silver cake baskets and the best china—perhaps Aunt Jeannie's? —with delicate flowers, looked very pretty indeed. Often I handed round the sandwiches and cakes and shortbread lending an interested ear to the conversation. The most successful At Home days from our point of view were when not too many ladies attended—straying fingers and later our supper benefited.

Besides these recurring secular occasions one religious rite was solemnised in the drawingroom. This was the mass christening of the three eldest Chisholm children. When my parents were married in the Windsor Hotel, Glasgow by a minister of the United Free Church of Scotland, my father was a Baptist. Although my mother did sometimes attend Baptist services and played the piano for my father's Sunday youth classes I do not think she was ever tempted to become a member. When I became of church-going age, quite early as with my father's absence in the army I was company for her, we attended St James's United Free Church, two doors from us and when away from Edinburgh, any Scottish Presbyterian church as I fancy he did too. As a young man he had enjoyed his work with the various boys' organisations but probably came to find the Baptist church too restrictive in its outlook. My parents enjoyed visits to the theatre, Barrie being a favourite dramatist and on their rare trips to London they saw light opera and musicals—'No, No, Nanette', 'Katya' and 'The Merry Widow' from all of which they brought back the music. In Edinburgh we saw D'Oyly Carte productions,—I remember 'The Yeomen of the Guard',—'Lilac Time', 'Rose Marie' and Harry Lauder—beside attending Usher Hall concerts. My mother would have enjoyed more serious drama too, she records them both attending 'Faust' but also her husband sleeping his way through 'The Tales of Hoffman.' The Baptist Church however frowned on all theatre and indeed it was a boast among many devout Scots, not only Baptists, that they had never darkened a theatre door. I doubt if my Uncle Ernie ever did. He did go to concerts as he was intensely musical ('Could come home and play ever note he heard' so ran family lore) so he presumably would at least have enjoyed opera. But then again he might not have—the loose behaviour on stage would not have been to his taste. A man of multitudinous narrow views he was rather against kissing—a peck on an avuncular cheek was all right, but never on the mouth.

Our father by the time of Marjorie's birth was a member of the Church of Scotland, perhaps he changed when he had to declare his religion during his war service, I do not know. What however was clear, was that there were now three little Chisholms waiting to be called into a state of grace. I used to think that in our circumstances it was such a good thing we had not had to wait to be christened before being given a Christian name which was almost a necessary thing to have. In my childhood people looking into a pram never seemed to ask, "What is her name?" but always, "What are you going to call her?" which seemed to put the poor child's existence a little in jeopardy.

On Tuesday 9th April 1918 Mr Maclellan, who had been my mother's minister in Sherbrooke Church Glasgow and had been the chief of the three who officiated at my parents' wedding, came across from Murrayfield where he now had the charge of Roseburn to conduct a service in our drawingroom. Mr Maclellan was of great interest to me as he was often held up to us as a walking cautionary tale. He had only the sight of one eye having been blinded in the other when a nail which he was extracting from a packing-case with the claw of a hammer flew out and struck it. I have been wary of hammers ever since.

I felt rather proud of being involved personally in a christening at the mature age of seven and self-importantly handed over a note requesting that I be permitted to leave morning school half an hour early—we had no afternoon classes. I hurried home and after dinner was cleaned and brushed and dressed in my brown magyar-sleeved velvet dress and brown stockings. Ian wore his knitted blue silk jersey which, like my frock, had been made by our mother. It had a chequer-board pattern of different types of stitch. He also wore his blue corduroy 'knickers'. He stood even better than I did. I was thought to be self-conscious. Baby however stole the show. She was dressed in the fine white cotton Victorian christening robe with daisy motifs in which my mother and her brothers and my grandmother Mary Jane and Great Aunt Barbara and the rest of their family had all been christened. My sister Moira also wore it and daughters Rosemary and Caroline and Katy, the last just caught in the nick of time to be inserted into it before she outgrew it. Penelope at five and Terence at nearly four had definitely outgrown it when, owing to flittings and parental inertia, they shared Caroline's christening, the one in a blue and white striped gingham the other in a brown hand-knitted sweater with Fair Isle on chest and cuffs.

'Baby was awfully good and lay in my lap smiling up at me. She smiles a great deal and started to do it when she was barely a week old. Mr Maclellan said she looked a very wise little person as if she had been here quite a long time.'

The water for the christening was in the silver rose-bowl which had been a wedding present. According to my mother's journal it was a simple but impressive little ceremony. Matching the simplicity, there was for the following pleasant and friendly tea only a plain cake—no icing on account of wartime restrictions. Aunt Barbara had come through from Glasgow to share in the occasion for which, noted my mother 'I was very glad as only Annie came down from Claremont Crescent'. As the date must have been fixed for quite a while to allow for the minister's commitments and my father's leave from the army this rather suggests family 'feelings' perhaps over our change of religious allegiance. Aunt Annie, however, for all her vagueness was possessed of a vein of gentle obstinacy in the face of intolerance.

My first piano lessons took place in this room, first from my mother and then from Minnie Burton, daughter of Dublin Street adherents. She looked rather stern as she had straight brown hair parted in the middle and drawn severely to the sides and wore glasses, but she was not. She was a very nice person and a good teacher whom I liked very much—not only because she straight-away gave me a proper music book with proper tunes for both hands. We did use some Adam Carse books of exercises but I had also Walter Carroll's 'Scenes at a Farm' and the one she first produced which I thought looked really grown-up. I think every piece was the whole page not just two lines as in the early Walter Carroll books. I have forgotten both title and composer, perhaps it was Thomas H. Dunhill, but it had a buff cover with a picture on it of scarlet poppies and golden sheaves of corn. I think Minnie Burton must have been quite a psychologist in a quiet way. I continued with her for some years, going to her parents' house in Queen Street, but eventually it became too difficult to fit in her times with the demands of school. She once gave me a delicate bracelet of pink and white glass twisted like barley-sugar sticks which for some reason I have always thought came from India.

Another memory of the Inverleith Gardens drawingroom is of my mother and myself singing at the piano with Ian in attendance. He was far from sharing our cultural tastes ('had to be dragged against his will to the Scottish National Gallery' a later journal entry records) but let us pass unhindered from old English to Scots to drawingroom album music. Among our favourites were 'The Shepherd's Cradle Song' and 'Ma Curley-headed Baba' but the one we really enjoyed was 'Rothesay Bay' which we both loved, she no doubt because it spoke to her of girlhood and I because it spoke to me of the happiness of holidays with Aunt Barbara and the Uncles. Ian never cared for it, possibly our sentimental rendering had sickened him, and in later years dismissed the bereaved hairst-lassie as a careless peasant who mislaid all her relatives. At this time there was however one song he always joined in and kept on demanding, Arne's arrangement of 'Where the Bee Sucks.'

'Merrily, merrily, shall I live now
Under the blossom that hangs on the bough...'

He was only three or four and looked so sweet chanting away, "Meddily, meddily..." that we made the dire mistake of applauding him. He became quite above himself and ever afterwards, throughout the last verse and reaching into the silence which should have succeeded our tasteful rendering of Shakespeare's lyric, his determined, tuneless and unstoppable drone hammered on, "Meddily, meddily, meddily, meddily...."

CHAPTER TEN

Out and About...

THOUGHTS of the garden hold as many memories as do those of the house. We passed through the front garden only when going between gate and door. It had a square of grass and by the side of the path a sycamore tree. The back gardens were long between their spiked railings dividing each from its neighbours. That of the Roses to our right was well tended with many flowers besides the fine sweet-peas. We had sunflowers in the bed bordering the Roses and roses and other flowers on the opposite side and in the bed beneath the stone wall at the bottom of the garden. Here too was rhubarb and some vegetables and a rubbish heap which helped us scramble up the wall from which the Castle and the hills could be seen. My mother in her journal records planting new flowers and bushes but in those days she evidently had her priorities right for in the same entry as that in which she extols the benefits of whole milk for babies she writes

> 'Elaine and Ian are making forts, dug-outs etc in one of the flower borders, a nice messy occupation.'

A wooden summer-house in which Aunt Barbara used fleetingly to sit, she was an active lady, stood half-way down the garden. It was rather sinister. A rat had once run under it. I envisioned him still there, his sharp eyes on our ankles. Outside the parlour and kitchen windows, flanked by the wash-house and coal-cellar to the left and a privet hedge to the west, was a sparsely gravelled rectangle containing a meat-safe, a large slatted and meshed wooden one on legs, and a wooden folding garden seat of uncomfortable design.

Here it was I embarked on my first attempt at world travel. There is a photograph taken of me that day. I was four, equipped with a wooden rifle and wearing a toy officer's hat. I had set all my animals, Buphba, Mappy, Little Teddy and their mates on the seat to watch me, then taking up my spade (wooden), I started off to dig down through the hard-packed ground to Australia, to see for myself those odd beings under us who must walk about head-downwards. By dinner time I was losing strength and impetus and desisted. The failure of my attempt made me feel the Antipodes to be really another world so I am in no way surprised that even now I have not set eye on them. At a later date in the garden, inspired by *Alice Through the Looking-Glass*, I determinedly walked away from objects hoping to fetch up against them and also practised flying from the wall. Neither experiment was outstandingly successful though I brought myself to believe I had floated down the stairs. Perhaps I did.

It was in the garden, earlier than this, that my mother called me to see my first aeroplane, two of them actually, small, because they were reasonably high above me and of course in those days they were small. They were travelling much more slowly than such things do now so I was able to watch their progress at leisure while she told me there were men in them. Not that I had asked. I do remember once standing in the bathroom making myself quite giddy with the thought of eternity—for ever and ever and ever andeveraneveranever ...... and ever ......but on the whole the poor Indian with untutored mind (? Lo) was an eager speculator compared to me. My younger sister was the one with the enquiring mind. I remember hurrying home from a Sunday walk to proudly boast to our mother of the question she had propounded in the Cinder Path, "When God made the world out of nothing, where did He stand?"

For me, I was quite content to see those two black specks as two black specks. Mankind would not have travelled far along the road of knowledge had surmising been left to ancestors like me.

But I am in good company— '...If the sun on some portentous morn were to make his first appearance in the West, I verily believe, that, while all the world were gasping in apprehension about me, I alone should stand unterrified, from sheer incuriosity and want of observation.' So Charles Lamb in the guise of Elia. Of course when my mother told me about the men I went into my accustomed routine.

"No! Men! Don't tell me! There can't be!"

I remember it as clear as day and, for what it is worth, the clothes I was wearing, a crotal-coloured stockinette dress with sunflower-yellow braid round neck and sleeves and knickers to match. A snap-shot of me in this dress gives my age as two.

Apart from sister Marjorie taking her first quite confident step and Mr Rose's leap, one of the more dramatic events in that garden, the build-up to later less pleasant scenes in the house, took place one sunny morning when Ian and I, having balanced a clothes-pole on a kitchen chair, were taking turns practising walking up it. Suddenly Ian, trading on the leniency usually accorded him on account of his tender years and winning smiles, pushed past me to take an out-of-order turn. I, not being a gullible adult, naturally pushed back, whereon he sank his teeth in my upper arm. I yelled and hit him and he yelled and rushed into the house shouting, "She hit me! She hit me!" My mother hustled me upstairs and put me over her knee. Maddened, not so much by pain as the unjustice, I thrust my arm at her. "He bit me! He bit me!"

She could indeed see that he had—I was able to exhibit the evidence for quite a while—so bustled back downstairs to the kitchen where my little brother was looking beatific. Before he saw my mother's expression he gave me a triumphant smile—then for the first and only time in my life I saw a smile being wiped off a face—as he in turn was invited upstairs. The odd thing that has stuck in my mind about this scene is that Mary, stirring something in a pan, must have been transfixed by the rapid maelstrom of yells and passages up and down the stairs for she was standing amazed, in exactly the same attitude when I descended as when I had been dragged up.

It was not only in the garden that we got our ration of fresh air. My mother was a fiend for it and we were always being taken walks.

60

This suited me. I enjoy urban walks and did as a child. In our neighbourhood besides parks and nursery gardens there was a great variety of houses and gardens about whose inhabitants one could speculate and whose dogs one could greet through their gates. The long stretch of Inverleith Place was worth it for two magnificent russet Pomeranian friends. Shops too were more individual and interesting then than now when the bulk of them are chain-stores or carbon copies the one of any dozen other. Most shops then 'delivered' and customers could find their messages home before them. The message-boys had specially adapted bicycles with built-in carriers for their large baskets. I envied them what I saw as their free life, whistling as they cycled through the streets and meeting gangs of friends at street corners.

There were a great number of shops at Goldenacre, at least three grocers, two green-grocers, three and later four bakers, two chemists, two stationers, one with a good lending library, two butchers, a fish-shop, two drapers, two sweetie shops and a post-office and dairies and many others all with their own specialities. Many of the shopkeepers were the owners, so over the years we got to know them and they us and they took a real interest in our lives and purchases. The nearest of the drapers was a great favourite with me. Besides elastic, wool, thread, needles and thimbles and so on—all sold to the customers' needs and choice and not in nasty little tightly sealed plastic packs in the numbers or amounts decreed by the wholesalers—there were shelves of desirable Christmas or birthday presents for mothers and maids—or me. There were well-stocked and attractive needle-cases, tape-measures springing in and out of decorative holders and ornaments. I still possess a Bonzo and a charming blue china pussy. There were all manner of pincushions, some round and tightly covered in shiny chintz, some made like china birds, ducks and even a kingfisher, whose stuffed backs were decorated with multicoloured pins.

Nearby there was also a cobbler. We thought, perhaps truthfully, that he was a hero from 'The' or some other war because he had only one leg and used a crutch. When the bell over his shop-door rang

61

he limped in from his workroom at the back and unerringly picked our mended shoes from what looked like a jumble sale of chaotic footwear. The only shop I disliked was the butcher's with its smell of death and Peter Rabbits and Benjamin Bunnies and beautiful pathetic hares hanging around the door. An enforced visit to it was made endurable by the odd fact that the butcher himself was a friendly man who never fussed when I messed up the sawdust on his floor, making castles or drawing patterns on it with my foot.

Of the bakers, our favourite, so far as goods were concerned, was Mackies, although the girls in MacVitties were more generous with free buns and 'one for baby'—how diet-conscious mothers of today would hate them. In most bakers too, 'the bakers' dozen' (thirteen) was still standard custom. Standing in Mackies we would debate what we would have for tea—individual creamy cakes were only for Sundays though that treat was sometimes marred by nasty scenes when a quicker eater grabbed the one your heart had been set on. Of plainer cakes, a general favourite was what we called 'volcano cake'. Circular, it had a hole in the middle and the thin water icing was sprinkled with coconut. Then there were 'Double-U's', flaky, sticky pastry in the shape of W's. Custard-slices came into the category of tea-party cakes (as a larger school-girl I regularly made them from a packet for one special friend and her daughters) but Windsor biscuits—I never remember calling them so—soft round biscuit with a filling and half a cherry on each iced top—were reckoned plainer. Their real, pre-1914, name was German biscuits as the real pre-1914 name of the North Sea was the German Ocean.

Our own grocer was in Inverleith Row but we occasionally went to a nearer one which was a roomy corner shop with big windows and a lot of floor space more like a country than a town store. It kept brightly polished apples in barrels and the owner had an odd name, Pitkeathley, almost as odd as the one a cousin of my father's had, Plenderleith, but he was just called Plen. There was a Barber and Hairdresser with striped red and white pole over his door but whose best, uncapitalised, advertisement was the sight of his two daughters with shining luxuriant heads of hair. Other shops showing the traditional badges of their trade were the chemists with pestle and mortar swaying above their doors and large coloured pharmacist jars in their windows.

In the days of the First World War there were still in the Granton and Inverleith districts of Edinburgh many rural walks. There was scarcely a house between us and the village of Davidson's Mains two miles to the west. It is now an enlarged suburb between which and Granton are contiguous housing schemes. There was a mainly disused works' railway (to Bruce Peebles) passing under a curved bridge over which we hung every year to admire the wild roses along the embankment. The lawn of the farm at Drylaw produced masses of the earliest snowdrops, target for a spring walk. We never picked either the roses or snowdrops, just admired. Over from the Ferry Road and round by Craigleith Quarry was all country and there was the shore road by West Granton Pier and the gracious seventeenth century house of Caroline Park with its elusive ghostly lady and memories of Lady John Scott although the ghost was not of her. This was a pleasantly diversified walk with us first picking our way over rails and between wagons and sniffing the strange, not entirely disagreeable, smell from Caroline Park's incongruous neighbour, the Gasometer. Sometimes we strayed aside and went right out the West Pier to the Esparto Grass ships from the Baltic with their foreign speaking crews. Beyond Caroline Park, still on the landward side, were the remains of Granton Castle and the submerged quarry. This had been a viable concern until one night the sea rushed in, taking half the Quarry Master's house with it. Fortunately he had wakened with a feeling of unease, noticed a crack widening in the ceiling and hurried his family out so there was no loss of life. Usually we turned up Gypsies' Brae, near the mansion where Chopin had once visited, to Crewe Toll where under the railway bridge we could call up echoes. Occasionally we continued along the foreshore to Cramond, a rough walk before the part-way esplanade was made. Cramond, with picturesque tiled houses, church and tidal estuary with low-tide access to Cramond Island, and memories of the Romans and the Guidman of Ballengeich, was another world. There was a ferry with

63

boatman who would row you over to the grounds of Dalmeny House with its springtime snowdrops and haunted Barnbougie Castle. When unencumbered by the youngest members of the family we sometimes continued along the five mile stretch to the Forth Bridge at Queensferry where fiction was scarcely to be distinguished from history in mingled memories of the Sainted Queen Margaret and David Balfour and his villainous Uncle Ebenezer and Captain Hoseason of the brig *Covenant*.

A favourite Sunday walk was to the Breakwater. Down Granton Road we went, perhaps visiting the farm in Rosebank Road on the way, till at the top of Granton Steps we looked down at the Forth, the Breakwater and harbour and East and West Piers and beyond to the Kingdom of Fife. The Paddle steamer *William Muir* sailed from the East Pier to Burntisland. A line of railway ran to a platform on the berth for from 1850 until 1890, when the Forth Bridge was opened, the world's first train ferry crossed from here to Fife. Opposite the entrance to the piers was Granton Square where the cars (trams) turned although a few continued along Lower Granton Road towards Pilrig and Leith. During the 1914 war huts stood here, canteen and rest-rooms I suppose for the various naval and military personnel on duty at the harbour which was barred to civilian access. Voluntary groups gave entertainments and I remember one at which two of my friends recited their pièce de résistance party verses, one with 'Great, big, beautiful, wonderful world' and the other with 'Little Orphan Annie' and 'The Whistle that the Wee Herd Made'.

At this time there were not many houses in Granton Road—some villas and the inevitable nursery garden were near the south end with the suburban line Granton Road Station. Halfway down on the east side was a block of tenements which I remember for the semi-circular windows above their main doors whose shape I admired and was told were fanlights—a pleasing and appropriate new word. Before the Steps, to left and right, were two roads with large houses in their own grounds. I did not know then but have learned since that my great-great-grand-uncle the eminent artist Robert Scott Lauder made his last home in Wardie Crescent to the left. However we did know that Challenger Lodge in Boswall Road to the right (formerly Wardie Lodge and now St Columba's Hospice) had been given its name by Sir John Murray to commemorate the ship in which he had sailed in the *Challenger* 1872–76 expedition to obtain scientific data for the drawing up of navigational charts. To be truthful, we did not know all this then but we did know that this attractive Grecian-style house had belonged to a famous sailor explorer. Nearer the steps was the headquarters of the Royal Forth Yacht Club marked by an enormous anchor, a relic of the 1564 siege of Leith. Again details were obscure but the ambience of great deeds was there. Boswall Road stood high above Lower Granton Road and the railway line, and the houses there encompassed views from the Forth Bridge to Inchkeith, with Inchcolm, Aberdour and a large part of Fife with what a home-sick maid called the High Binns and Low Binns above Burntisland, and beyond them the Fife Lomonds. In clear conditions Ben Ledi and other Highland hills could be made out as indeed could glimpses of them all from our own top windows while further east was Kirkcaldy famed to us not for its Wemyss pottery or manufacture of linoleum but for a consequence of the latter—in the words of a poem by M. C. S. 'its queer-like smell'. When our holiday train bound for the more salubrious air of Crail and the East Neuk drew near Kirkcaldy we opened the windows wide and sniffed in rapturous anticipation. It was I suppose a form of glue-sniffing of which the inhabitants must have involuntarily and perpetually partook, though I never heard of them 'going on trips' or suffering from delusions other than the quite reasonable one that they as Fifers were among the salt of the earth.

On our walks to the Breakwater we went down the steps to the Granton Hotel, crossed the road and a few yards to the west passed through an archway made by the railway line. We rarely played on the beach there though it was pleasantly sandy, it being one of the many places my mother thought not quite clean. As to that she was probably right comparing it as she did with the quiet shores of Bute, although even with a harbour to one side, the fishing village of Newhaven to the east and the port of Leith beyond, its state then would probably compare very favourably with the nowadays polluted shores of this island and the seas world-wide. Occasionally her longing for the sea must have overcome her apprehension of germs for we did spend some happy afternoons there, after one of which she admitted to her journal, 'it was really very clean'.

The object of a Sunday walk, however, was to walk and we went along, either on the giddy-making smooth outside stones with the steep slope of unhewn stones below to the sea, or skipped and jumped on the rough blocks in the middle. Halfway out were steps from which men, and in those days only men, could bathe. They left their clothes in heaps and to my admiration swam about out of their depths. Some had quick dips even in January.

Our parents, their minds no doubt on domestic matters like dinner or the maid's day out, often turned before the end. It was best when we had time to go right to the harbour light on the wooden platform where men fished or sat and smoked, their lines fastened to the rails looking after themselves. Crossing the slatted footbridge gave a feeling of adventure for you could look down and see the tide running below. In later years this feeling was to return when the wind caught the sails as we left the shelter of the harbour for the open firth in the *Wana*, the small sailing boat, with marked lack of amenities, which my brother sailed with two friends. They raced her but we had leisurely cruises too, up to and under the Forth Bridge and across the Forth to land on Inchcolm with its twelfth century abbey. The Fife volume of *The Buildings of Scotland*, 1988, edited Colin McWilliam, describes it as 'now a popular resort for seals and the more discriminating tourist'. On the day I best remember, it was, apart from two unobtrusive strangers, ours alone. We swam from the boat then went ashore and wandered through the sunlit ruins.

Contrariwise, it was often a great relief to slip back past the light into the still waters of the harbour and feel the sails lose the wind. Particularly was this so after the annual Ladies Race (of the Almond, not Royal Forth Yacht Club) which took place on a midweek evening come wind, come weather. And blustery weather did often seem to come. It was with sinking feelings that during the day I watched strong trees bend and toss their branches. The main rule of the race was that the helmsman must be a helmswoman. Unless this helmswoman was more experienced than were the majority of the dragooned sisters or girlfriends this caused great frustrations among the normally male crews. In the case of the *Wana,* Ian and Michael and Pat, a pair of brothers, were all skippers and always argued anyhow at the top of their voices as to whether to go about or luff her or (at the same moment) to gybe/don't gybe her. In desperation I implored them to drop the nauticalese and simply direct me to Fife or Lothian.

On the last day of one season, in October, we did not return to Granton at all. Although what could have been described as a stronger than strong wind was blowing and a more than boisterous sea stirring, so inured was I to perpetual arguments and friendly recriminations that it did not occur to me that this was anything other than a normal, late season, Sunday afternoon sail until I realised that, for once, all voices were speaking as one and what they were saying was that we would never make it and had better run for Leith. When we eventually reached the shelter of the docks I was despatched home to assure our families of our safety while the others remained to berth the *Wana.* Rain-streaked and sticky with salt, I climbed a vertical ladder and rose into the gaze of the well-dressed after-lunch strollers at the very spot where, as a plaque on the wall revealed to me, King George the Fourth on the fifteenth of August 1822 had first set foot on Scottish soil. Since Charles the Second he was the first reigning monarch to visit Scotland and he had had to be invited. I wondered if he looked as storm-tossed as I, as I made my stiff and yellow-oilskinned way to the road to a car-stop.

All in all, these sailing summers of the 'thirties gave me some of the most profound pleasure I have ever known. Mind and body were, if not always in tune with, always in touch with a power beyond ourselves. At times we had the deep satisfaction of achievement or as on one June evening a sensation of utter content as we moved leisurely homeward over a whispering sea before a light, following wind whose every puff breathed the warmth of summer.

A Breakwater walk I did not go, also occurred on a Sunday. I heard my father and mother repeatedly call to me to come and get ready and finally to threaten they would go without me. Being engrossed with brick-building on the parlour floor I paid no heed except occasionally to mutter, "I'll come jusnow". Jusnow was a great word with me. It meant soon, when I feel like it. I was always going to do things jusnow.

Suddenly I realised that the beseeching voices were silent and as I raised my head I heard the click of the front door closing. They HAD gone without me! Furious, I rushed to the door and in an outburst of tears and rage hammered on it, my anger intensified by the sparkling rays shining through the red and blue and yellow glass telling of the lovely day outside.

This cold-blooded treatment was supposed to 'teach her a lesson' but like all lessons imparted in this way failed of its purpose. I hated them for it and were it worthwhile to keep up such an old grudge would still! It is of little comfort to reflect now that possibly they were equally miserable on their walk!

CHAPTER ELEVEN

Mabel and the Three Bears

A WALK to the Botanics—the Royal Scottish Botanic Garden—provided a variety of pleasures, too many for any one visit. These Botanic Gardens are in age, in Britain, second to those of Oxford and I would dare to say one of the most beautiful, if not the most beautiful, in the world but this, as I realised during a tour of Mauritius, is a delicate matter. I was in a group being shown over the gardens there when the guide, a young girl, suddenly said, "These are the second most beautiful botanical gardens in the world".

Intrigued by this assured statement, someone of course asked which were the most beautiful. She shrugged and confessed she had no idea, she had just been told to say that. Immediately the mixed bag of cruise-ship passengers, American, German, British, French and others, forgot the tortoises and water-lilies to sing the praises of their favourites. I felt it might be a piece of information she would drop for succeeding tours.

The Edinburgh gardens are laid out not all on one level but with sloping lawns massed with trees and banks of rhododendrons. From the upper walk is the same long townscape as from my bedroom window. After the births of my brother and sisters it was always difficult for a time to make this a regular walk as there was a ridiculous regulation banning prams from even the gravelled walks. When the occupant of a pram was at length able to stagger it could be released and the pram left with others in care of a keeper at either of the two gates. The infant was then free to collapse into flower-beds, scatter gravel on the grass and generally become more of a menace out of than in its baby-carriage. When we did go on a Sunday to the Botanics it was difficult to decide which part to visit. In spring the pond was first favourite with tadpoles and frogs and moorhen. The steamy hothouses always attracted though often they were turned down, "Not today I think. You might catch cold coming out of them into this bitter wind."

There was a serene little wood of conifers near the rock garden which in early May was awash with the blue of wild hyacinths. It had the cool remoteness of gardens of antiquity and I thought of it as the Garden of Gethsemene or the garden of the first Easter.

When I was little, the rock garden was my favourite place. Not just a slope with stones, it covered a large area with twisting paths among the boulders and unexpected steps running up and down. There was also a water-fall (trickle) which I always hoped would one day turn into a torrent. Best of all in the rock garden were the Bears' Houses. These were circular, well, houses—the reverse of those children dig in the sand for the walls were rocks standing perhaps three or four feet high. Each had shelves and a table—or if you will, a rough rock—in the middle and of course an entrance. There were no bears. One did not actively play in the Botanics, the Keepers discouraged that, though occasionally I brought Buphba to share my homes. For the rest, imagination did all. I was the Baby Bear and my parents the Father Bear and Mother Bear.

Our more workaday family walk was to Inverleith Park, a large open space of about seventy acres like its over-the-road neighbour The Royal Botanic Garden. It was surrounded by an open iron fence backed by a spindly hedge and trees, beyond which was the bark and tan-chip riding track which we had to cross but on which, despite its pleasing texture, we rarely lingered lest we be cut down by passing flash of hooves. In my day the Park was a splendid place for children, with extensive acres of rough grass quartered by the four carriage-ways leading from the main entrances, three of them with fine stone pillars and iron gates. We went in by a pedestrian swing gate at the corner of Inverleith Place and Arboretum Road. The

Inverleith Place gate had over it the inscription 'Manners Makyth Man'. My brother swore that a class-mate of his, living across the road, was regularly, when in disgrace, haled there by his mother to read those noble words. The carriage-ways were never used for traffic other than that of prams, scooters and tricycles apart from the park-keepers' occasional slow-moving equipment. At their intersection was a drinking fountain up whose steps we always scrambled but whose waters, particularly if from its chained iron cup, never passed our lips. (We knew that you never knew what you might catch.) An inscription told us that the fountain had been erected by public subscription in 1900 in memory of John Charles Dunlop, a Magistrate, who had died on the 4th of February 1899. He had himself commemorated his wife on the Arboretum Road Gate. It was for hygienic reasons too that we were discouraged from using the swings and see-saws near the tennis courts but this did not greatly distress us as apart from racing round and round our chief interest in the Park was the Pond with its open-billed ducks and swans and flotillas of model yachts whose skippers, mainly elderly men armed with long bamboo rods, made their vessels tack to and fro from one shore to the other in the most masterly way, never having them ignominiously turn on their sides to drag sodden sails under water as was always happening with our string-controlled craft.

When frost came, children had to be restrained by the keepers from prematurely 'trying the ice' then, when the pond was finally pronounced bearing and the harassed men were able to stop waving threatening sticks and blowing intimidating whistles, we went sliding while more skilful—and indulged—children skated. We never had skates "because by the time we buy them the ice will have gone and by next year your feet will be bigger". It did not seem to strike us that with four of us there was something wrong with this line of reasoning but sliding, after all, was fun and few of our friends had skates either. The long slope above the pond made a distinctly hazardous sledge run, ending, unless you braked, on the path or stone declivity leading to a freezing ice-bath. The only one of our family to make such intimate acquaintance with the pond was

71

Marjorie who toppled in while sailing her boat and had to be rushed home weeping in the pram where she dripped on her baby sister.

If our mother or Mary stopped to speak with friends we might play with the children in their charge—if we all approved each other. Then it would be one of the varieties of Tig—plain tig, lame tig, stone tig or the more complicated French Tig. Steps and Statues were more static games suitable for when our elders sat down to chat and of course there were all manner of ball games like Donkey. One of our favourite counting-out rhymes was regrettably racist although in those days no one noticed the overtones.

> 'Eeny—meeny—miny—mo
> Catch a nigger by the toe,
> If he squeals let him go,   [humane really]
> Eeny—meeny—miny—mo.'

Unexceptional was the brisker

> 'One potato, two potato, three potato,
> Four,
> Five potato, six potato, seven potato,
> No more.'

Sometimes we digressed into a rose garden, but rarely, as from it the direct way to the pond was down steps, unnegotiable for a large pram. It is still a retreat—now a scented garden. After our time the Park may well have given more pleasure to more people than just to children and model yacht enthusiasts, but it lost something of its spacious quality as it became fragmented with football pitches, muddying up 'our' grass, a pitch-and-putt course and war-inspired allotments. Today it is still as it was then part of the oasis of greenness and space which stretches from the Gothic romanticism of Fettes College, through Park and Botanics, along the valley of the Water of Leith and beyond to Heriot's playing fields and the ordered wastes of Warriston Cemetery.

One walk popular with us despite its length was to George Street, a considerable climb up the slopes of the New Town but made worthwhile by the visit to Henderson's Bazaar, a treasure house of a shop, of a sort less common then than now. It stocked Oriental cups and dishes and bales of chintz and cotton and silk from which my mother chose material for furnishing and dress-making. (Much more interesting than Cruikshanks, in Hanover Street, which supplied flannel for nightgowns and pyjamas, also coats for which we had to stand still while being measured.) Henderson's smelled of incense and spice and on its shelves could be found intriguing toys of thin wood and coloured paper. There were wooden puzzles and trick boxes and painted fans and Japanese or Chinese lanterns and almost best of all mysterious pieces of paper which when floated on saucers opened out into flowers.

The best walk of all was probably that down the Cinder Path to Arboretum Road to Stockbridge, either through the Park to the west end of Raeburn Place or straight down the hill to the Water of Leith across which lay the Colonies, one of the several housing complexes built about 1861 by the Edinburgh Co-operative Building Company to provide reasonably priced homes for artisans. This, on account of the setting, is the most attractive. The houses are stone, sometimes flatted with outside stairs, and with craft and masonic symbols decorating many of the gable ends. With gardens, most of the streets run at right angles from the main Glenogle Road down to the Water of Leith which at this point on its attractively rural way to Canonmills has passed through Stockbridge and the valley of the Dean. This district is part of the Georgian New Town and has gone up and down in its fortunes over the years. Today on an 'up' it has antique shops and boutiques and houses are sought for and 'improved'. In my childhood it was an area of mixed housing with some very poor properties since demolished. We liked the shops there. Their difference from the Goldenacre ones made them seem more interesting. They were also cheaper but that was not my mother's aim in going to them. She was not one to wear out shoe leather seeking bargains, like some of her friends. It would in any case have been pointless as, like me, she could add a column ten times and get as many answers though I daresay she felt a Good Housekeepingly glow if she found she had saved a penny or ha'penny or even farthing. On the Raeburn Place expeditions any profit to her purse

73

would soon have been wiped out as, because these outings were treats, it was tacitly understood that as well as buying necessary things we would also buy unnecessary ones. Besides its 'making a change' her prime motive was to pay a nostalgic visit to Coopers, a grocery store whose business was mainly in Glasgow and the west. Here we always bought dried bananas. I daresay other shops in Edinburgh stocked them but we never came across them. After that routine call we went to a greengrocer and then to a baker to get a selection of tea-bread different from the Goldenacre varieties. Last came the highlight of the afternoon, the delightful searches round a newsagent cum toy shop and a china shop cum ironmonger. My mother would pick up some kitchen gadget or dish or jug and I would choose packets of beads to thread or perhaps a frame like that of a slate but with obscure roughened glass through which you could see outline pictures on paper below and trace them on the glass. Once I lost my heart to a tea-set and was given it. The cups were smaller than coffee cups but my brother and I could drink from them. The set was made of tin, painted red and had pictured on it various adventures of Mother Hubbard and her Dog. My mother seemed to enjoy these outings as much as we did for she was always happy and relaxed on them. In memory I still can savour their delights.

When going to Stockbridge I preferred the approach by the Colonies but as with the Erskine Ferry road it was not unalloyed bliss. In this case it was not a baleful notice that worried me but a huge padlocked wooden chest standing outside a lodge-like cottage in an enclosure near the bank of the Water of Leith. It contained, I now imagine, a Corporation Gardener's tools. Then, unfortunately I had other information. I knew that Mabel was incarcerated in that box— Mabel from the Lord's Prayer. Who other? No one should ever laugh at children's notions, no matter how weird. I was mildly terrified she might burst out and was sorry for her but not, I regret to say, to the extent of dreaming about her or demanding that her box be opened. I classed her on the black side of magic. The Lord's Prayer evidently reckoned her a menace. If you have yet to identify the lady she figures in a petition near the end, 'Deliver us from Mabel.'

CHAPTER TWELVE

The Crescent

NUMBER 7 Claremont Crescent, to us simply 'The Crescent' was, until my Grandmother sold it in 1925, almost as important as home. As with 39 Inverleith Gardens I am boringly able to recall almost every inch of it, not so much in the basement although even of it I have pictures of a laundry and very hot kitchen with red-faced cook Lizzie. I expect Lizzie was also temperamental for apart from, for more obvious reasons, the walkway behind the third floor parapet, the basement was the only part of the house that my cousin Kathleen and I were discouraged from visiting. Actually we were rather scared of her even when innocently nipping down the steps to the back door to rescue a ball.

There were to me puzzling features about this house. As a start although it stood first in the Crescent it was numbered seven, but despite being the first it did not stand where one would expect a first house to stand, at the corner where the Crescent debouched from East Claremont Street, but some way along presumably to leave room for the missing six houses. And where were they? Their spaces were partially occupied by the Drill Hall, the much later and out of keeping premises belonging to the Territorial Army whose entrance was on East Claremont Street. I wondered what quirk had made my grandfather site his house where he did and not label it one, for to add to my bewilderment I had grown up in the belief, acquired I know not how, that he had built it with his own hands and that it had been for some time the first and only house there. He could have been excused miscalculations in his measurements for it would have been an arduous part-time job for the busy owner of a well-established jeweller's, silversmith's and goldsmith's business as the Crescent had a basement and stood three storeys high. When sanity took over and I relegated my silver-haired grandfather with mason's trowel and hod to the same realm of fancy as the Clyde-paddling Glasgow merchants, I thought for years that he had at least been the first owner. Quite recently from paper ephemera come into my possession, I find it was not a Chisholm house at all but had belonged to my grandmother's parents, William Gibb, Printer, and his wife whom he married in 1853, Jessie Plenderleith Wilson. He died in 1865 and his wife lived on in the house until her death in 1909. Her daughter, Agnes Helen Gibb, was married in the house on the 8th of October 1873 to Alexander Wyse Chisholm. After their marriage the young couple lived at various addresses in Dublin Street and East Claremont Street where my Chisholm great-grandfather had also lived, then in 1888 Agnes Helen with her husband and growing family returned to her girlhood home where they set up a joint household which from all accounts was very harmonious.

On the 15th of June 1888, Mrs Gibb wrote to her son-in-law,

'My Dear Alick,

I think it is better to put in writing, for your consideration, what we have often joked about, viz, the idea of your taking up your abode here. I have for long thought about it, but now seeing the change which is about to take place in Willie's and Lena's circumstances has determined me to broach the subject.

There are many things of course to consider, once your mind is thoroughly made up that it is the right thing to do and I would like you to give it your serious consideration now that if it is to be matters may be gone into between us. I quite understand you may have a feeling about it, but you need have none so far as I am concerned. After you thoroughly consider it, I will be glad to have a talk, but I thought it was best to write in the first instance.

With love

Your affectionate Mother,

Jessie P Gibb'

Willie and Lena were son and daughter-in-law who had married in 1879 and by this time had three of their eventual family of four.

Willie, who had been I think in his late father's firm, sometime
Morrison and Gibb, never seems to have been a successful man of
business. As late as 1907 a member of an accountant's firm, but also
from the tone of the letter a family friend, wrote to his mother 'Willie's
affairs have troubled me very much, because at one time, at all
events, they seemed so perfectly hopeless. But the one thing I am
more than thankful for is that we have been able to save him from
sequestration... That his late partners are entirely incapable of
conducting the business is patent to anybody...' so although they
may not have been his fault 'the circumstances' mentioned in the
letter seem unlikely to have been favourable. At some time he
severed his connection with the Edinburgh firm and went to London.
This Lena was my dream Lena of the poppy-garlanded hat. As a little
girl I used to hear elder members of the family distinguish her by
using her maiden name which was indeed Anderson.

Given this understanding approach by Mrs Gibb, the matter must
have been thought and talked over for on 27th September 1888 from
East Claremont Street went a letter from Alick to his mother-in-law.

'Dear Mother,
   In view of our going to 7 Claremont Crescent the following are the
proposals I have to make.
   I.   That I pay you the sum of Seventeen Pounds, ten shillings,
(£17:10/-) monthly during the first week of every month, commencing
November 1888. This sum to include Food, Coal, Gas with necessary
house expense. This sum to be altered if found necessary.
   II. That four servants be kept, you paying for two and I for two.
   III. That for necessary repair of furniture, you pay for your own
Bedroom and the Library, and I pay for our own Bedroom, Nurseries
and Schoolroom. That for Dining-room, Drawingroom and spare
Bedroom, we should pay in the following proportions: you pay one
third and I pay two thirds of expenses.
   IV. That I pay for Tenants Taxes, so soon as my own house sells or
lets.
   V.   The above arrangements to remain in force until Whitsunday
1890.
                              A W Chisholm'

At the end of this letter Mrs Gibb added and signed a note on the
28th of September and an exact copy was signed again on the 14th

of February 1889.

'I, Jessie Plenderleith Gibb of 7 Claremont Crescent agree to the foregoing conditions and accept the sum mentioned therein.'

Having as I thought tidied my Great-grandmother away into her marital home, two slim pieces of paper fluttered out of a box of assorted documents again to disturb my conceptions. One is the birth certificate of a younger son, who did not long survive, who was born at an address in York Place, possibly that of her parents but the other is a letter dated 6th February 1863 from 17 Gayfield Square, which seems to have been the Gibb home, in which case William Gibb Printer can have enjoyed his new house in Claremont Crescent for only two years before his death. He very well may have been the first owner and occupier for although the crescent was started in 1823 only half the intended houses had been erected by 1852. Eventually all save one and the two projected wings were completed. (*The Buildings of Scotland,* Edinburgh volume.) I had done right to be puzzled.

We have a charming four-generation family photograph in which the three ladies, mother, grandmother and great-grandmother all faultlessly attired in beautiful, figured, tucked, ruched and lace trimmed gowns have their eyes on the centre of interest, my cousin Ralph Chisholm Newman Darling who—also in frills and lace—is seated on his mother's knee. He has been 'shortened' and must be about four months old. His great-grandmother seems to have been of the generation that always wore a lacy cap indoors for we have no pictures of her without one. Ralph, who looks as if he throve on all the love and devotion he was obviously given, is looking up at her with the trusting air small babies so often have. In this instance the trust was well bestowed. Gaga, as rather unhappily with regard to today's terminology she was known to the family, was loved by them all and by a host of friends. It was probably she who set the family pattern of hospitality and concern for the less fortunate. Obituaries are perhaps suspect but I could almost vouch for the truth of this one from the *Scottish Baptist Magazine* of March 1909. It is a fact that while all her grandchildren spoke of her with love, the youngest, my amusing though often spitefully tongued aunt, went out of her way so to do—to me conclusive proof.

THE SCOTTISH BAPTIST MAGAZINE.

THE LATE MRS GIBB.

On January 27th, at the house of her son-in-law, Mr A .W. Chisholm, Mrs Jessie P. Gibb entered into rest.

Mrs Gibb, who was born on January 29th, 1830, was a daughter of Mr Robert Wilson, for many years an office-bearer in Bristo Place Church. She had as maternal uncles the celebrated artists Robert Scott Lauder and James Eckford Lauder, with the latter of whom she was a great favourite, and in whose pictures she frequently appeared.

Mrs Gibb had for so many years been an active and leading worker in Dublin Street Church and among Edinburgh Baptists, that it is hard to realise she has passed away. Her connection with the Baptist Church takes us far back into last century. From a deeply interesting notice in the "Bristo Place Church Magazine," we learn that she became a member of that church on July 8th, 1849, her father having been then a member for forty years, and a deacon for over twenty. Some years after her marriage to Mr Gibb, who was an elder in Lady Glenorchy's Free Church, Edinburgh, she became a member of that body. In 1865 she lost her husband, a man much esteemed, and in 1871 joined the church in Dublin Street, in which she continued to live and labour until the end.

With the death of Mrs Gibb has passed from us one who was truly a mother in Israel, of whom the words might have been written: "Our sister… who is a servant of the Church… a succourer of many". She was given to hospitality. How many have had church life made attractive by her gracious kindliness and unfeigned interest will never be known here. Young people in lodgings, students, and those in business life who were severed from home, all strangers and lonely folk, found the most unconstrained of welcomes from Mrs Gibb, and at once felt at home in her genial presence. All her interests were expansive and unselfish. Her last hours of activity were characteristic of her life-long sympathy with all sorrow and need. Dying in the early morning hours of Wednesday, the 27th, as late as Monday evening, the 25th, she wrote two letters to friends who had suffered bereavement, and two others to Councillors in Edinburgh soliciting their support in behalf of an applicant for a charitable fund. Mrs Gibb was one of those who are the welding power of Christian communities. She had preferences, doubtless, but no exclusions. And her affection, time, means, and interest were at the disposal of all with whom she came into contact. One mark of the Christian, by no means obvious in all who bear the name, was truly hers: "We know

79

that we have passed out of death into life because we love the brethren". The fact of finding in any one a fellow Christian overrode entirely the world's barrier of class distinctions. She moved a Christian gentlewomen among rich and poor with the same gracious kindliness, and with the power of putting all at ease which only comes from a large-hearted sincerity of nature. She was the centre of all the social life of the church, and was mistress as none else of all the details of the ever-recurring soirées. She was the prime mover in the Dorcas work, and bore the burden and heat of the day in Mothers' Meetings for many a long year. And in thus coming into contact with all sorts and conditions of people, she found the reward of the liberal soul. A language too proud to borrow remains for ever impoverished. Similarly, the exclusive nature shuts out much which would add to its individual worth. Mrs Gibb welcomed the chance of intercourse with all, and from humble folk she gleaned much. A keen sense of humour, a true mother wit, and a wealth of pithy Scotch expressions were hers, and they lent vividness to her conversation. One is safe in assigning to her humorous sense her dwelling upon the fact that in James Eckford Lauder's picture of the "Ten Virgins" he painted her in both groups! Her never-failing interest in others kept her young in heart, and she was as much the friend of the young people of a later day as she had been of her contemporaries. Surrounded as she was by her children's children, even to the third generation in the last year or two, she was never at any time out of touch with young life.

"Dwelling among her own people," and yet the friend of good causes widely spreading, she cherished always a love and loyalty to the House of Prayer, the Church that was her spiritual home, that a younger generation might well imitate. And now that she has gone, one recalls with thankfulness a course so faithfully pursued and a memory so gracious.

Committed Christian though she was, it must have taken all her reserves of charity, unless her sense of the ridiculous came to her aid, to forgive the writer of the following diatribe directed at her, a concerned church member and forty-one-year-old widow with two children, when she gave notice of her intention of leaving the Church of Scotland, which she had joined as lately as 1863 solely that the family might worship together, and of rejoining the Baptist Church which was the church of her youth. The Reverend Mr Davidson makes the most unctuous of nineteenth-century fictional clerics credible—though in the interests of publication their creators might have baulked at making them as long-winded. If my memory serves aright he lived in such a nice house too!

80

Ramsay Cottage
Trinity.   8th March 1871.

My dear Mrs Gibb,
    Your letter to me of yesterday has both astonished and grieved me.
It has astonished, inasmuch till this time I never once heard an
expression from your lips in favour of Baptist views as compared with
the doctrines of our church, while your own past history, I mean in the
change which you made so many years ago, and the hearty way in
which you have ever since entered into all our congregational action, led
me to believe that your mind had not undergone any second change,
but had continued to be fixed on all points of difference between the
one body and the other.
    And again, as I have said, I am grieved not only that in our close
pastoral relationship, (so close indeed that it had passed into a personal
and family endearment) is on your part, to be broken up, but that this
should take place at the instance of so young a person as dear Aggie
whose teachings of late have, with your sanction, been of a divided
kind, (which, as I think they ought never to have been,) and without the
slightest consultation with those whose position and relationship entitled
them to the first consideration and given them the first claim to be
heard, is both strange and disappointing.
    That Aggie has declared on the Lord's side and been spiritually
converted is indeed a most precious thing, and one in which all of us
must rejoice, and none more so, I am sure than her present Pastors, and
tho' we may not have been the honoured instruments, still, we must
equally rejoice in that accomplished fact. But why that should lead her
to give up all her former church and congregational connexions I am at
a loss to discover, where, as you admit, the same vital doctrines are
taught and taught I trust, in spirit as much as in truth.
    It is true that Baptist views are not held by us but these are not of
vital or of exclusively saving kind, or, woe unto us! nor did those special
views surely, form any element in the matter of her conversion.
    If Mr Grant has been the instrument in God's hand, in bringing about
that precious result, I should not so much have wondered that some
desire should have been expressed for her attaching herself to the
ministry of one who had been so honoured of God for her good, but
when it is not, as appears, such personal matter at all, but Baptist
principles at large which now prevail with her and have influenced her
decision I must say, I think it was hardly fair, that such a step should
have been taken and such decision been come to, without in a single
instance, submitting the matter to me or Mr (?) Cusin who in God's
Providence held the very responsible place of Pastor and Guardian of

81

her spiritual interests. She ought, at least, to have been treated to both sides of the question.

It is not even as if no opportunity or encouragement to speak out had been given her, for I have more than once reminded her of what might now, by God's grace, be expected of her and on the subject of communion I had expressed the hope that by and by she might be turning her thoughts seriously in that direction when I received no reply. I have also observed of late a shyness on her part, certainly never witnessed before, showing that something had been working in her mind which ought, in time, to have been ...... Considering, moreover, the more than mere public or official relationship which has so long subsisted between us, I am certainly more than surprised, I am deeply disappointed that so grave a matter should have been settled all on one side, without an opinion having once been asked of us, or a single interchange of sentiments been allowed between us.

I thank you, my dear Friend, for your continued kind and friendly expressions of attachment to myself and Mr Cusin—this I am sure has always been most cordially reciprocated hitherto—you are also pleased to add that you shall always feel ready to come to us or to either for advice and counsel—but what my dear Friend have we found in the present instance? Why, if such readiness should it not have been now? Why should it not have been showed at a time when above all others it had been so loudly called for? You knew well what an accumulation of influence lay on the other side—I am far from saying illegitimate or improper influence—I mean on the contrary, the influence of so much Christian worth and godly example in your own family relationships and otherwise—persons whom I most highly value and esteem still they were all on the Baptist side—and, I do not wonder that a young and affectionate girl like Aggie should, in such circumstances, have taken on impressions favourable thereto—but on that very account and in all fairness to herself, as well as in dutifulness to those who had been called, in providence, to be her teachers, the case, so long as it lay in the balance, should have been submitted to them, and before such a decision as you now announce, had been arrived at.

But as that decision has now been come to, and the responsibility been wholly taken out of our hands and lies therefore no more with us, I must just accept it as it stands.

That your dear child is a Christian, and a true disciple of the Lord Jesus in that I heartily and gratefully rejoice, but that by a mere side element, (certainly not essential to its birth or growth) it should be the occasion of the breaking up of a connexion which has so long subsisted, and been so very dear to us both—which was inaugurated at a very interesting period of your life and had therefore very sacred memories attached to it from first to last, is certainly a little trying to one's spirit, and will, also I know be a subject of lamentation to many.

Since however it seems to be a foregone conclusion and does not admit either of counsel or of argument (which, indeed have been all along unsought for) I forbear, and can now do no more than commit you and yours, as I most earnestly do, to the favour and good care of our Saviour God. May he bless you and keep you and cause his face to shine upon you and be gracious unto you. May he lift up the light of his Countenance upon you, one and all, and evermore give you peace.

I remain my dear Mrs Gibb,
> most faithfully and affectionately yours
> in the bond of the Gospel
> Geo. H. Davidson.

There went a man who loved the scratch of his pen and if he loved the sound of his own voice as much how congregations 'sitting under him' must have suffered. He had however met his match in the elusive dear Aggie who was a very determined and obstinate person. As she was married some year and a half later he may have had the forces of young love against him too. 'The influence of so much Christian worth and godly example in your own family relationships and otherwise...' was 'otherwise' a hit at Alexander Wyse Chisholm? It is a pity his attitude did not seem to teach my grandmother the virtue of tolerance if we are to suppose it was the memory of his officious sanctimoniousness still rankling some forty years on that kept her from attending our christening according to the rites of the Church of Scotland.

Crises of conscience (and the upsets they provoked) seem to have plagued my great-grandmother. Here is the rather insouciant letter she had written when leaving the Baptist church in 1863 for the Reverend Mr Geo Davidson and Lady Glenorchy's Free Church. Mr Anderson must have realised her decision was irreversible.

My dear Mr Anderson,
I was sorry you had the trouble of calling so often and not finding me at home. I suppose you must have observed that I have not been in church for some months, and I ought to have communicated with you or Mr Dickie before this, but circumstances have prevented. I now feel it my duty to resign my connection with the church and worship with my husband and children. This has cost me for some years serious and

prayerful consideration, and I have after much struggle come to that conclusion. Of course those that have not been placed in the same circumstances cannot judge, but it is not, I think for spiritual benefit that a family should be divided. I may say that for some years I have held free communion views, and that in leaving Bristo Street I am not sacrificing any principle by connecting myself with any other Christian church. I believe the gospel is purely preached and their doctrine sound and in all my intercourse with the members I have found them to be sincere and consistent Christians.

I shall ever feel a warm interest in all that concerns Bristo Street Church, and I do trust that our Christian friendship will still be continued, at least nothing shall be wanting on my part to maintain the same. As my mind is quite made up on the subject I trust you will see the propriety of intimating my resignation to the church without further proceedings on the matter.

       Yours,
          Jessie P Gibb.
17 Gayfield Square
6th February 1863.

I have long known there was good reason for me to admire my Great-grandmother. Family lore credited her with a sense of humour and much tolerance both of which she must indeed have had to live for many years in apparent harmony with a daughter, son-in-law and their growing family. I like the sensitivity in her approach to her son-in-law over the prospect of a shared home, but it was when I read her letter to Mr Anderson of Bristo Place Church mentioning though in no way apologising for her many months' long absence from church that I took her to my heart. Who could better that throwaway line, quite bold considering the religious climate of the times, 'but circumstances have prevented'?

CHAPTER THIRTEEN

Wafers and Walls

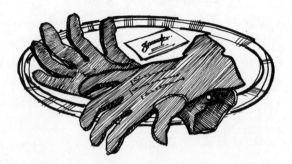

WHOEVER built 'The Crescent' built well. As with most terraced houses of Edinburgh's New Town, two or three shallow stone steps led to the bridge-like approach over the area (the yard in front of the basement) to what to me seemed a massive door opening on to a tiled hall. The hall was square at the front but narrower at the back on account of the stairs at the right-hand side. To the right of the main hall stood two white busts on pedestals. In an old photograph of the Mackay and Chisholm double-windowed shop front in Princes Street there were in the right-hand window two busts, perhaps these very ones. I have no idea whom they commemorated but think they were classical rather than modern characters. There was a top-hatted individual in the photograph too with a second man, my grandfather I think with one of his staff. Against the wall on the left stood a high mahogany table for the accommodation of visiting-cards and the hats and gloves of male guests. I played under it. My slightly older cousin Ralph would be busy with his own concerns and neither cousin Kathleen nor brother Ian at the playmate stage, if indeed they were born, but I had no need of any of them. "Edie! Annie!" I can hear my grandmother say, "call the Child for her tea," and the Child would reluctantly crawl out leaving behind Saddold, Glomo, Sye, Bodo and Kalunken, her intimate but invisible friends.

Beyond the table, first on the left was the Library with dark curtains and furniture and a huge walking-in cupboard into which my grandmother would retire with as many of her recalcitrant family and staff as she could dragoon during thunder-storms for she had an irrational dread of those noisy outbursts of nature. According to Dedae, my younger aunt Edith, her mother had chosen to have an autumn wedding thinking that by then all risk of summer storms should be over. Alas! It was a case of the best-laid schemes ganging agley. On the 8th of October 1873 when Agnes Helen Gibb became the wife of Alexander Wyse Chisholm (in the upstairs drawing-room?) it was to reverberating peals of thunder and flashes of lightning.

Behind the Library was the diningroom, an even larger room with the customary Victorian furniture of dark table and chairs with their back-of-knee-pricking horse-hair, enormous double sideboard and on the mantelpiece black clock and classical ornaments. This room also had a huge cupboard, two actually though it was only the nearer one that concerned us, holding happy memories of the decanters and bottles of home-made ginger wine which my grandparents, in the interests of the many young people who visited them, used as their only social drink having in their mission work seen the multifarious evils that could follow over-indulgence in alcohol. The wine was delicious and was generously dispensed by my grandmother and aunt who considered it a healthy harmless beverage. My mother for some reason did not agree so my pleasure in the draughts was enhanced. One wall of the room was lined with almost ceiling high glass-fronted bookcases with cupboards below. The cupboards held a medley of things, ping-pong bats and balls, jigsaw puzzles of the British Isles and the Holy Land and gourds of all shapes and sizes which seemed mysterious to me and which I loved handling. Oddly enough I remember no books in the Library but these deep shelves held enormous green bound classics, Henryson, Dunbar, Chaucer, Dryden and other giants of literature, products of my great-grandfather's printing firm in Tanfield Lane, Murray and Gibb forerunner of Morrison and Gibb. In later school and university days these shelves yielded me much pleasure in desultory reading. Many of the books I would have had to borrow from the Carnegie Library, ("Are you sure these books are clean?" and indeed in the old brown bindings many of them did not look as well-tended as do Library books now, "You don't know where they have been") whilst a great many of the minor classics I would not have known of to borrow, clean or unclean.

It was in one of these bookcases that I came on Bishop Percy's *Reliques*. The English ballads did not stir me as did our own Border ones but from them I realised that the 'false Southrons' had their point of view, considering themselves worthy Borderers even though their Battle of Otterburn was prosaic stuff compared with our Otterbourne.

> 'But I have dream'd a dreary dream
> Beyond the Isle of Skye;
> I saw a dead man win a fight,
> And I think that man was I.
> ....
> My wound is deep; I fain would sleep;
> Take thou the vanguard of the three,
> And hide me by the braken bush,
> That grows on yonder lilye lee.'

I remember being shocked by Robert Henryson into a new awareness of poetry. Until Robin and Makyn I had liked my poetry to be what I considered 'poetical', more than just pretty but still euphonious. Robin 'on gude green hill kepand a flock of fe' had seemed to promise a pastoral idyll but it was revealed as something quite other. I fought my way through 'my dule is derne bot gif thou dill' and appreciated 'The man that will nocht quhen he may Sall have nocht quhen he wald'.   This astringency was something new in my experience yet it was undeniably poetry. It was probably with Henryson that my love for 'sweet, sour; adazzle, dim;' was born.

Another heavy volume explored one day of summer sun as I lay stretched out on the diningroom floor pointed a spine-chilling finger at me from Maister William Dunbar, 'Timor mortis conturbat me'. From him it was but a step in my Saturday afternoon reading to Thomas Nashe with again the authentic touchstone of shivers up the spine,

> 'Brightness falls from the air,
> Queens have died young and fair;
> Dust has closed Helen's eye...'

In my very early days, underneath the diningroom table was one of my refuges and after being allowed to 'get down' after finishing my share of the family breakfast I crawled into the shelter of its white starched damask walls. Here it was that I gathered from the tone of the exchanges above my head that Aunt Annie's husband, my English Uncle Tom, was not entirely persona grata with his in-laws. This seemed to be, I learned from the comments of my sharp-tongued aunt as I pursued my innocent leg and shoe-strewn way, because he took sugar on his porridge. I myself have never sunk to taking sugar or even syrup on my porridge but I would not condemn a man for it. To the end of her days though, Dedae was a racist, disliking all of alien blood and none more so than the English. Not surprisingly in this case the antipathy was returned.

Out of the diningroom to the left a small flight of stairs led down to a lavatory—for the times the house was well provided with these conveniences, closets we called them. We had always understood that this was because our grandfather was forward-looking in his ideas of house design, but this is an attribute we have to transfer to an earlier unknown, possibly the architect William Burn. Halfway down the closet stairs another short flight led to the right up to the schoolroom, a small square room with one window over the outer world and an interior one over the stairs. At one time young female Chisholms may have studied there—the boys went to good day schools, the Academy and the Institution—and all of them foregathered. In my schooldays it was given over to my cousin Kathleen for entertaining her friends, particularly the Triple Alliance, a loosely cohering secret society frequently torn by strife, consisting of Kay and myself and our friend Verna. Here, after school tennis, or afternoon classes we sat in peace, after an initial scrimmage for the favourite chair, an outsize version of a Victorian baby-chair which took some squeezing into, at a table set out for us at my aunt's instigation by Alice or Daisy, pleasant sisters from the Granton district. We had our own pot of tea and we wolved sandwiches, paste or egg and cress in bridge rolls (an appreciated luxury for me as we had them only for 'occasions') scones, buns and packets of

THE JOURNEY BEGINS

Elaine Mary Chisholm

born 2nd February 1911

with her mother

Elaine Mary.
2nd February 1911.

Mrs William G. Chisholm.
returns thanks for kind enquiries
and congratulations

Strathearn,
33 Inverleith Gardens.
Edinburgh.

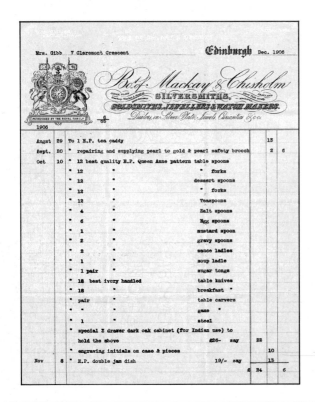

Mrs. Gibb   7 Claremont Crescent   **Edinburgh** Dec. 1906

Bo.of Mackay & Chisholm
UNDER PLATE   SILVERSMITHS   FROM THE TRADE
GOLDSMITHS, JEWELLERS & WATCH MAKERS.
Dealers in Silver Plate, Jewels, Curiosities &c.
PATRONISED BY THE ROYAL FAMILY

1906					
Angst	29	To 1 E.P. tea caddy		13	
Sept.	20	" repairing and supplying pearl to gold & pearl safety brooch		2	6
Oct	10	" 12 best quality E.P. Queen Anne pattern table spoons			
		" 12 " " forks			
		" 12 " dessert spoons			
		" 12 " " forks			
		" 12 " Teaspoons			
		" 4 " Salt spoons			
		" 6 " Egg spoons			
		" 1 " mustard spoon			
		" 2 " gravy spoons			
		" 2 " sauce ladles			
		" 1 " soup ladle			
		" 1 pair " sugar tongs			
		" 18 best ivory handled table knives			
		" 18 " breakfast "			
		" pair " table carvers			
		" " " game "			
		" 1 " steel			
		" special 3 drawer dark oak cabinet (for Indian use) to			
		hold the above £26- say		22	
		" engraving initials on case & pieces		10	
Nov	8	" E.P. double jam dish 19/- say		13	
			£	34	6

MACKAY AND CHISHOLM

Established 1835

THE CHISHOLMS

(left to right)
Dedae
Ainslie
William
Ernie
and Annie

[M]C's grandparents
[Ale]xander Wyse

[Agn]es Helen Chisholm
[wit]h their
[chil]dren

THE AUTHOR'S PARENTS

Miss Stewart of Ardenlee
Annie Macdougall Stewart
before her marriage in 1908

William Gibb Chisholm
Goldsmith
and Soldier, 1915–1918

multicoloured pink, yellow and white wafer biscuits, uttering no words but engaged one and all with one or other of the very many school or adventure stories from the well-stocked bookcases holding relics of my aunts' and uncles' and father's childhood mixed with some belonging to my cousins. We each had our favourites, fortunately different. V liked Pixie O'Shaughnessy and a fanciful one with a title about the snow-stairs and K was as addicted to *The Pemberton Twins* and *Seven Little Australians* as I to Amy le Fevre's 'Us' books—*Us and our Donkey, Us and our Empire* and *Us and our Charge.* We read the same ones over and over again which added to the pleasant security of the tea-time ritual, a security which may have helped to mask the potentially traumatic, but for books of the age fairly usual, fact that in nearly all these stories the children had lost at least one, if not two of their natural guardians—and they were lucky if it were just by marriage or service overseas. Once one of us read a book about Tibet and discovered that Tibetans added butter to their tea so we did too. The result was so disgusting that we rushed down the stairs and emptied our cups in the hand-basin, probably the only time that anything of the school-room feasts was wasted. There could well have been a disinclination on the part of my grandmother and aunt to share their peaceful drawing-room teas with three giggling school-girls—like most children we were at this time often completely incapacitated by uncontrollable, unreasoning, stomach-holding fits of laughter, most irritating to the beholder—but I tend to give credit to the understanding of my aunt who had not forgotten her own young days and at this time was very good to us.

Back from the entrance to these two stairs, left turn led to a long flight down to the right and the angry cook but left turn again was the pantry, a long passage-like room, leading to glass door and outside wooden steps, the usual way to the garden. In the pantry there was a small churn and often a pleasant house-maid willing to demonstrate the large knife-cleaning machine like a ship's wheel or the hoist for sending food from the kitchen and back.

The garden was large, mostly town grass on two levels surrounded by sparsely gravelled paths with flower-beds running below the walls and at the far end a copse—or even forest. Later years revealed this as a sooty shrubbery with laurels and a few sycamore. One bed grew something colourful, peonies and in spring daffodils, but the family were not keen gardeners which was all the better for us. When we were small we often played in a tent, left over from some earlier activity of father or uncles for an adult could stand upright in the middle of it but as we grew we took to the walls and the trees. Restrained as we were from wandering far afoot, travelling upwards, even more than working a swing high, gave us a sense of freedom.

> 'Up into the cherry-tree
> Who should climb but little me?
> I held the trunk with both my hands
> And looked abroad on foreign lands.
> ....
> If I could find a higher tree
> Farther and farther I should see,
> To where the grown-up river slips
> Into the sea among the ships, ...'

I cannot now understand how we were allowed to do the things we did. Two of the walls would be a normal five foot high but the one on the Drill Hall side of the garden where the best trees were was considerably higher. I can only suppose that my aunt having been a tomboy herself sympathised with us and managed to divert her mother from going too often to the window to look out at us for my grandmother was always apprehensive about our physical safety, anyone's physical safety. My father's rugby playing had been covered up for him for months by the family's old (old when I knew her) nurse who, when it was eventually discovered, talked his mother round to accepting it. There were of course often tea-time visitors to the Crescent who took up her attention. Sometimes these guests before setting off again for the mission-fields of China or Africa would express a desire to see dear Annie's and dear Willie's children. Then it was a collection of sooty-looking objects that paraded in the drawingroom for this was before Clean Air Acts and there being, besides house chimneys, those of Breweries, Tanneries and Mills not far distant, the stout willows and poplars were absolutely black. No doubt the mission workers were to come across even more disreputable creatures.

Once on the walls the world opened out for us. We could travel right round the garden, past the shrubbery, rather difficult this with branches sticking out to catch our skirts and hair, then a step down and up on the gate leading to Mr Hoy's nursery and so to an easy run along the wall to the steps up to the pantry. For various reasons we did not do this last part very often. Our elders with thoughts of neighbourly susceptibilities did their best to discourage us from taking a public survey of the next garden where the ladies might be out gardening or resting and regard us with disfavour. In itself this might not have deterred us but at least one of the three sisters was a school-teacher and she Head of the Academy Preparatory and as such we felt might inquire after our state of learning.

On the opposite wall we were less visible and could climb high into the trees or drop down into the wilderness of rough grass at the back of the Drill Hall, always damp and covered with cuckoo-spit. Sometimes we crawled over the Drill Hall roof to where we could peep through a skylight. This we considered very daring and it had a not unpleasant frisson of terror about it as we were completely ignorant of what rifle practice involved and felt we might be struck by stray bullets.

It seemed to be a fact of life in those days that if you had a garden wall you had children on top and these not necessarily yours. Few can have felt in a position to complain about other people's children when their own were probably travelling the length of the street on other walls. It strikes me that people must have been generally more tolerant of children then than they are now when they have become accustomed to them being tethered to video or television. Of course during the war and for a year or so after, it was largely a woman's world and grandmothers, mothers and aunts, besides their natural affinity with children, are in general more liberally minded towards them than are the majority of male relations whose sometimes regrettably macho mind yokes women and children together as women are well aware on other than life-saving occasions.

91

The land behind the Crescent was referred to as 'The Sandpit' a fragment of which remained. The Bellevue Tennis Club where the family had played and of which my aunt was still a member was situated there. For several years our school rented some of their courts and although I never enjoyed tennis it was reckoned a social asset so I 'took' it which is why I was able frequently and with a clear conscience to escape from home—since the 22nd of May 1919 Number 4 Wardie Road—to the laxer atmosphere of the Crescent with Angela Brazil, bound copies of *The Captain*, tree-climbing, ginger wine and packets and packets of wafer biscuits.

Between the tennis courts and the Crescent lay 'Mr Hoy's', a nursery garden. Edinburgh in those days was as full of nursery gardens—at least four lay within the possible purlieus of a family walk—as is the country-side now of Garden Centres. A happy feature of nursery gardens is that they are criss-crossed by paths splendid for rushing along in games of tig and hide-and-seek and it is not unknown for the beds themselves to be sometimes narrow enough to be cleared in flying leaps. Mr Hoy must have been a very good-natured man for we treated his grounds as a legitimate extension of the garden. Possibly he did not wish to antagonise his customers in the Crescent for although it is true we did no harm all that unasked-for activity must have been distracting. Perhaps a bit of a philosopher he reasoned that all ills pass and that in time we would grow to be ladies. If he ever did complain I expect my aunt soothed him. She despised many of her fellow creatures but her friendly manner concealed that and she was generally popular.

Mr Hoy and members of the tennis club entered the grounds by a gate at the far side of the Drill Hall on to East Claremont Street, one of the widest of the New Town's cobbled streets. There was a terrace of good stone houses on the north side where my Chisholm great-grandfather had lived and before they moved to the Crescent my grandparents also. I think my father and the rest of the family would have been born there. On the south side there were newer tenements with some shops, including a sweetie-shop. Occasionally when we had a few pence between us, not many needed in those days, and when adventure really beckoned, we would leave by Mr Hoy's gate and cross the road in giggling and furtive haste and make some surreptitious purchases. We stuffed them in our mouths or about our persons and scuttled back, our eyes darting from side to side for potential informers in the guise of family friends. It was a fairly pointless defiance of authority. Had we asked permission it would have been given but would have engendered a fuss, ("Wipe your faces and take care crossing the road,") and would possibly have been coupled with the suggestion that we just help ourselves from the jar in the diningroom. It was the secrecy that appealed to us and the one-upmanship of defeating even the kindest of adults. It was most fun for my cousin. I after all, when I came to go home (generally after a phone call from Wardie Road) was used to walking two miles alone through Edinburgh evening streets, but she, living in her mother's absence with her grandmother and aunt was escorted to school long after younger children went on their own. As my grandmother was very often heard to say—

"It is a great responsibility... having another person's child."

CHAPTER FOURTEEN

The Golden Bowl

TO REACH the main staircase from the housemaid's pantry we retreated past the diningroom—and Saint Sebastian. My grandparents had a good collection of paintings, many of the Scottish school, probably on account of my great-grandmother's connection with Robert Scott Lauder and James Eckford Lauder her uncles, both of whom used her as a model. My aunt occasionally waved a hand at a wall saying, "That's said to be a Scott Lauder." She explained no more than that he was some kind of relation and famous but as schoolgirls we were not interested enough to enquire further.

Like the furniture many of the paintings in their heavy dull gold frames were huge, challenges for Dedae and the maids and later occupants at spring-cleaning time. One that I remember with pleasure I thought was of Edinburgh but it could have been of some Italian city. Though I did not realise it then it was faintly reminiscent of Claude. Saint Sebastian on the other hand had been a bad buy. I hated that picture. 'In the Italian style' one could have said. It was painted in dark oils. "It's supposed to be good," my aunt said with a singular lack of conviction. The saint, bearing a sad expression and a resemblance to the worst of second-rate religious Christs, was almost, apart from his loin-cloth, completely naked but liberally bestuck with arrows. Why anyone should have wanted to buy, hang or come to that paint it, I could not and still cannot understand. If it were a wedding present it was a most unkind one.

Haste past then to the bottom of the stairs where on dark evenings we used to sit making spooky noises and daring each other to climb alone to the nursery floor. Having reached the top landing, with no gas-jets lit, even although you knew the howls and wails emanated from your cousin and friends you could still work yourself up into a very satisfactory state of terror, without be it remembered any extraneous help from television or horror films. A round of Russian Scandal having once resulted in the message, 'This room is full of ghostly beings' being rendered as 'full of croony beaks' we seized on the expression. For all they lacked of substance, croony beaks were not comfortable beings to be alone with on the top landing.

At the head of the stairs on the first landing came first a spare bedroom over-full of furniture too big for it. It was half filled with a very high plumped up bed and had the stuffy smell of a perfume that had once been. A text hung over the bed.

Next came the drawingroom. This was a lovely large room with windows over the garden and looking into the trees. I have a memory of my grandmother, not yet an old woman but in voluminous widow's weeds, seated at the left-hand side of the fireplace singing, with Kay and me leaning against her knees and chirping in chorus,

'When He cometh
When He cometh
To gather His jewels,
All His jewels, precious jewels,
His loved and His own.
Like the stars of the morning
His bright crown adorning
They shall shine in their beauty,
Bright gems for His Crown.'

"Mother's favourite hymn," said Dedae and we knew Gram was thinking not only of her husband and Uncle Ainslie but especially of her first-born child Jessie who had died in 1881 at the age of seven, far too young and long ago to be thought of as an aunt.

There was a long black jardiniere in the middle of the room in which rampaged my grandmother's precious vine. I could not think why it should be called a vine—no grapes. For my aunt it was rather an incubus. She had to water it regularly and periodically sponge its

95

leaves as it worked away in its endeavour to take over the house. Like the massive pictures and bookcases the vine accompanied my grandmother and aunt from house to house as their need of living space became less. My aunt's voice again comes suddenly out of the past, "Jim Milligan always said it wasn't Mother he had to find a house for, it was her bookcases". A typically incomprehensible adult pronouncement it made sense years later when I realised he was the family lawyer. Thanks to Jim Milligan and the bookcases the two succeeding homes, though ground-floor flats, were in the same type of spacious Victorian building thus preserving for my generation a sense of continuing security. A different marble fire-place had the same fender and long fire-side stool before it and the same huge gold-framed mirror above. Always there was the grand piano and the glass-fronted display cabinets. In them were ivory chess-men and small objets d'art. When I was little the one I gazed on most and was occasionally allowed to finger was a set of dolls' house chairs and couches made of red thread woven between the pins that formed the legs and backs.

Next the drawingroom was a large cupboard whose shelves held the household linen. It was a favourite haunt of Kay and myself and of our friends as stimulated by the books we took in along with the wafer biscuits we were convinced that somewhere in this house there must be a secret passage. This cupboard struck us as being the most likely—or least unlikely—place for its hidden entrance. Round and round its walls we went, disturbing the piles of freshly ironed sheets and table cloths, our legs scratched by the wicker clothes-basket, tap-tapping and hearkening for the authentic 'hollow sound'. Later in the concealing darkness we whispered knowledgeably and ignorantly of Sex. Over the years I have had a recurrent dream of climbing through a hatch in this cupboard into a dream house whose interior though fictional is known to me.

Next to the cupboard was my grandparents' bedroom whose mantelpiece, rich brown tallboys and chests were stacked with framed family photographs more of which covered the walls. In one of my few memories of my grandfather at home he was in bed here, not really ill as he was pleased to have us perch beside him. He was a kindly man, not as forceful as his wife, moderately well-read and moderately well-travelled. He died when I was ten rather unexpectedly I think at the end. I remember an early phone call and the drop in my father's voice. He had asked for Ernie but whether because he was a favourite—or doctor—I do not know. Even at ten I was still fond of dramatising myself and I remember on the lovely April evening of his funeral tossing a ball up and down in the front garden with sideways glances at the neighbours' windows and wondering did they notice how bravely I was concealing my grief. Was this sheer posturing or did it show a facility for standing outside myself?

I have few intimate memories of my grandfather at the Crescent because when I was there during the day, he was at business in Princes Street. There he used to take me through to the showcases at the back of the shop where there were clocks and porcelain vases and ginger jars from the East and up to the first gallery where were most of the antiques which were his chief interest. Besides elaborate clocks and more Chinese or Japanese vases was a curved glass case holding a beautiful masted sailing ship of ivory, also I think of Chinese creation. It was my favourite piece and the fact that I could go back there to look at it time after time makes me think now that he was not perhaps a very pushing man of business. Perhaps he was simply reluctant to part with things he loved and regarded the first floor gallery as a private treasure house of his own. This idea ties in with a memory of us having tea one day at the Crescent when an outspoken guest who was some kind of Chisholm connection but had nothing whatsoever to do with the business apparently criticised it—and by implication my father—as not being up-to-date. My mother was incensed and to my indignation I was dragged away from playing with my cousin and we departed for home. I had no idea of the reason for her behaviour until evening brought home my father who had the whole tale poured into his ears. He was annoyed and appreciated the loyalty but pointed out such behaviour was typical of the sinner. My mother never forgave her. To my relief the trouble seemed to have blown over the next day.

Certainly in my grandfather's day Mackay and Chisholm was a quality jewellers and gold and silversmiths. In later days when my father was sole partner and war and economic distresses had hit luxury trades the business had to become more fashionable to survive. I can see the deprecating look with which he once presented me with a jewelled evening clip. "What they call costume jewellery," he said, "but in its way quite attractive."

There were many jewellers' shops my father completely despised, 'cheap' he said they were though the goods inside may not have been. The attitude lingers on. Today when looking for a jewellers I size up appearances from outside, instinctively preferring one with darker solid look to a tinselly modern shop which I conclude, on occasion mistakenly, to be but a meretricious establishment over whose threshold the elders of our family would be hard-pressed to set foot. I cannot think what he would have made of those today with frontages plastered with red 'Sale' or worse, 'Reductions' notices.

My grandfather took me too on some of my earliest tours of the business whose premises stretched from the Princes Street entrance, opposite Sir Walter Scott and his monument to a lane off Rose Street. It had a basement, and I think three floors above the ground floor showroom. In the basement, a place of curiously assorted smells, were the craftsmen. I do not know what part they played at this time in the actual production of the salvers, bowls, trays and quaichs which they engraved for weddings, retirements and christenings. They certainly adapted the sizes of rings and repaired jewellery and re-set stones in modern settings. There was a lot of activity involving grindstones and machines not all of which was I encouraged to examine at close quarters. The men wore rough leather aprons and cleaning and polishing liquids and pastes, responsible for most of the smell, stood about on long trestles with soft bristled brushes. Products of this and of an even earlier workshop have occasionally greeted me in unexpected places. At an hotel in Devon three dessert spoons of the early nineteenth century were liberated from a showcase into my hands by a pair of receptionists so flatteringly excited at being able to restore them to a descendant of the maker that they could scarcely insert the key into the lock. In the Museum of Bridgetown in Barbados the custodian and myself were equally thrilled at finding my father's workshop had been responsible for the silver quaich presented to commemorate the Jubilee of King George V and Queen Mary.

Above the shop were the watchmakers—an altogether admirable kind of men. When any family watches needed more attention than could be rendered by my father, magnifying glass in eye, cleaning or adjusting the regulator, we handed them to him in the morning and in the evening they came back, cured. This preferential treatment makes it difficult today, should you actually be happy enough to find a watchmaker willing to repair your watch rather than advise you to cast it away and buy another, to become reconciled to seeing it vanish at the end of a white tab for possibly several weeks. Our watches came back at speed but if there was any doubt as to the efficacy of the repair to watches of real customers they were kept a day or two as in a convalescent home to be checked and regularly wound till they were running smoothly. This winding went on even at weekends and the staff took turns on a Sunday morning to visit the shop for this duty. We learned that a watch should be wound at the same time every day, never overwound and when being adjusted for even a few minutes' discrepancy always to put the hands forward and never back. And never, but never, to lay watches on a cold surface. That way led to chills in their springs. I accompanied my father on these Sunday outings when I was still a very little girl for he went off to the army when I was four. Besides the winding the errand included the letting-out of the night-watchman. This human equivalent of the electronic alarm was locked up with the shop and normally released with the morning arrival of the staff. As well as the phone I expect he had access to a key but that possibility never crossed my mind. I thought him rather brave—and lucky— in being able to stay up all night. The man I remember had a collie type companion, name of Rover, whose photograph he gave me.

One May Sunday, after the war, we had a different and most interesting outing, not to Princes Street but to the Palace of

Holyroodhouse where during the sitting of the General Assembly of the Church of Scotland the sovereign's representative, the Lord High Commissioner, holds court for two weeks. Mackay and Chisholm had provided some of the silver so a member of staff had to be in attendance. My father wanted to see that all was in order so we set off to be there while the company was at the service in St Giles Cathedral. Business concluded, my father was all for going home but this member of his staff was not at all inhibited by his surroundings and suggested we take the opportunity to go through the private apartments and view the tables set out ready for the official lunch and dinner. My brother and I were of course eager to do this, we had been often enough in the public rooms and seen the staircase used by Darnley and his gang of assassins to break in on the queen's apartments to murder David Rizzio and gazed half-believing at the stain on the floor—blood—which would not scrub out. We had also been bored by the rows and rows of Royal portraits, mainly imaginary and stretching back to the crack of doom. Some of the doors of bedrooms and private sitting-rooms stood open so we were able to glimpse inside but it was the sight of the State Rooms that awed us. Two were set out not as for workaday meals but as might be for banquets in fairy-tale palaces. Porcelain plates and sparkling crystal glasses were set out on starched damask cloths on which shone plenishings of gold and silver. It was for us but a gleam of splendour. My father was all the while mentally computing the Order of Service in St Giles and long before the ponderous roll of the Doxology can have stirred the banners hanging from the rafters he thankfully withdrew his family to the anonymity of the Royal Mile.

My grandfather, fond though he was of us and we of him, like most men of his time was rather remote from our day-to-day affairs. Certainly with wife, daughters, nurse and maidservants he had no need to concern himself with the minutiae of our lives. I do have a picture of him setting off for work in the mornings. A horse cab with usually the same cabby called for him and brought him home at night. We stood at the door with my youngest aunt and waved and then were allowed to race the horse to the pillar-box at the end of the Crescent. There was another participant in this ceremony who at this stage of his career did not run, but waddled behind us. This was the much loved Snap, a low-down-shaped ginger-coloured dog like what might have been the offspring of a beagle and a dachshund. The most unsnappish of beasts, he may have been christened on account of his colouring which did resemble that of a Ginger Snap.

Next to my grandparents' bedroom was a smaller one, then another closet with skylight window a storey above like that in our maid's room. This lavatory though not 'en suite' was near enough the main bedroom to have been intended as the 'master' one for it was the most impressive in the house being made of dark wood with as I remember a brass handle instead of a chain from a cistern. The bowl was circular and discharged the water in an impressive way. Unfortunately there were no floral designs on it as there were on some of that time as they would have cheered it up. With the inadequate window so far away it was rather dark and frightening. Next came a housemaid's pantry then round to the nursery stairs. They had shallow treads as befitted short legs and in our early days led to Nurse Merrylees. She had been the Chisholm family's more than nurse—confidante, friend and tactful smoother-out of problems between children and parents. She now came in daily to mend and do other small jobs and since my Aunt Annie came back from India with Ralph and his soon-to-be-born sister Kathleen had been able to take over again something of her old activities. Aunt Annie was forced by the First World War to stay on with her parents until my demobbed, sugar on his porridge, Uncle Tom set up in medical practice in London. Ralph had the distinction of being born in India but Kay was Edinburgh like all of us. There was still a nursery gate at the head of the stairs for the nursery door opened immediately off to the right. The nursery was where my bed had been put when Ian was born. There was usually a fire burning behind a nursery fire-guard under the white mantel. The chairs were wooden, painted black with deep blue cushions tied on with tape. Before we advanced to our own school-room teas, Nurse gave us tea here. An odd memory of a nursery tea concerns Kay, aged perhaps two or

101

three. Upset about something, she was crying quite copiously but silently, the tears coursing down her plump cheeks. She was also, to my great interest, for I had heard the expression but never seen it in action, 'wringing her hands'. I was most impressed by her silent control.

Here was a most magnificent dappled rocking-horse not on rockers but on parallel hinged bars which slid back and forward and an equally magnificent three-storey Victorian doll's house.

When the nursery was no longer Nurse Merrylees' domain left-overs from other rooms filtered in. A pile of my gynaecologist Uncle Ernie's text books had us searching, ears acock for footsteps on the stairs for more comprehensible information regarding sex than that afforded by the early books of the Old Testament. Particularly were we intrigued by the mysterious monthly flow of which we read and imagined as being much more dramatic than the reality. That being so we were completely flummoxed as to how no evidence of it was ever apparent to our eyes. We were not so stupid (quite so stupid) as to imagine all senior girls in St Oran's to be medical freaks. When one morning I was surprised by finding my pyjamas and sheets blood-stained it for some reason never entered my head that this was the answer to our cerebrations so I went—not very comfortably—to school. In the afternoon I crossed the road to check a French exercise with a friend but increasing discomfort made me realise this problem was beyond me (and apparently here to stay) so I went in search of my mother. One of my friends told me later—but she had been prepared—that when she had broken the news her mother turned to her and said "Oh good! Now you really are a grown woman". It was not so in Wardie Road. I found my mother on her knees beside the Michaelmas Daisies by the water-tap. I do not know why this spot seems to have engendered family confrontations, it was the very place where some years later my father was to make a Pronouncement. On this occasion, not wishing to alarm my mother, I tactfully mentioned that I seemed to "have become a little red between the legs". My mother rose, brushed down her frock and took off her gardening gloves. "Bother!" said she, "I was afraid this would happen!" Leading me to her bedroom she opened a drawer in the bottom of her wardrobe and taking out an armful of roughly cut and unstitched strips of terry towelling thrust them at me with two safety pins and told me to affix one fore and aft to my vest. She then added some information. "Everybody has it," says she, "Margaret has it," (she added a few more names of my friends) "have it—but don't talk about it—you don't need to tell anyone you have it". So like a fool, and feeling one of the curst not for months did I tell anyone I had it, thereby leading to all kinds of troubles with my friends who, similarly afflicted, did not much discuss the business but naturally wondered why I had to be so devious. Some time later my cousin also had It and being my grandmother's very special charge (she reckoned her super-sensitive and stayed her nerves—teetotaller though she was—with brandy before music examinations) was kept off school for a day. I actually was told by my mother and despatched to the Crescent to visit (and I suppose condole). After this that particular adolescent worry fell into perspective. The secrecy of elders in any generation is hard to condemn, conditioned as it always is by their upbringing and in the early twenties, beneficially perhaps, their evasions kept our imaginations on a perpetual and not unpleasant qui vive. Thus Kay, having her hair brushed by our aunt, is told that this year on holiday she must not go on cycle rides in the country by herself to which Kay's natural response was "Why?" Our beleaguered aunt replied mysteriously, "I cannot tell you now but you will understand when you are older".

But back to the nursery in the Crescent where through a connecting door was the pleasantest bedroom in the house which, with a view to the faraway Firth, was large and light enough not to be overwhelmed by the usual massive furniture. It had a beautifully designed washhand basin like a shell. As schoolgirls, far above adult nerves we played Kickory, lifted from the Katy books, in this room. A game of silent seeking in the dark, the peace was punctuated by wild yells of 'Kickory' as one after another escaped to the sanctuary of the lit passage. The door to the passage was opposite a housemaid's pantry and to the right was the only bathroom in the house with built-in bath and what was not so expected, a covered in coal-bunker. Quite a sensible location really. If you became dirty stoking up the nursery fire with all your little charges helping, there to hand were the means of cleaning everybody up again. I suppose in the days of Queen Victoria and her son, coalmen having shot hundredweights of coal down chutes or humped sacks down area steps saw little out of the way in being asked to carry more up several newspaper-covered flights to a bathroom. I remember the ca'fuffle involved in Inverleith Gardens, laying down old rugs and newspapers over the floors and carpets from front door to back to minimise the mess made by 'the coal' as he and it passed through. His arrival was as much to be dreaded as that of the sweep. Ian and I did not help by happily scuffling through the papers.

There were two other bedrooms on this floor. To reach them yet another unpleasing picture had to be skirted past where it hung above a chest. It was a print of the Crimean or perhaps Boer War. Whatever battle of whichever war, it had resulted in a great many dead and dying horses and helmeted soldiers of the Queen now lying in considerable disarray. It was completely horrible. The rooms had belonged to my uncles, Ainslie and Ernie. When I first went to the Crescent Uncle Ainslie still had one of them. It was only after his death in 1916 that they became free for us to rampage through, Uncle Ernie having long since left home. They had each a door into the passage but also a door into a communicating space, both passage and hanging wardrobe—Uncle Ainslie's dressing-gown hung there for months—so should have had great potential for chasing games but for long I felt it an intrusion on his lingering presence. Our chief use for these rooms was for the access they gave by their windows to the narrow catwalk that ran the length of the Crescent behind the balustrade. It was an escapade frowned on as much for the risk of annoying neighbours as any real danger. Ralph and his friend Monty travelled long distances peering into other people's windows or so they boasted to us. Kay and I, if not more polite, were more timid and besides where we were concerned our aunt had a regrettable second sense and almost invariably turned up as we scrambled out.

CHAPTER FIFTEEN

Or Ever the Silver Chord

IT IS ODD that it is only now I come to mention Uncle Ainslie for he, with Aunt Barbara, are the two people I loved best in my childhood, in memory not lost to me today. It is also odd that he, Robert Ainslie, third child and first son of the family, should have been so christened for the most notable of earlier Robert Ainslies was a rather dubious character who bested Alexander Chisholm's father Robert over a disputed inheritance. He is reputed to have got control of the person and affairs of an elderly aunt and on her death to have acquired her entire estate. He resisted all claims on it, including that of his deceased brother's widow Elizabeth and young family. She wisely decided not to take part in the suit against him. 'In fact I have had so much to struggle through since my husband's death that I feel inclined to leave my own and my children's claims in the hands of that merciful God, who will avenge the rights of the fatherless and widow, and will not forsake them.' Although Robert had, besides his aunt's estate, sometime appropriated the title of Reverend and preached in dissenting chapels, it was clear he had not been chosen as God's instrument. The minister of the parish of Downe where he was residing, on being appealed to, wrote, 'What claim he may have to the title of Reverend I cannot tell nor any (one) else' and 'There are various unfavourable reports of his character and conduct'.

My Uncle Ainslie however re-habilitated the name for he was good through and through. My father and he were congenial companions enjoying holidays together. Once at least they made a foray north and crossed the Moray Firth by the long since defunct ferry from Fort George to the Black Isle. Dedae had nothing but good to say of him. Seeing me one day looking at the not very good water-colour portrait a friend had painted she stood by me, looking up, "Everybody loved Clainey," she said. He most unobtrusively suffered years of ill-health from a cancer, but was unfailingly patient. My mother has an entry in her journal dated 30th August 1910.

'Last Friday was my birthday—which one I shall not record.' [She never would divulge her age, maddening to embryo family archivists, but such coyness was common practice then.] 'We had quite a little party at night, Edie and Mabel' [Gibb cousin] 'Arthur McLean, Ainslie and last but by no means least, Miss C L whom we may perhaps be welcoming as a sister-in-law some day. She is certainly an exceedingly nice girl. The whole family is deeply interested in watching the progress of the affair but they are a very baffling pair. Nothing seems to be settled yet. Our mode of procedure was rather different and we have certainly proved the truth of the old saying, 'Happy is the wooing that's no long a doing'.'

This is all we know of Miss C L. Perhaps the romance faded naturally or perhaps Uncle Ainslie soon felt the stirrings of his illness for it was less that six years after that evening that he died peacefully in his sleep on the 18th of June 1916 when I was five.

During these early years my mother and I were frequently at the Crescent for tea. If he were not about she would ask, "How is Ainslie today?" and my grandmother would probably say he was coming down for tea. Sometimes he would be in bed and not appear and I had to be restrained from going up to see him. This annoyed me intensely for I felt he was in a special way, Mine. If he did come down it might be in soft slippers and dressing-gown. Sometimes he wore a black patch over one eye but never did he give the impression to children that he was a sick man. Always patient with us he took a real, not simulated, interest in our doings. Once I had a badly bruised and swollen foot, the result of having pulled a heavy piano stool over on to it and had to wear a snow shoe as I could not get my ordinary shoe on. (Shoe? It might have been boot as we used sometimes to wear lace-up boots when I was young, good for the ankles.) There was some trouble connected with the incident, I had been warned not to do whatever led to the disaster so the scant sympathy given me had been laced with remarks to the effect that I had only myself to blame. Not so Uncle Ainslie. No wonder everybody loved him.

"Poor wee wifie," he said, "look at the pair of us." (It was an eye-patch day.) "We're two wounded soldiers."

Besides his genius for sympathy I thought he had another—for drawing. When my mother and I 'went up to Princes Street' that is to Mackay and Chisholm to see my father, Uncle Ainslie would take me into his part of the glass-surrounded partners' and cashier's office where there was a very high desk of the type you must stand at or perch on a very high stool. Quite Dickensian. Having lifted me on to the leather stool which was rough to the backs of my knees he furnished us both with pencils and paper and we drew birds. Not until much later did it dawn on me that art was perhaps not one of his gifts for the birds were very rudimentary—Vees with curved sides—which I admired hugely and reproduced at school for years. Once having done them he was never allowed to escape. Sometimes he daringly put these flicks into a location in space by indicating houses beneath them, straight lines for roof ridges, slanting for the gables and oblong chimneys with straight-lined smoke.

After all those years it is a pity we cannot thank our grandparents, parents, aunts and uncles but most of all Uncle Ainslie himself for completely shielding Ralph and me and the younger Kathleen and Ian from a sorrow that must have grievously afflicted them all. To my mother's journal again,

'Mrs Chisholm has already received over 300 letters of condolence and cards. All the letters speak of Ainslie's great patience and pluck in his trying illness. It—his courage and patience, seems to have struck everyone who came in contact with him. It seems strange that a life like his, a nature so fine and thoroughly good should be taken away when so many 'wasters' are left to injure themselves and all who have any connection with them.'

She continues later,

'Elaine has never asked why I am wearing black as I thought she was almost bound to do, especially as she has seen a good many funerals lately, military or otherwise. Nor did she inquire very much as to what I was doing in Edinburgh,' (we were temporarily in Hawick) 'last Monday and Tuesday. On Wednesday when she was out with me she said quite suddenly, 'You look very pretty Mummy, in your nigger costume'.'

Children often intuitively suck in information about unpleasant events though they may be inhibited from questioning lest the answers confirm their dreads or upset the adults on whom they depend for emotional security. I was never told, "Uncle Ainslie is dead". But I knew.

In that year we were many months away from Edinburgh so more rarely at the Crescent but I clearly remember an incident on a visit home. I was standing at Goldenacre, near a chemist and the Post Office, fidgeting beside my mother and an acquaintance. As the interminable conversation went on above my head I was alerted by a change of tone. "How did she," (in a whisper and with a nod down to me) "Take it? She was very attached, was she not?"

"Well, oddly enough," said my mother, a wary eye on my unresponsive countenance, "she has never asked… or said anything… but children soon forget".

I knew they were talking about Uncle Ainslie, (to quote a daughter as yet many years unborn, "I'm not a FOOL, you know") and this child never has forgotten. Nor did my cousin Ralph for on mentioning Uncle Ainslie once to his greatest friend she immediately said, "He was a wonderful person, wasn't he? Ralph always said so."

So from the two of us I pass on to the limited immortality of a family, the memory of a favourite uncle and a much loved man.

CHAPTER SIXTEEN

Nodding Plumes

MY MOTHER was right in saying I had seen a lot of funerals lately. This was none of her doing for she had an abnormal horror of the mere mention of death, probably resulting from the shock, at the age of eight, of losing her mother, followed by the disintegration of the home, the separation from her two brothers and virtual disappearance of her father. She never, to us at least, spoke of these childhood years. Had she been able to do so she might have released some tensions and made it easier for her to live with herself and incidentally with her children. She did all in her power, in a rather ineffective way, to shield us from knowledge of death, even to the extent—inexplicable in a person of literary and artistic talents—of defacing a lovely Hans Andersen, bound in limp blue covers, whenever a mention of death was on its gold-edged pages. As instructions to our nurses, maids, relatives or anyone who might be 'reading out loud' to us or maybe as guide-lines for herself, whole lines and paragraphs were heavily scored out in black 2B pencilling and above the titles of many of the stories in the same 2B pencil were the underlined words in block capitals, NOT TO BE READ. Those knowing their Hans Christian Andersen will realise that not much was left to be read. Though an avid reader and since my chickenpox days with Fairy Bluebell, well able to read, so foolishly obedient were we as children that I never did read those forbidden portions till we 'did' Hans Andersen's Fairy Tales at school. The burden of guilt so easily in those days imposed on children, at least in our family, would have been too great.

Once I did, when about nine, read a forbidden book, or more accurately what I supposed from the circumstance of its being hidden away in a cupboard, to be a forbidden book. For days I sat in happiness, on the drawing-room carpet, concealed by the open cupboard door, ready to substitute for my engrossing find, should I hear my mother approach, a boring leather-bound and fringed book about British Columbia, a present from her brother Willie who had for a time worked in Canada. When eventually surprised, I found that the book had been intended for me as a Christmas or birthday present but laid aside for a later occasion as my mother thought it too old for me. True, it did mention death and the danger of death but scarcely seemed to qualify for being placed on even a family Index. It was Louisa M. Alcott's *Little Women*!

Again I recall in my early teens, while happily and haphazardly accompanying my own singing at the piano—with no transistors or Walkmasters we had to get music and rhythm out of our systems by our own efforts—moving from favourites of *The Scottish Orpheus,* 'The Rowan Tree', 'The Auld Hoose' and 'Leezie Lindsay', through more robust items from *The Scottish Students' Song Book,* 'Gaudeamus', 'A-Roving', 'Excelsior' and 'For To Admire', to 'The Wearing of The Green' and 'Drink to me Only'. The 'March of the Cameron Men' shook the piano and then it was the dramatic drawing-room ballads of Fred Weatherley and others to which with mutual satisfaction my father and I used to give voice of an evening. 'A Jovial Monk Am I' was tricky, we excelled in 'The Admiral's Broom' and 'When Saw You Last your Father, Boy?' There were so many others too, 'Linden Lea' and *The Indian Love Lyrics* with 'Pale Hands I Loved beside the Shalimar' and others with accompaniments evocative of bells— camel and temple—that the recitals were usually terminated only by hoarseness or flagging fingers. One evening I had advanced to the *Church of Scotland Hymnary* of the day, an edition far superior to any of its too frequent revisions and was drawing to a close with an impressive (to my mind) rendering of Crossing the Bar, 'Sunset and evening star', when my father came charging up the stairs, uncharacteristically for him, really angry.

"Don't play that!" he hissed. "You're upsetting your mother! It Brings Things Back."

Disgruntled, I broke off in mid-voice, puzzled as to what tragedy I could be recalling to her. Like most young people living what they consider uninteresting lives, I was always hopeful of high drama, rich relatives in Australia (we had none) dying and leaving us fortunes or dark unmentionable skeletons in cupboards coming home to roost! Needless to say I never again dared tentatively to finger out anything in the nature of a marche funèbre, no matter how classical or celebrated. It might have been of course that my father, faced with a drooping wife, took matters into his own hands but even if not it seemed to me then, as it seems to me still, to have shown a ridiculous excess of sensibility. I was bound to stop soon—the hymn has only three verses.

Despite her shows of sensibility and all her 2B pencillings it was obviously impossible for my mother, during these years of the Great War to end all wars, to conceal the fact of death from her children. Not only were there more funerals than usual with men from the trenches being brought home only to die but death in those days was not decently, or, according to your point of view, indecently hurried away in a motor-hearse with the least possible inconvenience to the traffic of the living but from the drawing-down of blinds in all the neighbours' houses it was indulged with full panoply of black mourning coach with carved urns and magnificent black horses with well-groomed tails and plumes nodding above their heads. They led the procession of horse-drawn coaches and cabs bearing the soberly dressed mourners, veiled women and men with shiny black hats. The day of the Saulies was not so long gone. Uncle John, really my mother's uncle, wrote in November 1929 of his uncle Andrew Macdougall who had been Precentor at St George's Parish Church, Buchanan Street, Glasgow.

'St George's was at that period a very fashionable church. Over 70 years ago it was customary at the funerals of members of wealthy families to employ two or more Saulies to ride in advance of the hearse mounted on beautiful black horses. If I remember aright they wore evening dress

111

or Frock coats and black cloaks, top hats to which were attached long flowing scarves tied in a large bow, the long ends falling down behind the rider's back, black knee breaches and black stockings and black shoes with broad silver buckles.

Each Saulie carried in his right hand a black truncheon like a Field Marshal's Baton. Barbara thinks Saulies also walked alongside the hearse. I once as a boy saw Uncle Andrew acting as a Saulie and mounted on a handsome horse and sitting in the saddle as one to the manner born. It had a very stately and imposing effect.'

The cavalcades I was accustomed to watch in Edinburgh did not take advantage of their combined horse power but made a decorous way through the streets where the public, standing for a minute still, men raising their hats, paid homage to a soul's passing. I read once an hilarious account, I think by Bernard Shaw, of a Dublin funeral, when the horses took fright and went galloping along the roads, the hearse rollicking behind them. Funerals in the Ferry Road and Inverleith Row were never like that. I stood on the kerb beside the prams and listened to Mary and Ella commenting in muted voices above me on the turn-out and speculating as to the identity of the late-departed now making a last journey through native streets in possibly greater style than ever in life. I too speculated on the identity of the late-departed but in my case it was on the identity of the soon-to-be-late-departed. Ever so often nowadays when I contemplate the apparently inborn knowledge of so many things in my children—and even more so in my grandchildren—am I struck not by the ignorance and innocence of myself as a child but my sheer abysmal stupidity. For years I thought the grace before meals that we gabbled three times a day, afternoon tea being exempt, was not 'For what we are about to receive ...' but 'For a quarter of what we are about to receive may the Lord make us truly thankful.' I thought it showed the Lord in a pleasant light as a Being of unsuspected gastronomic discrimination—did he perhaps dislike rabbit and tripe as much as I did? —but I wondered how he had arrived at such an exact measure for our thanks. So it was that now I peered into every conveyance as it passed, wondering which of all those sombre but quietly chatting persons was the dead person and marvelling that he or she could travel so peacefully when soon to be put underground.

A caring child would have suffered agonies on their behalf but the plain truth is that I did not. As I remember I reasoned that all God does is right and if this was the time He had ordained for someone's departure to the Happy Land there was nothing to be done about it. A faint misgiving did occasionally strike me as to God's criterion for wedding the person to the hour but I brushed that away with the comfortable thought that only the old died and as soon as the knots of men, women and children with bicycles, prams and scooters dispersed and the built-up traffic began to move, I went off skipping happily along the pavements—taking care only to not step on the lines.

CHAPTER SEVENTEEN

Buskers, Bands and Bankers

IN THOSE DAYS of the First World War 'well-brought-up' middle-class children had more sheltered and no doubt healthier existences than had those whom we called, quite simply with no thought of patronage, 'poor children'. The word class and the conception of it was never in even my adolescent consciousness and certainly never in connection with any of the acquaintances of our childhood. 'Poor children' were a different matter. Their disappearance, for the focus of poverty has moved, must be the biggest single difference I see between the Britain of today and that of the first quarter of the twentieth century. They were marked out by their appearance as much as is a foreign ethnic group today. Often poorly or not at all shod, with jerseys matted, skirts and trousers skimpy or several sizes too big, frocks bearing the stamp of the jumble sale, from necessity not for period cachet, heads cropped, they have vanished from our streets absorbed into the well-dressed chain-store norm.

Despite all adults said of their disadvantages they did seem to have more fun than we had. They were free to roam the streets, playing in them all those exciting games, peevers, bools in the gutter, skipping with the rope tied to lamp-posts, tossing home-made diabolos, clattering rough iron hoops from barrels along pavements, paddling in Puddocky or other stretches of the Water of Leith and in the parks swarming all over the swings and round-abouts and see-saws with no thought of who had been there before leaving goodness knows what dire germs. We were not allowed to play on

114

the road or pavement outside the house, this at a time when traffic-wise in suburban Edinburgh it would have been almost completely safe to do so. What was our garden FOR? Besides we did not want to go making nuisances of ourselves. Making a nuisance of oneself was about the worst crime a child could commit. True, the mores of a nearby family must have been different for with balls and ropes and prams they played on the pavement until, it seemed to my jaundiced ears, all hours. I envied but never joined them. They were anyway mostly younger and I would have been shamed by being called in for our ridiculously early bed-time, for years half-past six. I must have been nearly eleven when one night in the bathroom I savoured the delirium of finding I was still up at ten minutes to nine. Naturally I fought and argued and wrangled over this issue of bedtime, occasionally winning a grudging extension of a quarter of an hour but when won this was as dust and ashes for after I had made all the fuss and received all the opprobrium my little brother shared in the triumph, a good two years before it was his due. "Don't be so selfish, Elaine. Why should Ian go to bed when you are up?"

The other long-running battle was over pocket-money. I realise today's children have pocket-money troubles too but theirs are about the amount. We quite simply had none. We were lucky children, in a nice house with caring parents, bed and board provided—"What do you need pocket-money FOR?" Our weekly comics were on the paper-bill and we did not need nor often get sweets (bad for the teeth). All true though the last deprivation did little for the family teeth and the sweetest toothed of us perversely had the best ones, but how frustrating. 'Poor children' definitely scored here. Bands of them turned up on our doorstep, guising, at Hallowe'en and Hogmanay from miles away, Canonmills or Leith, to be given pennies and ha'pennies and praise for their ill-rehearsed but determined performances of verse and song before clattering away into the dark.

Birthday and Christmas gifts of money were not popular with us as they were immediately taken away to be put in the Bank to swell our savings until we really needed them. When if not now? We never thought of attempting to release it. That meant bankbooks (mother's wardrobe) a walk to the bank on the Mound where, chins scarcely up to the high broad polished counters we would have had to try to crack the mystique of banking. It was a project not even contemplated.

The appropriation of our cash on birthdays and at Christmas was irritating though on those occasions there were gifts in kind to mask the disappointment. It was the purloining of the casual out of season windfall that was so exasperating as when our great-aunt and great-uncles visited us. Uncle Harry could always be depended on for the odd coins and so could Uncle John. Despite being an inventor or perhaps because he was an inventor (of a marine valve still travelling the seven seas) he often seemed a little vague yet he had obviously heard that tipping the young was an acceptable thing to do. He would say goodbye, get as far as the gate, then stop and putting a hand in his pocket draw it out with a sixpence or two.

"Perhaps you could do something with these. Would they be of any use?" His apparent vagueness had not swamped his scientific acumen, the whole performance was an elaborate joke. We would thank them, following to wave them away in the taxi, or on good days in their Daimler, John, Mr Carswell to us, at the helm then turn towards our mother in despair.

"I'll put your money safely in the Bank," said she.

My parents do not seem to have been alone in their attempt to inculcate their children with the virtues of saving. My brother's wooden tank, ranged along with the Red Cross ambulance, was in reality a money-box bearing the words

'If you would the Kaiser spank,
Put your money in your tank.'

My money-box was in the form of a small wooden stool fit for a teddy. It bore another rhyme—

'Our wee Bairn
Is no fool.
She puts her money
In the stool.'

Bankers! How I hated them. Small wonder that in later years when

116

my father was trying to impress on me the desirability of having a good job (with a pension) and eventually marrying a good man (with a pension)—who at nineteen wants a pension?—I burst out indignantly that whatever happened to me I would never marry a banker.

Bankers are still with us and have on the whole turned out to be a perfectly agreeable type of person but people who have largely vanished from our scene, apart from musicians in the London Underground and theatre buskers, are the multitudes of entertainers who used to enliven our walks. If the Punch and Judy man was at the Mound I used sometimes to try and persuade my mother to cross and watch although like many small children I found the show repellent rather than pleasing. The Organ-grinders, churning out their bright mechanical music, with their monkey companions sitting a-top in cap and jacket, I loved. Like the Punch and Judy men, the Band Stand Orchestras and the mistily remembered German Bands marching cheerfully through our streets, they were of a superior caste, dying relics of a Victorian breed of true professionals, very different even to a child's eye from the thin, ill-dressed, often disabled musicians and pavement artists, sad legacy of the war and post-war poverty.

Although I regularly admired the blues and green, pinks and purples of the brightly chalked drawings of flowers and castles and ships at sea of a pavement artist, I felt disturbed as I stepped carefully over his one good leg, that he, surely in need of care, should have to sit there on a sack in a windy street. Among other regular local entertainers was a raucous red-faced singer who bellowed his way through our neighbourhood. I imagine the coins tossed to him to hurry him on his way were mostly exchanged for liquid comfort. Quite other were the elderly blind couple, perhaps husband and wife, a well-known pair in our part of Edinburgh, who made me feel very uncomfortable as they passed singing in wind or shine, and once I remember in snow with hopeless upturned and rather angry faces on frequent slow journeys through the streets of Trinity and Inverleith.

Along with the Organ-grinders and Bands the other most colourful travellers to frequent the streets of my childhood were neither Buskers nor beggars but the hard-working Newhaven Fish Wives in their distinctive blue and white striped skirts, part gathered over their hips and with white cap and shawl. They carried wicker creels on their backs, a broad leather band round the forehead taking the strain. Mostly fair-haired, the result some thought of an ancestry in the Low Countries, they were renowned for their lovely complexions, supposedly from their contact with the natural oils from the fish. True or not, they deserved this bonus, for the fish, cold with ice, must have been most disagreeable to handle in Edinburgh's frequent east winds. The same family, first mother, then daughters came to us regularly every week for years, filletting our choice of fresh sea-food on the doorstep.

CHAPTER EIGHTEEN

Enter the Aulds

ON MY MOTHER'S side of the family we had no grandparents. We had the Aulds.

Sometime after Mary Jane died on the 5th of December 1889 Charles Edward, when or on what pretext I do not know, seems to have abandoned his young family who were cared for by his brother Jack and wife Janet in Cardross with their own son. When my mother was about fourteen she went on a visit to her mother's people in Dennistoun and thereafter her home was with them. The two families did not agree so for several years the sister and brothers rarely met. When they eventually did it was from my mother's initiative but they never made up the missing years and she knew her Graham cousins better. People are forever surprising but I find it difficult to reconcile the somewhat selfish woman my mother became with the ardent and attractive young girl she must have been. Life, or her approach to it, had someway failed her. Her health may have been to blame. She always described herself as 'highly strung' and she certainly suffered badly from post-menopausal troubles which today would have been understood and alleviated. Perhaps it was the frustration, the being 'only a housewife' for she wrote and had published poems and stories for both the adult and children's markets and painted in water colour and on wood and pottery. These two last activities gained her membership of the Craft section of the Society of Scottish Women Artists. Tensions may no doubt have risen off and on in what initially I am sure was an

119

extremely happy marriage. I have a memory from very early days of hearing her address my father not as Willie but what my ears heard as 'Julius' obviously, however misinterpreted, a private endearment.

Certainly—apart from invariably throwing cold water on any of our schemes!—my mother had always a more open mind than had my father. She for instance sympathised with the Suffragette movement although she did not feel called upon to be active.

'Minnie' [cousin of mother-in-law but more of my parents' generation] 'is very keen. I am quite in sympathy with their ideas but I don't believe in the militant policy of breaking windows, throwing ginger-beer bottles at Cabinet Ministers etc.' [Later] 'Minnie Hislop came in to talk about the Suffrage—as usual. She is very keen. I really sympathise with the cause but somehow I can't work up very much enthusiasm about it. If they get it will it do any good. It is one of their contentions that it will make a great difference in the moral and social status of women. I believe in Norway where they have only had it three or four months they have already got a bill passed about the custody of children, giving the mother equal rights with the father over the guardianship of the child in marriage, and in the case of children born out of marriage giving the child the right to bear its father's name if the mother can prove within the first few months whom the father is. If granting Women's Suffrage could do such things in the social and moral life of women then the sooner we have it the better.'

She goes on to discuss the case of Lady Constance Lytton who when arrested under her own name 'was simply fawned upon in prison' and released without being subjected to forcible feeding by order of the Home Secretary 'but in Liverpool when supposed to be a plain Miss the prison doctor resorted to slapping her face'. Minnie must have been pleased to have found a sympathetic listener among her young relatives, the less seriously minded like our contemptuous aunt scoffed at her, but my mother, less than two years married, ends

'But there are two sides to every question. I can't quite agree with the way they abuse the poor men. Perhaps I am prejudiced in their favour because I have got such a splendid darling husband.'

As children we went two or three times a year to have tea with Minnie and her mother An Taggie and aunt Aunt Alice, familiarly known as Dido. Despite this she was a little alarming as she had been an eminent schoolmistress, Lady Superintendent of George Watson's

Ladies College and had still something of the manner. One of them, I think Dido, left me an attractive small pink velvet lined silver trinket box. Minnie and An Taggie gave me a book every Christmas bought from a scripture book-shop but of no particular religious slant. Often they were written by a woman with the odd name of Theodora Benson Benson. I think she wrote the one I enjoyed about the travels of the Apostle Paul but not the even better one of stories from Longfellow's *Golden Legend*. I never saw as much of Cousin Minnie as I would have liked for I have the happiest of memories of her. She presented my daughter Rosemary with a handsome hand-knitted and stuffed orange and brown Humpty Dumpty. Without a new baby in the family he might have found his way like most of her handicrafts to the stalls of some Dublin Street Baptist Church Bazaar for which she was an indefatigable worker. Her summer holidays she usually passed at a resort where she could collect Scottish gem stones which she later sent to Cornwall to have polished and mounted as rings and brooches for the same charitable destination. The outbreak of war in September 1939 found her in Nairn and she decided to return home immediately. A lesser person would have jettisoned the stones she had collected but not yet sorted over. Minnie just put them all in a suitcase and struggled back on a journey involving at least one change of train, the weight of her luggage surprising porters into ribald suggestion of spies and bombs. Not a person to be perturbed by any ill-informed critical judgements of her relatives whom she regarded with cool and tolerant eye. She gave up two of her afternoons on one of her highland holidays to keep me company as I lay at home recovering from a miscarriage and entertained me with her very sane comments on the lives of her and my relations of two generations. Her claim to fame in the family was that she was one of the first Norland Nannies. I was an unimpressed baby for my mother said I always cried when she took me over and subjected me to the soothing technique of what my mother called the 'Norland Bumps.'

Art, literature, drama, music all interested my mother. Her husband, without much understanding of it, admired her artistic bent and carried about in his wallet copies of her prize-winning poems which he proudly showed to friends. Being the eldest of the family I certainly found in her more than could my younger sisters of her earlier happier self though in my young adult years she was difficult indeed. All our sympathies then were with our father, a patient, kindly, conventional man who, where we saw her as selfish saw her as sensitive. I have thought since that the troubles that were always arising over my choice of friends, usually because of their (supposed) lack of social standing stemmed from his attitudes rather than from hers. He was occasionally capable of the most shaming though one had to admit entertaining remarks. "By gad! Had such a fellow come after one of my sisters, my father would have kicked him down the front steps!"

He was such a temperate sensible-seeming man that it was difficult not to be drawn into confidences with him. I remember standing idly beside him in the garden of 4 Wardie Road between the still-flowering Michaelmas daisies and the falling apples, so it was late autumn, probably into November and rhapsodising about my new University life.

"It's all so interesting, not only the work but," said I naively, "meeting all those people from other schools, Gillespies, Royal High and Boroughmuir" (we were Academy, Institution and Private) "and finding they are just like us." My father moved his pipe from his mouth. "That" said he, "is the Trouble about University."

In later years my mother could talk disparagingly with friends over erring or errant servants, but in earlier days she had always a good relationship with them and many who left to better themselves financially came back to visit or corresponded. It took the years after the first World War when the flighty young things having had a taste of freedom in Munition Factories or the Services turned their noses up at the potential slave labour of domestic service preferring regular hours and wages in office, shop or industry, to find her thinking in terms of 'the servant problem.' I remember overheard snatches of conversation on the phone, probably to Dedae, "...do you know, she actually asked to see the room she would be sleeping in! I felt I was the one being interviewed!"

My father's side of the family were much more class-bound though I must in all fairness say that my extremely snobbish aunt, prone to writing off numbers of her own acquaintances as 'not quite out of the top-drawer', had the most friendly relations with her mother's servants and in later years when they were married stayed with them in their Highland homes and on occasion helped with the lambing. Whether she originally viewed them as might a benevolent plantation owner his favourite slaves and then came to spy out their merits for herself I do not know. I am sure she was appreciative of the company of Alice and Daisy and other young girls in an aging household. During my formative years it was certainly never suggested to me that the various Marys, Marthas and Chrissies who lived with us and shared every aspect of our lives were in any way inferior to us. For that credit must go to my mother and beyond her to Aunt Barbara whose rapport with her staff seemed perfect.

After the Stewart family disintegrated with the death of their mother I am sure that both sister and brothers were happier and more fortunate in their new homes than they ever would have been in a household run by Charles Edward Stewart whose behaviour seems to have given cause for concern before his wife's death. His father-in-law had I believe to come to his rescue financially more than once and my mother has a revealing journal entry dated 23rd July 1901 which makes me understand more why she was so reticent with us. During this Glasgow Fair she and the Aulds were yachting nearly every day.

'We had a weekend at Tarbert, the first time I ever slept on board and also went to Inveraray, Inch Marnock, Loch Ranza; round Bute and Gairloch etc. ...... At Gairloch we saw the cottage where 13 or 14 years ago, Father and Mother, the two boys and I spent, what was destined to be, with the exception of a few days at Skermorlie, next year, mother's last holiday at the seaside. Had anyone told me then, that I would not set foot on Gairloch Head for 14 years and that it would then be, alone as far as father, mother and brothers were concerned, I should not have believed them. As I went ashore in the yacht's dinghy, with Uncle John, B Graham and her father, I could not help contrasting this visit with my first one. Then, we went as a united, if not extremely happy family, now—Mother dead, father a mere memory and not a very pleasant one at that, at present, to all accounts, living a life of utter degradation; a social outcast, my brothers not seen for years—what a change.'

I wish I had persevered with the few questions I did ask her or had thought to interrogate Aunt Barbara (or better, Cousin Annie Graham who knew everything) but what to me, a schoolgirl of the twenties, were grandparents who had died so long ago?

We had no need for a second set of grandparents—we had the Aulds.

Aunt Barbara, Uncle John and Uncle Harry were in our youth the surviving members of the nine children of Ann M'Dougall and David Auld, Ironmaster and Foundry Owner of Glasgow. Ann Auld died on the 29th of November 1874. This I have long known as Aunt Barbara gave me the mourning ring that had been made for her, a simple gold band with three seed pearls and ME MO RI AM spelt round it in gold lettering, the spaces between being filled with tightly woven hair. Engraved inside is the legend, 'My mother died, 29 Nov. 1874'. I had always supposed that Aunt Barbara had from that date taken over the care of the house and of her father and five brothers. There were two other daughters, Annie and Mary Jane but both were married, my grandmother only a year and half before her mother's death. There seems to have been an interregnum of second wife for in 1876 David Auld married Annie Naismith. She did not die until 1898 but as there is no further mention of her it would look as if the marriage were not a success and they were living apart.

Until I started probing in the family history I knew only one thing about my grandmother, apart from the fact that she had died when my mother was a child, and that was that she was very pretty, with large blue eyes, "the flower" as Aunt Barbara poetically and rather uncharacteristically put it, "of the flock". This knowledge was acquired in a memorable way.

One of the charms of the Aulds to us children was the unpredictability of their visits. We never knew when we would not be happily surprised by their arrival at our gate, on foot from the car (tram), more rarely by cab or taxi and occasionally in Carswell's Daimler. Strictly

124

speaking the Daimler was not Carswell's. It belonged to the Aulds. Carswell was their general factotum, chauffeur, boatman and handyman but so careful of the Daimler and its welfare was he and so jealous of its comings-in and goings-out, especially in bad weather, that we felt it to be his. My mother was not so charmed by her relatives' habit of erratic appearances. Like us she was fond of them and it was irritating to come home from an afternoon's trivial outing to find that not only had they been—from Glasgow—but also gone, for Aunt Barbara was an energetic lady who rarely sat long. Once Mary, who knew them well, did prevail upon them to come in and wait. Casting the baby to the girl in the kitchen she sped up to Princes Street with what speed the cable-cars indulged in and retrieved us from the store in which she had rightly suspected we were shopping. There was initial panic as my mother jumped to the conclusion that some ill had befallen Marjorie but it was a great excitement for Ian and me and provided an unusual jaunt for Mary.

There came an afternoon some years later when we not only knew they were coming but also when they were likely to arrive. They had called in at Mackay and Chisholm, probably to order a wedding present—the Glasgow connection was very good at making such purchases from my father—and he had phoned to alert his wife. She despatched me with Marjorie to the car terminus at Goldenacre to meet them and escort them home. The cars, being on rails, did not run in to the kerb-side but stopped in the middle of the road. Most passengers passed over the intervening cobbles as expeditiously as possible to avoid the onslaught of penned-up bicycles, motors and horse-drawn vehicles. Not so Aunt Barbara. As we stepped from the rather high pavement to greet her, she stopped dead, took my sister by the arm and gazing into her face uttered the mystifying words,

"You're Mary Jane!" (What did she mean? She was Marjorie Annie.)

"She was the flower of the flock."

We did not know that some years earlier when Marjorie was four a cousin of my mother, Johnnie Graham,

'Had astonished me and everybody else by saying that Marjorie is the

125

image of my mother. He seemed very struck by it and said he noticed the resemblance whenever he saw her. We have never noticed any resemblance to anyone in the family in particular in Marjorie but of course I don't remember my mother's appearance tho' Johnnie would. He seemed surprised to think the others hadn't noticed it before.'

Poor Aunt Barbara. She lost her mother in 1874, a younger brother in 1877, the youngest in 1881, her sister in 1889, the winter her sister-in-law and baby niece also died, her father in 1899 and another brother in 1909.

Poor Mary Jane too. She seems to have danced happily into marriage but unless hers was the sort of happy heart that is also light and sees no ill in those she loves or has loved, I fear it can have brought her no lasting happiness. In 'family archives', a cardboard box of odds and ends, are four pieces of paper ephemera relating to her. One is a note agreeing to meet her and together to visit a mutual friend, signed 'your affectionate companion M Colquhoun'. This is dated 11th November 1864. Another, post-marked 5th March 1864 is not in the same handwriting but looks to be from another affectionate companion as it bears a family resemblance to the decorated envelopes young people of today send their friends as they probably have done throughout the ages. This one is white, narrow and addressed in very beautiful calligraphy to

> Mifs Mary Jane Auld
> Bennie Place
> Glasgow

There is an edging of narrow green ribbon like a frame round the front of the envelope. At the back the ribbon makes a diagonal cross the centre of which is held down by a red sealing-wax seal. A piece of yellow ribbon is pasted on the top flap and piece of purple at the left-hand edge. Traces of gum on the bottom flap and at the right-hand edge possibly indicate that other strips of ribbon were there. Written across the right-hand end of the back in small, but still elegant letters, are the words, 'You will rue the opening of this note.' The note had been opened notwithstanding, slit along the bottom so as not to disturb the ribbon adornment. I wonder what gossip or ominous news it had conveyed? The defection of a swain perhaps? When I looked inside it was empty apart from a piece of yellow ribbon. Was this a message in Victorian young ladies' colour language, meaning jealousy, or envy threatens or was it just a missing scrap of decoration?

There are two letters written by Mary Jane. The first, on pink note-paper from Ashbrook Cottage, Garelochead must have been written on the first day of her honeymoon, which would be the 6th June 1873.

'My dear Mother,

I hope you are well and none the worse of last night also that Father is well and happy and able to laugh. If not tell Barry to give him a good scolding although I hope he is not requiring it by this time. We have been very fortunate in getting this place they are very nice people and could not be kinder to us than what they are. Last night we had had one marriage supper from Mrs Bennie [perhaps Rennie] so you see we did not miss all the good things. When we arrived last night Mrs B presented me with a bouquet of flowers which I took to be very thoughtful of her and kind. She remarked at the time that she had read in the papers of one of the Princesses being presented with one at a similar time so she thought she would make me a Princess for the night. We many a time thought of you all last night wishing you might have a happy evening also that you received the telegram. I came away without my mantle which I missed as it was wet. Some of you might come down on Saturday as it is a holyday anyway try and come as it is so very pretty down here and if any of you do come please to bring my mantle. Charlie wishes me to convey his thanks to one and all of you for complete arrangements for the wedding he is never done speaking about it. Also he wishes Barry to gather up all the presents as he has got a note of all them so she need not try to cheat. We intend going to the fishing in the afternoon and if we can spare a boxful of them we will send them up. You need not concern yourselves about us getting our meat as we have plenty and to spare. If none of you are down on Saturday Charlie expects to be in town on Tuesday or Wednesday and will be most happy to arrange with any of you that would like to come next week if you get a day like what this is you would enjoy yourselves. Tell Father that they feed cats on mussels here there was a large potfull of them boiled this morning for them. Wishing you all well and happy.
                    I remain
                        Your loving
                            Daughter
                                Mary Jane'

127

Her next (preserved) letter is dated June 27th 1873 and headed from Mount Pleasant. Where that is or whether it is a house or a place, I do not know. They are still out of Glasgow. Possibly after the honeymoon they moved to a seaside home of their own. I hope the move was planned and not occasioned by Charlie 'falling out' with the kind Mrs Bennie, 'falling out' appearing to have been one of his characteristics.

'My dear Mother,

I am very sorry that I have disappointed you in not writing before this time but I expected to have been up this week so that is the reason I did not write. You should get better quick and come down and see this house Barbara is quite delighted with it, it is such a fine roomy house. If you were down today you would get a bit of plum pudding Barbara has made one so you see we are not starving Andrew. We received Ann's letter yesterday and we are glad to see from it that you are all so happy. We have had very wet weather this week although it has damped the ground yet it has not damped our spirits. I could scarcely get doing any work this morning for Andrew is so full of fun and nonsense and gives me a carry on his back whenever he can get the hold of me it is time you were down to keep us in order so you better get well as soon as possible or I doubt you will find it hard work to tame us so mind what I am telling you and get better. Andrew and Robert are away out with Colin. Barry and I are going round to see the Brownlees. Wishing you all well and happy expecting to see you next week.

I remain your
Loving daughter
Mrs Stewart'

There is a slight flourish under the signature so I suppose the assumption of matronly dignity was to make her mother laugh. Indeed the whole tone of the letter with its rambling trivialities may be not so much an index of Mary Jane's nature as a deliberate attempt to boost her mother's spirits. The cause of Ann Auld's death is given as 'Disease of heart 10 years. Disease of Brain 4 years. Bronchitis 14 days.' Could disease of Brain mean a nervous illness, perhaps depression.

Andrew and Robert were the two youngest sons of David and Ann. At this time Andrew was seventeen and Robert fourteen. Both were delicate. Andrew died at the age of twenty-one in 1877 and Robert in 1881 at the age of twenty-two. Charles Edward and Mary Jane Stewart had a son (Charles Edward) born in Rothesay in 1880. He died in Ingleby Street Glasgow at the age of 11 months. There were miscarriages and perhaps another birth in Rothesay before the move to Glasgow and as in her letter Mary Jane seems to assume that her mother will know of the Colin and Brownlees she refers to, it is possible that Mount Pleasant was in Bute.

The fortuitously preserved scraps of paper and Aunt Barbara's and Johnnie Graham's spontaneous recognition years later are almost all the personal contact we have with Mary Jane. Such as they are they clothe in pleasing form the slight human semblance of a grandmother barely emerging from the mists of the unknown.

CHAPTER NINETEEN

And Now the Stewarts

IF MARY JANE has been until recently a shadowy ghost in our knowledge of the family's past, Charles Edward Stewart, rarely spoken of, was to our imagination not so much shadowy as shady. Without being told in as many words, we sensed that he was not approved of by his wife's relations. Whether this had been an instinctive reaction from the first—why else did the bride of a day so anxiously hope that 'Father by this time was able to laugh'?—or whether it grew from his repeated financial failures or discovered character deficiencies I do not know. Myself I have the idea that although attractive, probably a charmer and handsome as the Stewarts were—Uncle Willie and my mother were both dark and striking-looking, she with a fine complexion and true black hair— he was possibly something of a light-weight, unreliable and maybe a bit of a poseur.

As children we had the beguiling idea that he 'travelled in stays'. He is described in various documents as warehouseman or stay manufacturer with premises in St Enoch Square and at other Glasgow addresses, with at times fifteen employees, so this statement was entirely correct but in our imaginations did little to enhance the idea of him as a sober reliable citizen. Also in my mind, stays, besides being the figure controllers concocted of whalebone, laces and linen, chiefly the province of women, spoke to me, as a result of Henty, Ballantyne and Kingston, of ships' rigging which made him seem more flighty still. As there was in this case, as in so many of my ideas about the family arising from half-understood overheard remarks in my childhood, a substratum of fact, it may be that my reading of my grandfather's character is not so far from the truth. There was almost certainly financial inequality between the families—the Aulds though far from pretentious, indeed rather plain-living, were sufficiently well-to-do to own both a Glasgow and a sea-side house and to commission the building of their own yachts.

When the death of one parent and the apparent desertion of the other left the young family with no natural guardian, I had always supposed the boys went to the father's brother and the girl to the mother's home but according to a Stewart cousin things did not go so smoothly. The Aulds were willing to be financially responsible for the care of the children but in an institution, not living with them. John Tytler Stewart, Charles Edward's brother, said his brother's family were going to no institution and he took them all into his own home. David and Willie remained with him but about seven years later the Aulds gave Annie a home. In extenuation of what seems on the face of it to have been very insensitive behaviour on the part of Mary Jane's family, I must, in fairness, point out that in this year, 1889, Uncle John lost his wife on the 7th of November and their three-week-old daughter on the 15th. So the added grief of the death of a sister and daughter on the 5th of December may have been too much for the bereaved family to cope with. At this time the father, David Auld, was presumably in control and he was possibly exasperated by earlier repeated calls for financial help for his son-in-law. Seven years later he may to an extent have mellowed and with increasing age left more to his sons and daughter. Aunt Barbara, I imagine, was probably coming to realise that her portion in life would be to care for her father and brothers rather than to marry and have a family of her own. Both she and Uncle John, who had come back to the family home, possibly saw in their sister's daughter some recompense for the children they did not have.

I do not think my mother was at all aware of the reasons for the lack of a good relationship between the Stewarts and the Aulds. She certainly missed her brothers and from her journal one can tell she sensed a reluctance on her Uncle Jack's part to their having much contact. The Aulds did not seem to have put obstacles in her way. Who can know now what emotions fuelled them all, those eighty to ninety years ago. I am glad Uncle Jack comes so well out of the story for I have a painting of his which I have always loved since I first became aware of it hanging above the dining-room mantelpiece in 39 Inverleith Gardens. He may possibly have given it as a wedding present to my mother. Signed J. Tytler Stewart it is of a pleasant autumn or early winter's evening, bare brown trees, softy tinted sky with horses being watered at a stream.

With Mary Jane's honeymoon letter to her mother there lies also one dated a day later from Ashbrook Cottage to Ann Auld from her newly acquired son-in-law.

'Dear Mother,
    You need not be surprised (as I think you will be when you begin to read this note) as I have taken a great fancy to call you mother and thus have what very few do have namely 2 mothers. I trust that you now are better or at least on the right side of betterness. I am truly fussed when I think of how long you have had this turn—But I hope that you will be all right bye and bye. We had some letters from Glasgow today but none from you and we think we will have yours in the afternoon. Mary has just told me a very nice bit of news which she now commissions me to tell you. Which is that Mr and Mrs Bennie will be very glad to have your company and Fathers any day next week or week following. You already know from Mary's last letter how comfortable and happy we are here and I must really say that we seem to have got the sun of prosperity shining along our path. I know you will be anxious about us but really you need not be for we are conscious of this that if it should always be as it is now there will never be a dark day although we do not expect our days to pass all sunshine. Give my sincere regards to Father and the same to yourself and I trust that both of you will never have any cause to grieve over me as a son-in-law of yours. Tell Father that as he goes away on Monday to Aberdeen to say that I wish him great success, big sales, kind friends, and good health and I think that if any traveller get all that he will come back a glad and happy man. Give my best love to all the rest and I do hope that now we will begin to know each other better and better. I am your affect. son-in-law
            Chas. E Stewart'

I wonder what his parents-in-law made of this communication. He may have felt genuine concern for Ann Auld who had been in poor health for some years but if his wife was endowed with more of the world's goods than was he, I can imagine this talk of the sun of prosperity could strike a wry note with 'Father.' Preferable to me are Mary Jane's loving if oddly punctuated letters. Perhaps he was just a socially insensitive young man but his professions read sadly in the light of his later history. His daughter has a revealing word to say of him in a later journal entry but first one for August 31st 1901.

> 'Since my last entry I have not only entered my twenty-first year; but also seen and spoken to one of my brothers for the first time for nearly seven years. I think my life is going to be rather eventful at any rate last Thursday's happenings were rather out of the common. On that day Uncle John and I went down to Cardross. I had been thinking of going for some time and at last made up my mind that if I ever meant to be any more than a stranger to my brothers it was quite time we were getting to know a little of each other. So we went. It was a dreary dull morning when we left Queen Street and rain was falling when we reached our destination. I felt rather depressed and the uncertainty of the result of our visit did not cheer me. Acting on information received from M Anderson in May, we went first to a nursery near the station...'

This information had been oddly acquired by my mother. 1901 was the year of what she calls the X—an International Exhibition held at Kelvingrove—about which her diary is full. Glasgow citizens were bewitched by it—Glasgow is famed for the excellence of its exhibitions—and with aunt and uncles or cousins and other friends she went to it repeatedly. On May 17th she writes,

> 'Yesterday a very strange thing happened. Kate Oswald [a friend who later married her cousin David Graham] and I were at the Exhibition— with expectations of course. We were sitting outside chatting of things in general and our men friends in particular as girls usually do when they get together—when suddenly a girl touched my arm and said "Are you Miss Annie Stewart?" I said "Yes" but I was completely mystified. "Don't you remember me?" she said, "I am Maggie Anderson." Even then I could not recall her for a moment when it dawned upon me who she was—a niece of my Aunt's in Cardross—whom I hadn't seen for ages. She told me that David was a nurseryman in Cardross, Charlie was in Denny's yard and Willie was coming out for an architect. Charlie and Willie had taken bursaries at school. Aunt Janet had quarrelled with her sisters and their families. She had had a baby which had only lived two days and was in very bad health. Maggie A is working in Grosvenor's

Restaurant in the grounds. She is about 15 or so but how she remembered me I can't tell. I would not have known her anywhere. When I saw her last she was a mere child of six or seven. Some girls might have thought it strange, my speaking to a girl of evidently the lower class like Maggie, but Kate is not one of that sort. I am afraid Miss Drysdale would have turned up her dainty nose at such an acquaintance. I hate people who only value you for what you have not what you are..'

So acting on Maggie Anderson's information—not all of which was correct—Uncle John and his niece

'first went to a nursery near the station, only to learn that David had never worked with them; they thought, however, that he had worked in another nursery in the village. We went there and discovered that he had left, but the Nurseryman thought he was now in Dunbarton. A little disappointed, we thought our best plan would be to go along to the house; we had not intended to go there as Uncle and Aunt Stewart did not give us a very good welcome the last time Annie [an older Graham cousin] and I went, and had in fact been fearfully quarrelsome all along. However we went... but Aunt seemed rather pleased to see us. She showed me a great many paintings of Charlie's [her son] and Willie's; for boys of their years they were really marvellous. Charlie's paintings especially were wonderful; he had taken some bursary or other at the Art School and intends to follow the career of artist. We saw him; he was upstairs painting. He has grown very handsome and tall; he wears spectacles. David we found was in Denny's shipyard; to become an apprentice fitter. He evidently inherits the Auld talents. He was only sent to a nursery because the doctor had advised an open-air life for him, until he had grown stronger. He must be strong enough now, as he has to walk four miles to be in Dunbarton by six. She offered me Willie's address. It is 37 Church Street Dunbarton. We were also invited to come down some Saturday afternoon to see the boys; and before leaving she gave me photographs of the five of them. I wonder if Uncle Stewart would think she had been too friendly. As Uncle John was going to Craigendoran—for Rothesay—we parted at the station and I went into Dunbarton. I felt rather excited when I found Willie's office and opened the door. There are three apprentices in this office under a Mr Denny. Fortunately they were all out except Willie. I recognised Willie by something about his eyes or expression. Our first words after seven years parting were not strikingly dramatic. I asked him if he did not know me. He said he was not very sure; then he told me that he could not get out until another apprentice returned from dinner. I went round the counter and waited. Willie showed me some plans he was making for a house. He is not so tall as I am but very broad-shouldered and sturdy looking; he is fifteen past. He will have a five years

134

apprenticeship but will perhaps be coming to the Glasgow office in West Regent Street where there are five apprentices. I think he was pleased to see me; but now I realised, as I spoke to him, what a five years silence means. How much ground we have lost, never, I am afraid to be regained. I would not have felt so strange with an utter stranger; and then I had always the feeling that he might have been taught to despise me, or at all events to keep me at a distance, metaphorically speaking. It was like looking for something one had mislaid in a dark room; or at least with a very tiny taper. And my little taper was very feeble. Had it been a sister instead of a brother whose acquaintance I was trying to remake it might have been a little different. Girls can generally find an 'Open Sesame' to each other's hearts somewhere; if they can't they make one. But to leave your brother a mere child of seven or eight and to find him again, at fifteen, almost a man; is rather a problem. I felt that, somehow or other, all I could do, at my first meeting at all events, would never get below the surface of things; still I felt more satisfied with my visit than I expected to be. I found that he is not, apparently, a smoker; is fond of reading; and so far as I could get is very intelligent, bright and clever. When his dinner-hour arrived we went to a little tea-room, and had something to eat; after which we took a short walk; and went to the station. We passed one of his masters, Mr Denny, outside; the principal partner is Mr Crawford but he is always in Glasgow. So after all Willie is the brother I have seen first, while somehow I have always thought about meeting David. I must go down and see him, someday soon. Willie had just recovered from a bad attack of diphtheria. Cardross is evidently very unhealthy but as this is the last years lease of their house, Aunt said that she thought they would be coming into town, so that, perhaps I shall see more of them soon. I wonder if David and Willie will ever guess how I have longed to meet them. Willie, at all events, seemed pleased to see me but he is rather shy or reserved; a mixture of both I should say—with a very well developed character of his own. I can't say whom he resembles. On the whole I think, he is more of a Stewart than an Auld; but his hair is dark brown not black like mine, and he has very nice deep blue eyes. I asked him to come and see me and wrote my address in a little note-book of his; I had to buy a pencil which I presented to him. At the station he bought a time-table which he gave me, after writing his address in it—so our first presents to each other were of a severely utilitarian and economic nature. I don't know if he will come up or not, I think he is a little afraid of what Uncle Jack would say to him, if he showed himself too friendly to me. However it won't be my fault, if we don't see a good deal of each other now. I think we will be proud of Willie yet; and I at all events mean to make him really a friend, as well as a brother.'

135

Brave words—but by January 3, 1902, after accounts of rendezvous at the X, holidays and outings to opera and 'mystifiers' with Aunt and Uncles and various junketings with Graham cousins and attentive young gentlemen, she had grown worried again.

> 'I have begun to be rather anxious about my brothers. I sent them cards at Christmas and also answered Willie's last letter. I am afraid Uncle Jack Stewart must consider himself slighted in some way and therefore won't let them return any. He is most hasty tempered. I am afraid we will never be on any more than speaking terms.'

I had never given much thought hitherto to Aunt Janet, being as she was on the periphery of the family, but I find my heart warming to her. She was contending with the death of a baby, poor health, an extended family enforced on her by her brother-in-law's irresponsibility, which no doubt made for economic strain, and one would suspect domestic strain too. She 'seemed rather pleased to see us'. Maggie Anderson's information seems to have had some nuggets of truth among the gossip and if, in all the circumstances she did no worse than fall out with her sisters I think Aunt Janet is to be congratulated.

John Tytler Stewart was an excellent amateur artist, of landscape and portrait and professionally excelled as a worker in stained glass rightly valued by his employers, both in Denny's Ship Yard Dunbarton where he worked in the Decorative Department and later in Wm Meikle and Sons, 19 Wellington Street, Glasgow from whom, on the 27th of November 1905 went this letter to *The Glasgow Evening News*.

> 'Sir, In your issue of Thursday 23 Curt., in the "City and Clyde" column, an article appears under the heading of "Glass Staining," which, interesting though it undoubtedly is, conveys a very erroneous impression to the public mind; and being perfectly satisfied that your only desire is to set forth correctly the facts relating to the matter dealt with therein, we crave space in your columns to make the necessary correction.
>
> Anyone reading the article in question would naturally infer that the two gentlemen named therein, gathering up the results of experiments extending over a period of 50 years, have now brought under public notice, for the first time, the method of producing stained glass windows by what has become known as the "Cameo Process," by which all surface painting and consequent liability to decay is entirely obviated. In this respect it does material injury,

not only to ourselves, but more especially to our chief artist, Mr J. T. Stewart, with whom the idea of the "Cameo Process" really originated.

We do not dispute the statement that etching on glass has been practised for a very long time, but what is material in this connection is that until the production by us of the five-light window erected in Bo'ness Parish Church, as a memorial to the late Queen Victoria, so long ago as September, 1903, no one had conceived the possibility of the production of such a window entirely without surface painting. That window, when exhibited in our studios, was recognised by leading architects and others interested in art matters, as marking a distinct advance in the production of stained glass, and on that account was widely commented on in the public press, as anyone can see for himself by reference to the newspaper files of the period indicated above, and on many occasions of later date in connection with windows subsequently produced by us.

We might have protected the invention by patent, but neither Mr Stewart nor ourselves desired any advantage other than the credit of being leaders in the development of the branch of art practised by us. It is rather hard, however, that anyone deriving benefit from this self-restraint on our part should seek, even inferentially or by suggestion, to deprive Mr Stewart and ourselves of the credit which is our due; and we are sure that no fair-minded person will deny our right to make this plain.

—We are, etc   WM MEIKLE and SONS.'

My mother continues, the gloom of the turn of the year intensified by Hogmanay,

'... and to think it is all caused by father's bad habits; Mother's death, the breaking up of our home, and the changing of a small but very devoted pair of brothers and a sister into a trio of strangers—for I am afraid we will never get to know David or Willie any better.'

I am afraid we are unlikely to get to know the truth of this part of our family history any better either. 'Mother's death' being charged to Charles Edward's account, should not, I hope, be taken literally but as an awkwardly worded reaction to the domestic stresses which even a small child seems to have sensed. From my mother's few journal references to this time I suspect she knew more than she ever said and that the disintegration of her father's character and behaviour—through temperamental instability or indulgence in some vice—had begun before his wife's death and had poisoned the atmosphere of the home for some time. I have always regretted that the rift between the two families was never healed for I would have liked to have known Uncle Jack and Cousin Charlie. I could have done, for John Tytler Stewart lived until 1930 and his son until 1974. Oddly enough, Charles Stewart and Uncle John Auld had in Spiritualism an interest in common but I do not suppose either of them knew of the other in that connection.

The Stewarts passed on an artistic legacy to their descendents but my grandfather's own was a sad story. A diligent researcher discovered for us—what his brother and the Aulds had probably known—that he died on the 25th of July 1905 in Busby Combination Poorhouse, East Kilbride. His death certificate describes him as 'Pauper formerly Packer' and gives his age as 69 whereas he was only 59. My researcher makes as good an assessment of him as any, "From the ten year discrepancy in age I think we can guess that he hadn't worn too well!"

From my mother's diaries comes another revealing entry. It was written on March 4th 1899, shortly after the death of her Stewart grandmother.

'I only remember seeing her once when I was a very little girl. I remember she had very black hair and piercing eyes. I remember dimly the large kitchen with its two beds behind. Then the narrow staircase and the room in which David and I slept during our visit and which is memorable for me by a strange occurrence. One night as David and I were in bed I happened to glance towards the room door where regarding me fixedly was a strange apparition—the figure was that of an old man wearing a large soft hat and bending slightly under a burden. I remember hiding my face under the blankets and peering out twice, the second time to discover the figure gone. Whether it were only a half-waking dream or a visitant from the other world I know not. I remember our visit was cut short by a disagreement between my grandmother and my Father who was always quarrelling with someone.'

Chapter Twenty

Doon the Watter

HAVING stirred up the ghosts of Aulds and Stewarts I never knew, I come now to flesh and blood Aulds I both knew and loved. But first there is the half-ghostly Uncle David whom I have only recently realised I did not know as he died in 1909. Some photographs of a bearded man, often in a hard hat and looking rather like Uncle John, I was told were of him, the eldest son of the family. He was actually the second son, an earlier John having been born after 1837 and before 1841. He must have died before 1846 as the son born in that year was also given the name John. In notes to my mother, Uncle John writes,

> 'By the way mother's first child was named John and he was a child of such surpassing beauty that mother was known as the wife wi' the bonny wean.
>
> John died in childhood of scarlet fever to the great grief of his sorrowing parents. 'Not as a child shall we again behold him, but beautiful with all the soul's expansion shall we behold his face'.'

It was because of the photographs and because I had been told quite a bit about him that I mistakenly thought I must have seen Uncle David, He wrote poetry. In a letter dated 29th September 1917 Uncle John wrote to my mother,

> 'I have now pleasure in enclosing copies of your Uncle David's Poems and hope you will like them and that Elaine in time to come will treasure them as a legacy from her Grand-Uncle David.'

They seemed to have vanished among other papers but I found them recently. Expectation whetted by the search, I was disappointed to find them no doubt sincere but conventional verses of typical Victorian religiosity. More than his brothers he appears to have liked a quiet life for when mentioning him in her journal my mother sometimes adds it was Uncle David's first time, as for instance in sleeping aboard the *Oransay*. In October 1901 she writes,

> 'Uncle David and I were in Carlisle one day lately in the beginning of the month. A memorable visit for Uncle D—his first in England. I have been there already—last year. We left Glasgow at 10' [she writes pm but I think she must have meant am as she makes no mention of sleeping] 'with Uncle Harry and David Smith who were going to London and left Carlisle at 3 pm so our visit was brief. We spent about 10 minutes in the Cathedral probably less in the Castle. Uncle David says he enjoyed it extremely—although he was evidently in such a hurry to return to Bonnie Scotland.'

He studied the heavens, no doubt through the telescope that stood in the window of the drawing-room at Dunira, Craigmore, Rothesay, Isle of Bute, through which Ian and I watched the schools of porpoises cavorting off-shore. He took his interest in natural phenomena to the extent of, during thunderstorms, standing on the lawn in front of the house, worrying neither about the lightnings nor drenching torrents of rain though his relatives and staff worried for him. For this reason if no other I felt akin to him for lightning fascinates me too. Like Uncle John and many another scholastically inclined gentleman of their day he learned Gaelic by the commonly approved method, from translation of the Bible, and practised it on the boatmen and fishermen on the shore. At the turn of the century Gaelic was not yet a foreign tongue in the southern parts of Argyll. Many of the people of Bute were native speakers and there were always during the season Islesman crewing the pleasure and racing yachts on the Clyde.

I remember going with my father and mother for a day sail on the *Oransay*. This seemed their favoured name for real yachts as all their Manchester terriers were Springs. I never knew why they were called Spring. I assumed the season was intended but perhaps the first had been a lively terrier and sprung! Uncle Harry used to address the one I knew best as 'Wee Spunkie' which may bear out this theory. On the *Oransay* I stood on deck, in a rather attractive pink knitted coat with matching cap and pink knitted buttons, the work of my mother, and fished. This activity, corroborated by a snapshot made me feel a useful member of the crew. The snapshot unfortunately revealed the fact that unknown to me, my fishing-line was a painter which did not reach the water.

I think on this occasion we were staying at Dunoon for a holiday and had come over on the steamer and gone to Hazelcliffe to join the rest of the party, then walked down to where the yacht's dinghy awaited us, a yachtsman at the oars. We walked over the pebbles to the narrow wooden jetty then along it, my parents, Aunt Barbara and an assortment of men all like uncles. One of the men stopped and spoke some words in an unknown tongue in a self-depreciatory way to one of the bystanders. He was bearded, with a shy manner and was probably Uncle John. The walk over the beach, with the cold wet smell of the sea and the damp stones, though remote in time is still clear to my mind—or more correctly my mind's nose. Clear also is the memory of the surprise I felt at us all, rather over-dressed as we were in the pre-1914 yachting style, stepping into a very unstable-looking contraption, floating practically gunwhale level with the sea. To my eye it looked most unsafe but even the well-attired ladies appeared to think nothing of it but embarked in their turns and let themselves be rowed out over an obviously perilous stretch of jobbly water to the sides of a boat on to which they were helped up a steep hanging ladder to a platform near the top. I was amazed when I saw those long-skirted, well-dressed grown-ups, my mother and great-aunt, seat themselves voluntarily on those hard wooden seats as if it were the most ordinary thing in the world— which indeed to them it was.

Sometimes we stayed at Dunira with the Aulds and then we were made much of, not only by aunt and uncles, but by maids too, especially Mary, whose years with them had made her almost one of the family though she never overstepped her selfset—fairly liberal—bounds. She admired Mr John for his intelligence and gave him due respect while gently teasing his vague ways and while respecting Miss Barbara had a happy friendly relationship with her. She realised that Mr Henry despite his jokey ways had a trigger-happy temper and could be sarcastic. When however Uncle Harry, who was an arch-tease, was in the mood, she would take liberties with him.

"Och! Mr Henry! You're an awful man!" Then looking at me she would chant,

'Patience is a virtue.
Obtain it if you can.
'Tis seldom found in woman,
And never in a man.'

Going to Dunira or any later holiday house, meant first the regular established preliminaries to any extended stay-away from home heralded invariably, at least after the move to Wardie Road, by my mother one evening saying to her husband as he was finishing his solitary meal to the companionship of the *Edinburgh Evening Despatch*—we had all eaten earlier,

"Willie! You had better get the silver chest out of the Mouse-cupboard."

However bizarre this request may sound to alien ears it was run of the mill to us. Willie obediently rose from the table, rolling his napkin into its silver ring with WGC engraved on it, made his way to the underneath-the-stairs cupboard in which a mouse had once briefly sojourned, and pushing aside coats, boots, golf-clubs and rackets and hockey sticks emerged with the stout lined wooden chest into which would be packed in their cases and green felt all of the family's store of silver, entree dishes, christening mugs, cruets, salvers, cake baskets, rose-bowl and dressing-table sets. When some days later we set off for the station, the cab or cart which took the luggage took this chest too and off-loaded it at Mackay and Chisholm where during our holiday the contents were taken out of the strong-room and given a professional polish.

Much more troublesome than the silver chest was 'the valise' my father's responsibility, the exact packing of which was his especial pride. The valise was a large area of brown canvas on which were laid all our coats and blazers and waterproofs. It could not be rolled up and strapped until the last possible moment lest a change of weather necessitated a change of travelling apparel. While our outer wardrobes were being assembled the hold-all lay flat on the dining-room floor, horribly impeding free passage. It was too a perpetual bone of contention as we were forever abstracting garments or adding others and slipping already banned objects into the pockets thereby upsetting our father's calculations as to its eventual size and weight. When we 'took a house' on the Kyles of Bute our luggage would also embrace at least a couple of trunks with clothes and towels and bed and table linen, and the other last minute item, a scratchy basket from which came wails from our irascible and vocal ginger cat. Later in our childhood the trip to the station would be by taxi but in early days it was by horse-drawn and straw-smelling cab, a cab which swayed slightly as you put your weight, even a child's weight, on the small step so you could not but wonder how the conveyance was going to support an entire family.

From Princes Street the train took us to the centre of Glasgow where we got our first sight of the Clyde under the bridge near Jamaica Street. In Glasgow Central we changed to the train for Wemyss Bay but first came lunch in the Ca'dora across the road where in the Ladies' Room I always became abruptly conscious of our transit from East to West Scotland, not only by the ear, the ladies themselves sounding heartier and nowhere near as refined as those of the Capital, but also because as opposed to those of Princes Street they displayed a friendly and uninhibited interest in us which as a small child I found embarrassing. Our father was an intermittent partaker of the meal, escaping every now and then to 'see to the luggage' which it may surprise present day travellers to learn had been left with a porter mounting guard over it, for an hour or longer until our train came in when he would stow it in the van and keep a carriage for us too, so well staffed in those days were the stations.

At Wemyss Bay there was the long rush to get good seats, down through the arcaded splendours of James Millar's turn of the century pier and on to the steamer, adults and child with Ginger tagging in the rear. A lovely burst of salt sea holiday air greeted us as we went awkwardly up or—depending on the tide—down the slatted gangway soon to be drawn in as the ship cast off for the well-known piers on the further shore. When we were going to Craigmore we knew when we had passed the white light-housed Toward Point that we were nearly there, and as we come alongside Rothesay Pier we always experienced the anticipated moment of terror as the steamer appeared to be about to keel over as a surge of passengers made for the gangway. We did not disembark at Rothesay but the majority of travellers, many of them being commuters, did. My mother was unperturbed. Now that I consider them, 'my nerves' no matter how miserable they made her and her family in later life, never afflicted her where the sea was concerned. True, she rarely bathed but that was on account of poor circulation. Down the Kyles we indulged in quite venturesome trips in rowing boats or one year in *Beowulf,* a small motor-powered one, without any thought of life-jackets or even belts. She of course had been travelling on the paddle-steamers for years so the tilt to the pier did not disturb her. Ian and I however did our unobtrusive best by standing back on the uphill slope of the deck to right the craft's balance. Saved yet again by our efforts or by good fortune the suddenly almost empty steamer would make for Craigmore Pier where Carswell waited to meet us and drive us off to Dunira whose pointed roof and balcony and flagstaff on the side-lawn we had already spotted from the sea, there to receive one of those heartwarming welcomes which even then we appreciated though accepting it as no more than our due.

From photographs of this period, due to the, to our eyes, old-fashioned clothes which they naturally wore with few concessions to informality for leisure, the Aulds look to be a trio of elderly respectable citizens which indeed they were. From memory however I realise there was a light-heartedness about them and an almost childish determination to enjoy, now, at once, the immediacy of any pleasure to hand which gave them their great charm for me and I should fancy for most children. In part of course, neither Aunt

144

Barbara nor Uncle Harry having married and Uncle John having lost both wife and child with the child's birth, they accepted us as the grandchildren they would never have. So it was with our arrival at Dunira things began to happen. The whole household was there to exclaim.

"My! Mr Ian! How you've grown!"

"He looks green! He won't want his tea! Did you give your dinner to the fishes?" (Uncle Harry this.)

A ribbon-bound staff with just-not-wilting-flowers at the top was thrust into my hand by Aunt Barbara.

"Here! I kept you this from the Fête." (What on earth was a fet?)

We had to check on everything. People seemed all present and correct. Spring, impatient for his walk, suffered himself to be patted, but where was Toots? "Cheetie! Cheetie!" called Aunt Barbara. No Toots of course came forward but she was found in one of her favourite haunts, a rather cat-smelling room next to the kitchen, looking after herself at her saucer.

On warm days she and I lay in happy companionship on the front lawn in the shade of a tree whose low branches made a concealment for us, I with a book and she with her thoughts and her purrs. She was an elderly cat now but my mother remembered her as an impudent kitten and used to ask her if she thought about how she used to tease 'my poor Angel', a white cat of her girlhood.

"Can we feed the pigeons?" and off I would go with Uncle Harry to the pigeon–loft with its odd but not entirely unpleasing smell. But what could be unpleasing at Dunira? Actually the fascination the pigeons held for me was not entirely of admiration, they did have such hard beaks when they pecked my hands as I fed them their hard yellow seeds and they looked at me with such hard appraising eyes but I was the only female of the household to show any interest in them and proudly ranged myself along with the uncles, Carswell and the gardener. Besides my uncles liked them and that was enough for me. The same spirit led me to share in the ritual of the eleven o'clock glass of butter-milk Aunt Barbara drank in the pantry in Ardenlee for her health and complexion. The taste wrinkled my face

145

but I gamely drank it down. Uncle Harry and Uncle John knew the pigeons as individuals. The only one I remember was Castor Oil, so called because he was greedy and deserved a dose of that nauseous liquid—an Uncle Harry joke again.

There was a fascinating toy at Dunira, in Toots's room, that I was allowed to play with. It was quite delicate and I thought valuable but could have been won at a fair. It was a Mandarin whose head was on a coiled spring and who nodded it deliciously when he was gently touched. There was eventually some disappointment connected with the Mandarin. Either he vanished, broken perhaps or I had assumed he was mine and was upset when not permitted to take him home. Either way he lives on in memory, nodding on top of the harmonium in the cat-smelling ante-room.

Outside the front porch grew a bramble bush which I often saw in flower but off which Aunt Barbara and I bewailed I had never eaten a bramble because although the pretty pink blossom had usually gone before the end of our holidays we were back in Edinburgh before it fruited. In this instance the whirligig of time has brought sweetness, for more than a half century later we now have at our own front porch a bramble, which while doing its best to impede entry and ensnare visitors provides us with all the fruit for jelly and apple-bramble crumble that we could desire.

Inside the porch was a Nile Lily which, with the light oak woodwork, gave a quite erroneously chaste atmosphere to the house. I remember trailing Mary round the landings and bedrooms as she tidied and dusted and going with her into the big front upstairs drawingroom where we found Aunt Barbara.

"Did you know your auntie could play schottisches and reels awfae well?" asked Mary. "Give us a tune, Miss Barbara, do."

Aunt Barbara obligingly sat down at the piano and dashed away into jigs and The Dashing White Sergeant and Petronella while I exhibited the fruits of my dancing lessons and Mary, waving her feather duster, hooched and pas de va'ed with me, till Uncle Harry, drawn by the merriment, put his head in to say this was a queer way to be getting on with the housework.

146

Once established in Craigmore we never thought of the summer ending. It seemed it could last for ever, endless in sunshine and bliss. Across the road was the sea and the beach, not a building sandcastle beach for it was stony with pinky-red safely-clamberable rocks and we paddled, me with my dress tucked into my breeks for I was too old now for the romper-style waterproof garments I had worn at Elie and North Berwick short years ago. I remember the hardness and tarpaulin smell of a black shiny pair and the black and white checks of another of softer material. I was shocked by one little local girl who played with no knickers on at all. My usual playmate was Johan the elder of the two little Carswell girls. We built harbours with the stones or ground them up for sugar and flour and cocoa for games of houses or shops. The shops were limited in their range of goods but always there was rhubarb—red leaf stems from a convenient sycamore—and tobacco—the seeds of sorrel or dock.

Sometimes we walked with spades and pails to Ascog where there was sand in the bay made by the small curving peninsula on which stood Ascog Church. The road lay alongside the beach with a low wall at its seaward side. This configuration of confined beach made for great excitement after a line of warships striped like wild beasts passed up or down the Clyde. They went at a great rate nearer the opposite shore so it was hard to believe their passage could have any effect on our side of the Firth. We would go on with our digging or wading but keeping a wary eye nonetheless on the innocent looking sea. Then when all danger seemed past suddenly in a flash the placid waters of the bay would course up the shore, scattering children and creating havoc among the rugs and deckchairs and legs of mothers and nurses who had been too busy reading or chatting to have noticed the swift faraway passage of the ships. It was fun, though momentarily frightening to be chased up to the wall by the unpredictable sea which after its first sudden surges of water would as soon seem to forget its rage and settle back into normality.

Occasionally we were invited to the Manse for tea which I enjoyed and remember for three reasons. One was the hitherto unknown to me name of the minister, Mr Winter, which made him sound like a

147

character in a fairy tale and the name, also previously unknown to me, of his very pleasant grown-up daughter Hetty. The third, also new, was a delicious caraway seed cake. Seedcake was I am sure known all over Scotland but the other caraway delicacy, carvies, was for us mainly a west coast indulgence though we occasionally found them in Newhaven and Crail, so perhaps they were a seaside speciality. They were caraway seeds coated with white sugar icing sold from large glass jars and we spread them on buttered slices of white bread. This sounds to be a dentist's nightmare at which the health conscious would shudder today—but tasted absolutely delicious, the food of the gods. As my mother was practically manic about the care of her teeth and ours I can only suppose they held such happy memories of her west coast girlhood that she was on occasion prepared to let her principles go.

"Does your mother let you put soap on your face?" I remember a little girl with whom I was spending the night ask me in an aggravatingly censorious manner as we prepared for bed. "My mother says it is bad for your complexion."

"It's teeth with mine," I answered morosely.

Taking the long view now, as I guard my remaining molars and incisors, I think my mother had the right of it. Complexion is more easily renewed from jars. Apart from the fact that my mother had a naturally good complexion, due perhaps to the softness of west coast water, sugar of course was not the bug-bear seventy years ago that it is today—we used to have sugar sandwiches and my little brother always demanded, and was given, a drink of sugary water after his dinner. He had a very 'sweet tooth' and never if he could avoid maternal exhortations willingly brushed either it or its companions. They all remained beautifully white and never did a hole appear in any of them. Regularly on our six-monthly visit to the dentist did he slip unscathed from the chair, beaming at the dentist's undeserved praises, while I, having mounted in my turn, was as regularly tut-tutted over as the drill went into operation. Never as a child did I need to have the unfairness of life spelt out to me!

CHAPTER TWENTY-ONE

Montford and the Kingdom of Fife

OUR FIRST summer holiday after the war, in 1919, was spent in a very pleasant house a few doors from Dunira. Montford was a small eighteenth century mansion house divided into three flats of which we had the ground-floor one and the run of the garden. There was a large front lawn surrounded with flowers of which I remember chiefly the marguerites and antirrhinum, my first meeting with that fascinating flower. They were true snapdragon which to our interest could be induced to open their mouths, not like some of the modern rounder varieties which are a sad disappointment. My father came at weekends, a holiday he could possibly quite cheerfully have foregone involving as it did two long journeys—further in later years to the Kyles—as he seemed quite pleased to camp out in Wardie Road or at the home of another temporarily bereft father and husband. Otherwise there were five of us in the house, my mother, my brother, my eighteen-month-old sister, myself and Gigi (hard g's), a pleasant but not perhaps outstandingly efficient middle-aged mother's help. But efficiency is not all and indeed the only helpers in our home that I remember disliking were usually markedly efficient. I could not understand why my mother scoffed at Gigi's habit of occasionally washing only the feet of her stockings—it struck me as good sense when she had the rest of her washing and ours and mending, and the care of three children. She was possibly a little eccentric but that added to her attraction and I liked her very much as I did most peripheral adults who offered me a change of

149

companionship from that of my younger siblings. Marjorie was too young and Ian, besides being a little young, was not entirely satisfactory being so much my mother's blue-eyed boy that he could do no wrong. Fortunately for my confidence and self-esteem at this time the Aulds, unused to small children, found me, being older, more companionable and I basked in their regard.

Gigi had, at the other end of Rothesay a married sister, Mrs MacFie, whom she went often to visit. She told us wonderful tales of the treasures of her sister's house for her brother-in-law was connected with the sea and there were all manner of interesting mementoes of sea-faring life, including shells in which you could hear the ocean roar. This I frankly did not believe but when she took us visiting at her sister's special invitation and I put one of these great conches to my ear and shut my eyes, there, standing in the hall-way of a villa in Ardbeg, I could not only hear the breakers but see their blue-green waters crash as my assorted reading told me they did do on long yellow beaches. In an odd way they did this with more reality than fifty years later did real breakers on a real Hawaiian beach.

For Ian and myself the chief interest of the MacFie household was their parrot who had once told a message boy to 'Shut up!' We could not wait to see—and hear—this reprobate bird. We lurked round its perch, made sudden forays from the sitting-room with its glass-fronted cabinets of curiosities, scarcely lingered over a very good tea though I remember we did manage to eat a lot, but sadly all the wretched bird deigned to say was a rather perfunctory 'Pretty Polly.'

After one of those enjoyable but abortive tea-parties we arrived back at Montford to be greeted by the simple-minded relative of our landlady who asked what we had been doing. Excitedly we began to tell her, "We've been to see Mrs MacFie's parrot..." but she was not interested in the parrot. To our fascinated delight she chanted to us what we considered a rather risqué verse which of course we credited her with composing there and then.

'Mrs MacFie
She caught a flea,
She salted it and peppered it
And had it to her tea.'

150

This we thought excruciatingly witty and giggled over it and quoted it for days. It left me with a feeling of unease too... did anyone? ...and if they did would they put it on toast or what... and which Mrs MacFie was this?

Gigi was a great success with my brother and myself and she thought our little sister a real character—which she was. Despite the part-washed stockings she was a great success with my mother too who put it on record that she did much more to help her than a previous younger nurse had done. I remember her looking a little flummoxed one morning when Gigi and I emerged from our rooms changed from the clothes in which we had breakfasted and attired now in garments of sanctity—in my case a tussore coat and gloves and a brown tussore sunbonnet—complete each with Hymnbook or Bible and holy expression.

"Where are you going?" she asked in astonishment.

"Church," said Gigi, equally surprised.

"But...but... this is Thursday!" (Presbyterians recognised only the Sabbath.) Crestfallen, we retired to undress and dress once again.

Continuing with Gigi she was still with us the next summer holiday, the first of two we took in Crail in Fife. Perhaps this was to make things easier for my father to join us or perhaps by now the Aulds had left Glasgow and the coast and made their permanent home in Bridge of Allan. Although there were no uncles and aunt and Mary and no Toots and Spring I enjoyed Crail with its sandy beach good for bathing and its picturesque harbour and the bluebells on the way to the East Neuk where my mother and I sat and produced rather unequal water-colours of the sea and rocks and flowers. Occasionally we took the bus to Balcomie to search for cowries. Selcraig, the house we had rented was at a corner in a square of mixed housing styles old and new whose gardens were mostly climbed over by the most luxuriant nasturtiums I have ever had the pleasure of seeing. It must have been a 'good' summer for my memories are all of gold and orange and light.

Selcraig was as a summer lodging should be, slightly old-fashioned with a faintly musty smell and no elaborate ornaments to worry us.

151

It had a piano with Songs of the North and a book of old Scottish airs. I recall letting myself go on 'The Mountains of Morvern' fff. and 'Robin Adair' sentimentalissimo. There was a garden with a shed in one corner from whose roof there was a fine view of the road and passers-by. My guess as its being a good summer is confirmed when I recall one day climbing up to find the tarred roof melt under me, after which the favourite pink dress I was wearing was never quite the same.

One morning on the beach we found ourselves sitting next to a family slightly known to us as the elder daughter went to my school. I did not really know her—she was in the class above and a whole year older!—but apparently she felt this no bar to a holiday friendship. She was quiet but of great potential as she became well known in later years as the actress Lennox Milne. At this time it was her more rumbustious younger sister Flora who filled the stage. She had come on an old door or similar piece of wood which she dragged to where between two ridges of rock at certain times of the flowing and ebbing tide a large natural pool formed, ideal for swimming in as the water became quite, but not dangerously, deep. Flora ferried us all over its surface, propelling her craft with a broomstick. One day we arrived to find it had been taken over by a local lad. She immediately went into spirited action—both vocal and physical, and triumphed despite the boy being bigger—to the great admiration of her pusillanimous companions on to whom something must have brushed off of our school's conception of lady-like behaviour.

One day, sewing on the beach, Gigi lost her—and our—favourite scissors, an embroidery pair shaped like a stork. We stirred up all the sand around but could not find them so Gigi decided to put a notice in the Post Office window, a proceeding my mother rather pooh-poohed as useless but Gigi went ahead and drew one up and after lunch on our way back to the beach we detoured to hand it in. Some days passed and nothing happened. Gigi continued to bewail her loss and we all walked to and from the shore with heads bent while our eyes searched the road and verges. Then Ian and I had what seemed to our simple minds an excellent idea. To cheer things up we would pretend the scissors had been found and use this as a excuse for a Thanksgiving Service (we were always giving entertainments on one pretext or none). We put streamers up in the hall and outside the front door and wrote out invitations to a Grand Concert given in 'Thanks for Recovery of Precious Scissors with Presentation of Reward' and rehearsed sketchily. For good measure we put an enormous poster on the outside of the front door—two paces from the road. Gigi made no objection to this premature celebration and she and my mother and the current maid, like us ready for diversion, settled down to enjoy the entertainment.

The highlight of the concert, histrionically speaking, was provided by Baby, who uninvited bounded to the forefront and recited a long poem no one had ever known she knew, learnt from listening to my homework, 'A Fairy Went A-Marketing.' Success goes easily to the head of the young and she proved difficult to stop. A year or so later she was completely to disrupt a pirate play Ian and I and some of my school friends were acting in the dining-room in Wardie Road. We had taken some trouble over it and rigged up curtains. Forced by the grown-ups not to be selfish but to give poor little Marjorie a part we had grudgingly permitted her to be a cabin-boy with one line. When her moment came she seized it, changed the line and argued with the captain when he gave her an order. "I won't!" was her mutinous reply. As the action depended on her obeying, the play could not go on. The audience thought it hilarious and applauded madly but the cast was furious.

Here in Crail at the height of the revelry over the Fairy's shopping, the door bell went and we all, except probably my mother, surged to answer it in expectancy of receiving back the scissors. This time they actually were there, in the hand of a scared-looking lady. What she made of the din, or of the notice with its apparently psychically inspired precognition of her find, I cannot think. We stood and gawped at her. Whatever her feelings were, we felt as ones who had conjured spirits from the deep.

Gigi went off to find her purse and after returning thanks somewhat regally, dispensed the promised Good Reward.

153

CHAPTER TWENTY-TWO

Montford and the Money Hill

BUT FROM FIFE back to Argyll and Montford.

My uncles commuted to 'The Works' most days by sea and rail and I used eagerly to look out for their returning steamer cutting rapidly over from Wemyss Bay to Craigmore for Uncle Harry liked a walk with Spring before his evening meal and after making due adjustments to his city attire would come along to Montford to collect me. Always we went up the fields above Craigmore, first through the Montford garden among the marguerites then over the stile to a sparse piece of hill pasture with cows. The weather had to be really bad for us to forego this walk. Sometimes a smirr of rain would wash the horizons of the Argyll and Ayrshire hills and a rainbow shine but mostly the evenings were clear and still, and then with the waters of the Clyde beneath us and the bog-myrtle and queen of the meadow scenting the air that hill-side on Bute seemed magical.

One piece of this country-side, known to me ever afterwards as The Money Hill, indeed was magical. Money in this connotation has nothing to do with the astute or dirty deals of financiers but with the innocent pennies and ha'pennies of a golden age. We strolled along, even the elderly Spring showing glimpses of the far-off days when he really had been Wee Spunkie and I, encouraged by an uncaring uncle who did not have to wash my socks, made hazardous leaps over cow-pats. Suddenly Uncle Harry would point with his stick, "What's that?" and bending down I would find perhaps a penny and once a silver threepenny bit among the heather. This could happen four or five times on a walk and I was enchanted. How lucky we were to be going along these tracks just after somebody had dropped that magic money. There was no one but us on the hillside and Uncle Harry inclined to the belief that it was the fairies, the wee people who lived underground, who had left it for me and I saw no reason to think otherwise. Not for years did I associate this largesse with Uncle Harry, not even after the occasion when the fairies varied their bounty and dropped a delightful little golden key. Uncle Harry must have hoped to retrieve it unseen but I of course spied it and picked it up. I was charmed with it. It seemed just the right size for a fairy door. Though I could imagine no foreseeable use for it I longed to keep it as a piece of authentic fairy equipment. Strangely, Uncle Harry, who had never showed any desire to share my money windfalls, acted quite out of character and after he had failed to persuade me that some woe-begone fairy would be searching for its house-key said he thought perhaps the fairies meant it for him. It took him all his powers of speech and persuasion to win it off me, saying the fairies must have thought it his turn for a present and wondering if by any chance it might fit his gold watch. How lucky if it did for he had lost the key and could not wind it. Interestedly I watched him try. How clever of the fairies! The key fitted as if made for it. This miraculous happening reinforced my belief in the wee folk and I remember the two of us telling my mother and Gigi and Aunt Barbara and Mary and Uncle John about it. They were deeply impressed. Uncle John looked quizzical but said never a word.

Only once do I remember this walk being spoiled by the addition of a third person, a great-nephew of the Aulds who by virtue of being male talked superciliously about machinery. Everyone thought how nice it was for us both to have a companion of roughly the same age, a pleasure neither of their young relatives appreciated. I could see that David despised me for being smaller and a girl and he laughed when my short legs failed to clear a cow-pat. He refused to compete—it was babyish.

Bute at this time had a tramway system across the island. Inaugurated in 1885 it was at first horse-drawn and then in 1902 electrified. Roofed, but otherwise mainly open carriages with long forward-facing reversible benches, it ran from near the pier on its own trackway through some of the principal streets and then out between woods and fields to Ettrick Bay, a wide stretch of sandy shore where there were refreshments and amusements. These were donkeys to ride and goat carriages. It was driving the goat carriages that we enjoyed.

A very great pleasure was going for sails in the *Colleen,* Uncle Harry's motor yacht, 'quite comfortable for short sails though nothing will ever equal the *Oransay,* Uncle Harry's last steam yacht. Elaine and Ian proved splendid sailors'. So my mother's journal. Among our paper ephemera haphazardly surviving is a cutting from, judging by scraps of advertisements, a Bute paper. Someone has dated it May 31st 1904.

'NEW YACHT FOR A ROTHESAY GENTLEMAN.

Messrs John Fullarton and Co, of Paisley, launched on Tuesday from their yard there a steel screw steam yacht to the order of Mr H D Auld of Rockmount, Dennistoun, Glasgow, and Hazelcliffe, Ardbeg Road, Rothesay. The yacht which is of about 55 tons, Thames measurements, is 75 feet long by 13 feet beam by eight feet deep, and has compound surface-condensing engines of 136 i.h.p. by Messrs Robert Montgomery and Son of Greenock. She has exceptionally large accommodation, consisting of commodious deckhouse, with galley, cabin, with double stateroom aft, saloon and two double staterooms forward, and accommodation for five of a crew in a roomy forecastle. The yacht was launched by Miss Auld, sister of the owner, and named Oransay.'

The occasion is captured for posterity in a snapshot in an album entitled Sunny Memories showing the yacht on the stocks, with beside it a man and four ladies the foremost of whom is holding a ribbon-decked bottle.

The two excursions I best remember were carefree ones, without either parent. My father did not really like the sea and fussed about us being warm enough. I may be maligning him but I could swear that in our later days at Tighnabruaich we could find ourselves out in rowing-boats in nap coats, certainly in gaberdines. One of those outings was memorable to Ian and me for a rather mean reason. We

156

sailed into Loch Striven, a long dark loch reaching miles into the hills of Cowal. Uncle Harry did not trust Loch Striven, perhaps there were no safe anchorages and it was certainly given to sudden squalls when winds swept down the steep gullies. On this occasion it was just after lunch when Mary was washing up the dishes in a basin set on the bunk bench in the cabin that the loch showed its mettle. The sea suddenly became quite rough, rocking the anchored boat from side to side and Mary, thrown off balance, sat down in the basin of greasy water, which to our warped sense of humour struck us as being excruciatingly funny.

On the other occasion we had anchored off Largs—an anchorage the uncles and Carswell did not trust either. When the wind was in a certain quarter there was little shelter and the bottom, as I understood it, did not make for secure holding. All this talk going on above our heads was I am sure just day to day exchange of differing opinions about anchorages and so on, but it sank down to us and made most of our enterprises seem pleasantly hazardous. This particular day was as calm as could be—"like a mill-pond" said Aunt Barbara. I knew nothing of mill-ponds but ever afterwards compared them to their detriment, as far as clearness was concerned, with the sea at Largs that sunny day. After Carswell had let go the anchor and we had discussed would it 'drag', he and Uncle John rowed ashore in the dinghy, Uncle John jug in hand for the Italian ice-cream he loved, from a well-known cafe. Uncle John bought ice-cream whenever opportunity offered and a great treat it was too for Ian and me, for our mother tended to equate ice-cream with dirt, with germs, with scarlet fever, so we had it rarely. On his return Uncle John handed the jug over to Mary and she dished it out in bowls and saucers. Uncle John was not a tease like Uncle Harry but he had a quiet sense of humour which we did not always understand. He was a mild-looking bearded man with innocent blue eyes, usually wearing, even on a yachting trip, a hard-brimmed grey city hat. (Uncle Harry wore a peaked yachting cap.) Now he sat supping his ice-cream and looking across at us in puzzlement.

"This ice-cream is very cold," said he, "You would think they would heat it up." Feverishly Ian and I would try to explain that it was ICE-cream, it was meant to be cold, but he would just re-iterate his words, "you would think they would heat it up". We knew that he was clever, an inventor of a marine valve, but at times like this we wondered!

There was no finesse about Uncle Harry's brand of humour. I remember being cajoled by him with a girl cousin into the big dining-room cupboard at Dunira and told to help ourselves to lemonade. Dimly we felt we should have permission from someone more in charge of us and domestic affairs than was Uncle Harry.

"Go on," he said, "if you shut your eyes no one will see you." Easy victims, we fell, till we encountered the difficulty of locating and pouring the lemonade blindfold and heard Uncle Harry chortling away to himself as he, eyes open, downed a mineral water.

In her journal my mother writes,

'They [Elaine and Ian] enjoyed being amused by Uncle Harry and had some great times on the boat. Fishing was a great pastime of the uncles and the children who were at first rather scared when a fish was drawn up soon became quite keen, though it was only at the very end that they plucked up courage enough to touch a fish. I loathe fishing myself, it seems so horribly cruel. Uncle Harry used to tell Ian to whistle when he felt a tug on his line to ensure the fish coming up and Ian would whistle most seriously quite confident that he was causing the fish to come up.'

On the *Colleen* there was nearly always on the boards by the engine a tin full of repulsive looking red bait. On the trip to Largs, just after we had enjoyed our ice-cream, Ian, who was at the accident-prone stage through which most small children go, tripped and knocked his mouth on this bait-tin. After he had been cleaned up and comforted the two of us knelt on the seat and leant over the side looking down through the clear water to the sandy floor where shells of all kinds lay—some even moved about leaving tracks behind them. Ian opened his mouth to tell me something and disaster struck again. Loosened by the knock on the tin out fell his first loose tooth and eddied its way down to the sand. Helplessly we watched its passage then Ian opened his mouth and roared again. In later years he grew quite boastful about his first baby tooth lying on the bottom

158

of the Firth but on that day he was not to be consoled.

Some forty years later, on a Sunday afternoon walk, I came on a motor launch called the *Colleen* in Inverness harbour. I looked at her as at an old friend and yet, like many old friends, she seemed not to be quite as I remembered. The open well behind the engine seemed not as big, scarcely room now to fall on a bait-tin. A man, unfortunately not the owner, was working on her, and to him I told my tale, remarking that she differed a bit from my memory of her.

"That's right," he said, "they extended the cover from the cabin". He told me too that she had come to the Moray Firth from the Clyde, so she really was my *Colleen*. It was an emotional moment as I looked at her rocking on the tide with her cloud of bygone memories. Thanking the boatman for his information I walked off wishing the *Colleen* good fortune in the future and blessing her for her bounty of the past.

'I don't think I shall ever forget the day we left Montford for Orcadia,' wrote my mother when after some happy weeks our let was up and we moved for a fortnight into a house with attendance, 4 Orcadia, a few steps nearer Dunira. This was a more typical sea-side lodging. I remember the oil-cloth smell of the cupboards in the side-board and the very big cruet with a bottle for vinegar. We were not allowed vinegar—bad for us. The diary continues,

> 'It was pouring to begin with. After all our packing was done, I sent the children to Dunira and went to the pier with Willie who was going up to town. The 'Iona' when it came in from Rothesay was crowded already and by the time the Craigmore people got in it looked awful. There is nothing more uncomfortable than a crowded boat in drizzling rain and a choppy sea. Going back to Dunira I found Aunt Barbara and Uncle Harry very upset over Spring who was slowly dying (they thought of poison.) He died that afternoon, poor old thing.

It is only a few years since I first read these journals of my mother's but long before I read them I could have echoed them from my memory... 'I don't think I shall ever forget the day...' was true for me too. I remember the cold mizzling rain of summer on my bare legs. I remember the unaccustomed gloom and misery of Dunira and its inhabitants. I remember tiptoeing into the warmth of the kitchen with Aunt Barbara to hang over Spring and wonder how anything warm and breathing could shortly be going to be dead. I did not so much grieve for Spring who, although perfectly affable, did not at his advanced age lay himself out to be particularly enamoured of young masters and mistresses. I did grieve for Uncle Harry.

We retreated to 4 Orcadia and the grey day stretched out. So long it seemed, (the clock on the mantelpiece had stopped, perhaps it never went) and we had no idea of the time, for my mother, sad for a watchmaker's wife, was one of those people who 'cannot wear a watch'. She did, a rather nice gold one, but on her it was completely unreliable, usually as on this day, hours fast. We were given dinner at one o'clock, then in despair ordered, and got, high-tea at three-thirty, the landlady must have thought us mad and Baby was put to bed about four, my mother being under the impression that it was well after six. Baby however was not and after a brief catnap woke and stayed awake, hurtling herself out of bed, till long after ten o'clock. Ian and I morosely played Tiddley Winks until our more or less usual bedtime when we went to bed and tried to stay there but this was the dreadful bedroom in which Baby's cot was wedged between the wall and our shared bed, so that when she did a hurdle escape over the bars of the drop-side she fell on a soft bed rather than on the floor. Of course when we were there we broke her fall and she crawled rapidly over us and dropped to the floor and then she was off. Normally it was up to an adult to catch her and restore her to her cot but at 4 Orcadia there was a steep staircase so one or other of us had to bound out of bed and try—she was very determined— to drag her back by the nightie before she precipitated herself down.

Apart from this one day when we moved to 4 Orcadia, this was a very happy holiday, even my mother, often so hard to please, recording her enjoyment of it.

'I think I enjoyed it more than any we have had lately [of course it was our first since the war]. It was nice being near Aunt B for a change. I think she feels rather lonely though she doesn't look it and is very popular at Ascog.'

160

FOUR GENERATIONS

Annie Darling, Agnes Helen Chisholm
Jessie Plenderleath Gibb
with the author's cousin Ralph, born 1907

THE AULDS

EMC with
Aunt Barbara
Uncle John and
Marjorie
Logie Aston, 1925

Seaside holiday, 1913

Campfollowers—
2nd Lieut Chisholm with Ian
and EMC, 1915

EMC aged 4
with meatsafe

YOUNG REVELLERS

*Oban holiday
1924
Marjorie, Ian,
Elaine and
Moira*

*Dainty Dancers at the Monks of St Giles Ball
(standing) Alison Waterston, George Waterston, Eileen Sanderson,
Nancy Sandeman, Phil Waterston,
(seated) Dorothy Sandeman, EMC, Leonora Waterston,
Kathie Waterston, Agnes Waterston
(on floor) Waterston cousin, Ann Waterston, Robin Waterston*

Uncle John, in a letter to my mother in October 1917 had confirmed, in his gently ironic way, his sister's popularity.

'We are all well here which is something to be thankful for as this is a terrible place for afternoon teas and evening parties and daily visitors so that Barbara and Aunt Annie need all their physical and mental strength to cope with sometimes burdensome social functions. In fact Pollockshields compared with Craigmore has not even a look in. However the time is coming nearer when we shall return again to the quieter seclusion of Pollockshields.'

I hope that Aunt Barbara, Uncle John and Uncle Harry had as much happiness from our companionship as we had from theirs. When I see myself on the *Colleen* or dancing to Aunt Barbara's strathspeys and wandering in the bright northern summer light on the slopes of the Money Hill all those seventy years ago I can echo the words of the old song which I found lying on the tinkly piano in Crail—

'They were blessed beyond compare,
When they held their trysting there
Amang thae greenest hills shone on by the sun...'

CHAPTER TWENTY-THREE

Things that go Bump in the Night

THIS STORY has ambled to and fro over the early years of an undistinguished life touching only incidentally on the historically most eventful part, the years between 1914 and 1918, the years after which nothing was ever to be the same again, the years of what will always be to me, The War. Although the lives of many of our friends and acquaintances were to be altered by it, we as a family were little affected. Three of our uncles were in the Services but all returned safely. My father was patriotic and inclined to the military life—it was said his young man's dream had been the Army rather than Mackay and Chisholm. He had served in the Territorials for several years and wanted to rush to the Front. Fortunately possibly both for him and us, a severe attack of rheumatic fever soon after his marriage had left him not in the A1 condition required at that time for Active Service and he had to settle for Home Duties.

'February 17th 1915.
Willie went to Linlithgow on Monday evening to begin service as a
Lieutenant with the First National Reserve Company attached to the 4th
Royal Scots. Their work is guarding bridges, oil-works (I think) etc.
That is the date on which the war really began for me.'

It was also the date on which began for Ian and me a very pleasant roving life as a species of camp-follower.

Our first temporary home predictably elicited from Uncle Harry many jokes as to penny-cooks and ha'penny buns as it was a villa in the Midlothian village of Penicuik, whose name far from being prosaic actually means the hill of the cuckoo. The house stood in a cul-de-sac, (my first encounter with this exotic word) leading to a foot-bridge over a burn into a park. Our father was with a detachment guarding reservoirs in the nearby Moorfoots. On first arrival the house apparently left much to be desired... 'in a fearful state of dust and the kitchen in particular in chaos'. The weather did its worst, first a haar, then sleet—in May. There was no hot water and the smouldering maid looked like giving notice. However after purchase of a kettle and a pudding-pot and some smaller articles— a carpet-sweeper and mop had providentially come with us in the taxi—things began to look up and the weather to improve. With commendable understatement my mother notes,'The land-lady is really very nice but I don't think housekeeping is her forte.'

Penicuik to me means making real mud-pies with another little girl under the sitting-room window where besides mud there was a forest of lilies-of-the-valley. It means the change in my little brother from baby to boy, a boy with teasing propensities and like most small boys not knowing when enough was enough. He developed a favourite game of hiding our possessions and when we inquired their whereabouts would look at us with wide cherubic eyes and simply reiterate "Not know". There came an afternoon when my mother really needed her glasses, "Where's Mummy's spectacle-case?" We entreated, wheedled, threatened and turned the room upside down, receiving only the same bland reply as vital moments passed. The 'Not know' game was never so popular again.

Penicuik means too the disappointment of Ian and me when a soldier brought him a present and put it on his pram. The ungrateful present, a young wild rabbit, very sensibly skipped off and we never saw it again. We were desolated and the soldier was upset too but Mary and my mother seemed insensitively unmoved.

I remember walks through the woods beyond the park, sometimes as far as the road round the south side of the Pentland hills. The woods were blue with damp-leaved wild hyacinth and the heavenly blue of speedwell. I was convinced they were the very woods in two of my favourite books, *The Dolls' Day* and *Finding a Fairy* by Carine

163

Cadby, and half hoped to see fairies and Tip the dog and Belinda and Charles and Baby (the dolls) round every tree trunk.

Uncle Willie had given me Belinda, a pretty china doll with real hair and opening eyes dressed in white broderie anglaise and a floppy hat. Some time later I was given a boy doll so of course I christened him Charles. Most dolls of those days suffered the hazard of china faces. Charles had blue eyes and painted on hair. Belinda despite her china body never ailed but Charles was accident prone. He was forever having to have his head or feet or hands sewn back on to his stuffed body or chips out of his head glued back into place. Truth to tell his accidents were thrust upon him as Ian absolutely hated him and stamped on him and ran his trucks over him. So intense was his hatred that when I once overlaid him in bed (where on account of his delicacy he was not meant to be) and his head wobbled yet again I did not even need to lie to have it assumed by my mother as she stitched him together that Little Brother had struck again.

Another memorable happening in Penicuik that summer was the Flood. Citizens more senior than the two of us would probably have described it more correctly as a spate. In any event it cut off both sides of the footbridge so that we could not get to the park, only stand and watch enthralled as the foaming brown water went swirling past.

May 1916 saw us settled in Hawick, the nearest town to Stobs Prisoner of War camp where our father was now guarding German prisoners. We had intended to go in a leisurely style for most of the summer but as things turned out we went in some considerable rush. I am in two minds as to whether to tell the tale in my own very vivid recollection of the event which sent us or to use my mother's equally vivid cliff-hanger journal, probably best both.

Sunday, 2nd April 1916 was warm and bright. I played in the garden all day, in the afternoon with Ralph and Kathleen whom Aunt Annie brought down to tea. My mother noted the first lark-song of the year and more disturbingly that it was the kind of weather favourable for Zeppelins. On their regular weekly phone call my father and mother both commented on the beauty of this early spring day, then,

164

'About a quarter or twenty minutes past nine the electric light flickered and went out and then went on again but only as a dull glow merely the filaments of the bulb being red but giving no light. We had candles in the house fortunately and as they were being lit I said to Mary, "I hope it isn't a Zeppelin," merely as a joke as I never dreamed they would ever come to Edinburgh.'

(So like people near nuclear installations who never seem to contemplate disaster but decry the CND and Greenham Women, or like the inhabitants of Sodom and Gomorrah or come to that ostriches.)

'The electric has occasionally gone out before but never for long so at first we were not very alarmed though I knew that the lowering of the electric light was to be one of the signs of a Zepplin's approaching the town. But as it did not show any sign of reviving after an interval I sent Mary next door to Mrs Rose to ask if their light was also out. Being told that it was and also the lights in other houses near us, I began to wonder if anything were up, though the mere idea of a raid seemed too ridiculous for words. We went upstairs and did not undress, I lit night-lights and gave Mary one. Then I put my rings and money into a handbag and hung it where I could get at it easily, I laid out my fur coat and shoes before lying down. Needless to say I did not sleep though at the same time I did not really think there would be a raid. We had been told so often that the Zeppelins would never reach Edinburgh. The silence was horrible, all cars and trains stopped. I got up every now and then to look out of the window but everything seemed as usual. The light however was still lowered. I began to think it had only been a scare after all when about 11.30 I heard a peculiar bumming and humming sound, rather like the propeller of a ship. I tried to make myself believe it was all imagination but something seemed to tell me that we were not to escape after all. About ten minutes to twelve came the first crash whether the explosion of a bomb or the crash of a gun I cannot tell. It sounded like the report of a heavy gun. In the awful stillness it was the most appalling sound I have ever heard. Another report followed quickly. By this time of course I was up and had put on my shoes and coat. Going into Mary's room I found her awake and terrified. At first I thought of a naval bombardment. I looked out of my bedroom window and saw a blinding flash of light tear through the sky immediately above the Castle Rock. (I heard after that a bomb did strike the rock and knocked a piece off.) Almost at the same moment I saw another bomb fall—glaring like a ball of fire—in the direction of Bellevue or Rodney Street. (This district suffered very severely, all the windows being shattered and other damage to property done though

165

fortunately no lives were lost here.) I saw also a bright glare as of a fire in what seemed to be the Bonnington district. I was too alarmed to look any longer especially as the Zepps seemed to be coming nearer us—that is judging by the direction of the bombs for I did not actually see the Zepps. My one thought was to get as far away from the roof as possible so Mary took Elaine and I took Baby and we stumbled down the stairs. How we got down I do not know for we were both trembling and almost sick with terror. All the time the reports went on increasingly— crash after crash—now louder and now less loud. It is the awful feeling of being so utterly helpless that is so nerve-racking in an air-raid. You feel so defenceless. The noise of the explosions is bad enough but the horrible feeling that at any moment, without warning, a bomb may come crashing through the roof is indescribable save to those who have come through it. Bombs must fall somewhere so why not on your house and the knowledge that the last explosion comes from a distance is no guarantee—so swiftly can the murderers travel—that the next may not crash through your roof. After a while the noise ceased and we began to hope the Zepps had gone away but it was only a lull. During it I went to the front door and found most of the neighbours in their gardens. Some people were on the opposite side of the street watching the course of the Zepps. I don't understand how they could. The fire in Leith was blazing furiously and must have made a splendid landmark for the raiders. We heard next day that this fire had started before the Zepps had even appeared and is supposed to have been set going to guide the raiders on their way but whether this was true or not I do not know. There are such scores of stories going about. Certainly it was blazing away at the very beginning of the raid when I looked out of the window after the first explosion. We were congratulating ourselves on the worst being over when I heard a man's voice from the other side of the street say they were coming back in a straight line for the houses. I went indoors at once. This time the noise of the explosions and the rattle of the machine guns was terrific. The Zepps seemed to be quite overhead. The windows shook but did not break. I stood in the nursery doorway simply shaking. Elaine was on the couch and Mary beside her. Ian was still asleep on two cushions at the fire-place. I couldn't have moved to get to him and if I had I certainly couldn't have held him in my arms. I know now what absolute terror is. After a time a syren was blown from one of the boats in the river I think to show that the raiders had gone but even then we sat listening to every sound. The whole thing was over in about an hour but it was the longest hour I ever passed.'

The Edinburgh raid cannot compare with the massive bombings of the Second War but aerial attack on civilians was new and terror is terror no matter how occasioned. A *Scotsman* newspaper cutting of December, year unnoted, gives a more factual account despite the language of journalism then being more flowery than that of today…

'Zeppelins over Edinburgh.

The Raid of April 1916.

Now that the censorship has been removed it is possible to give in detail an account of what actually transpired on the night of April 2nd—3rd 1916, when Edinburgh and Leith underwent their first, and as it happily proved, also their last experience of a Zeppelin raid.'

The writer goes on to say that precisely a month later warning came of another projected raid but in the mist the air-ships lost their way

'with disastrous consequences to one of them, which after an involuntary tour in the Grampians drifted out to sea and was wrecked off the coast of Norway'.

The result of the 'Edinburgh visitation'

'was astonishingly slight, considering the dire potentialities of the instruments of destruction employed, the ideal weather conditions on that serene Sunday evening, with its clear blue sky, shining stars and clear atmosphere, and the fact that the region was lit up by a fire caused by an incendiary bomb which fell on a bonded warehouse at Leith Docks. Beyond a considerable shattering of glass and the destruction of a few houses, there was no damage of any consequence. Scottish stone proved much more resistive to the effects of bomb explosions than English brick.'

Six people lost their lives and about eleven were injured. The *Scotsman* took rather a hard line towards the casualties of Marshall Street.

'The death-toll demonstrated the folly of people collecting together and seeking shelter in an open passage…

The German report that "good results" were obtained against "the docks on the Forth" with "extensive collapses" was not only a piece of imaginative inexactitude, but a ridiculous travesty of the real character of the attack.'

I first read my mother's account of the raid only a few years ago and the *Scotsman* report much more recently and was interested to find how they corroborated my five-year-old memories which were far from being a 'ridiculous travesty.'

167

I must have half wakened when my mother and Mary had their confabulation about going to bed with their clothes on above my supposedly sleeping head, for I remember their words and their moving quietly about with lights and thinking that was an odd idea and why, so contrary to our well-regulated regime of wash, teeth, undress, nightgown, prayers and bed. Rather sneaky too, many a time I would have liked to have been spared the trouble of washing and undressing. Next I remember being roused and assisted downstairs by a trembling Mary. It was like a dream—not yet as it was to my mother, a nightmare. I remember sitting under a blanket on the green ottoman at the back of the room with Mary beside me. She trembled, so as trembling seemed to be de rigeur, I trembled too. As yet nothing had occurred to frighten me, the whole proceeding, especially the picking up of a peacefully sleeping baby, risking its waking, just seemed odd. Ian however slept peacefully on, in the cushioned comfort of the creaky basket-chair. There was a time later on when the machine guns and windows rattled that I remember looking across at him and almost envying his oblivion then thinking, no, far better to be awake savouring the excitement of this peculiar night. I was allowed, briefly, to go to the window to see the search-lights criss-crossing the sky. Ian and I had often enjoyed watching them so they seemed reassuring. Gradually a touch of tension got through to me so I trembled some more, not this time in sympathy but in reality. The only time I was really frightened was when my mother abandoned us to go into the garden. For the first time I realised a sheet-anchor of life could slip.

Later I remember the welcome midnight picnic, with hot cocoa, again such an unusual happening quite against family tenets—no eating after you have cleaned your teeth.

CHAPTER TWENTY-FOUR

Teribus-ye Tyr ye Odin

OF THE NEXT day I remember nothing save for a visit I paid with my mother to the over-crowded Goldenacre Post Office. I expect I slept late then played my usual games but for the adults it had obviously been all go.

'We came to Hawick on the 4th of April. Had it been possible I would have left Edinburgh on the third, the morning after the raid. My nerves were so upset.'

Our mother's nerves were to become increasingly part of our consciousness as she more and more called on them, often as a form of blackmail to achieve her own ends. It was difficult for a growing family in those times— 'Honour thy father and mother'—to ignore, let alone defy such ill-defined yet potent, almost personified symptoms of ill-health, particularly in the teeth of a father who indulged them. Often did I think there was little chance of my days being long upon the land which the Lord my God had given me!

'I felt I could not endure another night. That day, Monday, was a perfect nightmare. I tried several times to get on to the phone to Willie at Stobs but couldn't manage it. The wires were over worked. In the afternoon I sent a wire but the girl at the Post Office had a whole pile of wires waiting to be sent off from people in the town to relatives in other places to tell them they were safe. I heard from the Crescent that they had been worse than we were—all the windows at the back of the house being shattered. The Hislop's windows were broken too and Miss Waterston found a piece of the bomb in her bedroom... I was too upset however to go out to see the damage as some people did. In the afternoon Willie phoned to say that he would come that night to take us to Hawick the next day... Perhaps I am a bigger coward than most but I simply could not go on living in Edinburgh... The Kennedies went away

169

the day we did also the MacGregors ...I never did such a hurried packing in my life and in the end it was all packed over again the next day. I seem to have left everything I really want behind, but my sole thought that dreadful day was to get away at all costs. I cannot express the awful BLACK desolating feeling that hung over me for days after. A blight seemed to lie over everything.'

To be fair to my mother in what may seem, with hindsight, to have been a supercharged over-reaction to the raid it must be remembered that the aerial and sea bombardments of World War One were the first direct attacks on the British Isles since Napoleonic years. She had inherited too, probably from her Macdougall grandmother, a psychic awareness if not measure of second-sight. She often had feelings of mischance to come so may well have been more than generally affected by those past. Certainly I, with the unexpected train journey after the excitement of packing, felt no blight hanging over me nor was I incommoded by any absence of semmits or socks when I found myself suddenly translated from Edinburgh to Hawick, there to pursue an almost halcyon time of happiness until December, broken only by equally happy weeks at Dunira in August. During these same weeks both my mother and Mary must have been less than happy for it was obvious to the Chisholm family that Ainslie was dying, he did indeed die in June, and Mary had to leave us for a time to nurse her mother who also was dying. We were told nothing of these troubles. Children in those days were considered not only as immature adults but as practically mentally defective immature adults at that and left to assimilate unpleasant knowledge—or not—as circumstances dictated. Mary's place was taken by Martha whom we liked almost equally well and who was in some respects better than Mary.

'I never saw anyone so good at amusing children—she taught Elaine a great many little songs and played with them at all kinds of games. It seemed a special talent she had.'

I had always credited Mary with teaching me the rivers of Scotland, beginning

'The Dee, The Don, The DeverON,
The Tay the Forth The Tweed.'

170

and the other geographical jingle,

'Scotland, England, Ireland, Wales,
All tied up with monkey's tails.'

but it may very well have been Martha.

The haunting topographical rhyme I learned some years later was told me by my mother. In the spring of 1919 we spent a few weeks in Biggar,

('Edinburgh's big
But Biggar's bigger.')

Here Ian and I had our first attempt at hill-climbing when with our parents we climbed to the top of a small nearby hill, Busyberry Hill, which I connected, owing to one of the peculiar ramifications of the mind, with Squirrel Nutkin. Further away was the higher and mysterious Tinto.

'On Tintock-tap there is a mist,
And in that mist there is a kist,
And in the kist there is a caup,
And in the caup there is a drap;
Tak' up the caup, drink aff the drap,
And set the caup on Tintock-tap.'

When we were in Biggar there was a tremendous blizzard, the worst for years. The Biggar Water ran beneath our house and on the opposite slope stood the old Parish church. On the first evening of the thaw we walked there in the sunshine and wandered through the old grave-yard—because of the melting snow, the sudden emergence of daffodils and the hillside becoming alive with waters—the first grave-yard not to depress me with the thought of rotting flesh but to hint at a continuation of the spirit.

It must have been Martha who made us our kite for Mary had never shown signs of such inventiveness. It was a proper kite, not made from a pack—I doubt if such things existed then—but from thin spars of wood lashed together with brown paper pasted over them. We flew it on what I remember as being called the Red Hill and watched proudly as it climbed, with the tail, made of twists of paper tied into string, the handiwork of Ian and myself, dancing gaily behind. On

171

wet days or in the evenings she showed us how to soak stamps off envelopes then gum them over empty Virol jars thus turning them into mosaic vases to hold wildflowers or our collections of grasses so much more plentiful and varied then in those almost pre-pesticide days. A magnificent vase full of them on the landlady's kitchen mantelpiece had inspired these works of art.

Owing to our sudden arrival in Hawick we did not go directly to the house we had rented for the summer but to temporary lodgings in a flat above a shop in the, or one of the, main streets. Ever since I have thought that an ideal place for a home.

'Bang-whang-whang goes the drum, tootle-te-tootle the fife.
Oh, a day in the city square, there is no such pleasure in life!'

All life flowed up and down the street and pavements and in and out the shops beneath my entranced eyes. The shop below us was my favourite kind, an ironmongers, I think the property of the people with whom we lodged. They were very kind to the refugees in their home and their school-girl daughter brought her toys into our sitting-room to show me. She had a mechanical toy which fascinated me. It was a rider on a bicycle which when wound up travelled all over the floor, the cyclist bowing forwards and backwards. Of even more interest was the mirror fitted to the outside of the window and so angled that would-be callers would be scrutinised without the trouble of a trip downstairs. This I considered a very tricky contrivance. After all too short a stay in the city square we moved to a plain letting villa (with mice) and would there have continued our usual quiet life of walks and stories had it not been for two Pollockshields sisters who had married two Hawick brothers who were mill-owners. They were daughters of a friend of Aunt Barbara's and my mother had been friendly with a younger sister. They were very hospitable and invited us often to their beautifully appointed homes which my mother said made her 'gnash her teeth' with envy. She appreciated artistically designed surroundings but lacked the means to achieve her aims in her own home. When she went to drawingroom tea we children and Mary went to nursery tea so we all settled happily, my mother getting introductions to other women and to the Red Cross while Ian and I sampled an alien life-style, for one of those families lived a nursery life as children did in books with nurses and under-nurses so Mary (or Martha!) made friends too.

We visited our father quite often for tea for Stobs was just the right distance away for a (Chisholm-length) afternoon walk. This POW camp had been set up for interned civilians but they, in preparation for the (expected) Great Push had been transferred to the Isle of Man, escorted by, among others, 2nd Lieutenant Chisholm. I do not suppose the inhabitants of the camp were meant to fraternise with their captors but some of them always waved to us as we crossed to the Officers' Mess. I suspect many came from Bavaria or the Black Forest for they produced beautiful wooden artifacts. My mother acquired a tray with chipped out decoration, Ian a dachshund with jointed legs and I a Grimm's Fairy Tale-like representation of two bearded wood-cutters who alternately raised and let fall their axes. Knowing nothing of the probable economics of my father's transactions, we naturally assumed that the kind Germans had made these presents especially for us (perhaps they did have us in mind) out of the goodness of their hearts and found it difficult to reconcile this behaviour with the fact that as they were prisoners, behind strong fences, they must necessarily be bad.

Another fence comes to mind. About the height of a fruit cage it separated a shrubbery from the path leading to a tennis-court in the grounds of the children with the nurse-maids. We had gone for a walk, three nurses and at least five children to be shown the court which was kept locked. The key had been entrusted to the eldest child a, to my eyes, 'big girl' of about seven. For some unexplained reason, revolt against her nursery status perhaps or mere devilment at being able to show off before a younger and rather naive visitor, she suddenly tossed the key over the fence into the scrub. There was the most terrible fuss, consternations and recriminations—but no apologies. I was shocked at such behaviour but could not help feeling a guilty admiration for the sinner.

Happier events with them were a real Hallowe'en party (I forked three apples) and once an after-tea visit to the scene of the grown-ups drawing-room tea there to admire with them and the nurses and all the children a magnificent celebratory cake. It must have been for some family event and it was made in the shape of an officer's cap and covered with what looked like khaki icing. This was one of its wonders for at this time, as at our christening and our wedding in another war, icing was forbidden. The cook must have exercised all her ingenuity to produce with margarine and semolina, 'butter'-icing and marzipan for this triumph of confectionery. I think it must have been the memory of this masterpiece that fuelled the succession of decorated cakes in the semblance of ships, cars, cricket-bats, crabs and cuckoo-clocks with which I have marked family birthdays and Christmases over the years.

The cousins of these children, two boys, lived in an equally beautiful home. I remember arriving at it and walking up a drive thick on the left-hand side with marguerites. Beyond the marguerites was a pony on which the father held me for a ride. The elder boy and I quickly became friends and he led me off to a summer-house in which was a beached flotilla of model boats many of which were made of tin and had sharp pointed ends. Inspired no doubt by the same devil of showing-off as his cousin and having acquired an accomplice in crime he collected a basinful of them and had me do the same. Supervision was not as tight in this household but it was still surreptitiously that we made our way to a bathroom where he filled the bath and we launched the ships. We had a good time in this beautifully appointed white, white, bathroom, making waves, (slosh slosh over on to the floor) propelling the sharp and rushing fleet from one end of the ocean to the other, crashing them into each other and into the gleaming porcelain of the bath before we were discovered and bidden take all back outside.

With my mother I often took afternoon tea with various kind ladies one of whom presented me with Topsy, especially made for me from stuffed discarded woollen stockings. She had curly black woolly hair and flat white linen buttons for eyes. She wore a bright gingham dress and cap and curtain-ring earrings. Neither the Topsies nor Little Black Sambo nor Epaminondas—a current anti-hero in the children's section of *Home Chat*—gave adults of those days complexes of racist guilt nor did I despise the two fictional little boys for their blackness and certainly did not think their foolishness stemmed from it. In my experience little boys tended to be foolish in real life be they ever so white and simple little boys (all but the youngest brother) were a perfectly normal stock in trade of European folk-tales.

Mary took us to the Shows—a fair held in what could have been in happier times the week of the Common Riding when the Cornet and his retinue would have ridden the Marches and Hawick's ancient slogan been proclaimed. We had never sampled a fair before and delightedly explored its pleasures while my mother muttered half-heartedly of dirt and germs and scarlet fever. There had been heavy rain and in some of the passages between tents we had to walk over the mud on duck-boards. It taxed my credulity to think that ducks ever did. On an evening visit with friends Mary won a coconut which she had to relinquish to Ian as he conceived such a passion for it that he took it everywhere, even to bed. He had a penchant at this time for uncomfortable bed companions, another being Elent, a wooden elephant on rockers.

Mary and I had a craze for 'talking Hawick'. To the best of our ability we mimicked the Border town's unique accent, speaking of 'coups of ty'ee for yow and my'ee' and requesting eachother to spell 'Egypt' which emerged something like 'Eye'ee jiy'ee y'ee pie'ee ty'ee.'

One of the keenest disillusions of my life occurred in Hawick. Of the medicines we had in those days, one was too pleasant a remedy, more like a party drink, to be offered often. Even its label promised well bearing a bunch of grapes and if I remember aright a happy naked babe or cherub or one of Bacchus' train. This was Eno's Fruit Salt of which we were given to believe that too much was not good for us. Then there was spoon-licking Syrup of Figs, gritty-smooth Milk of Magnesia which made you pull a face and Dr Gregory's revolting pink (and gritty) mixture. Infinitely worse than Dr Gregory's brew was the occasionally administered Castor Oil. I shuddered when I thought of the two little girls a friend of Mary's had once cared for. They were the recipients of a regular week-end dose,

175

the benefit of which, apart from the one routinely expected, was said to be that it made their hair grow long and shining. I could picture the poor nerve-racked wretches, with more than waist-length hair, like the lady in the Harlene advertisements, which when it came to washing and brushing must have been more trouble than it was worth. Though we were not persecuted to that extent I had sampled it often enough to detest its nauseous oiliness so judge of my excitement when looking into the curved window of a chemist's shop at the end of a block of buildings I spelt out the miraculous message—'Tasteless Castor Oil.' I tugged at my mother's sleeve and suggested that next time we had need we bought this kind. "That," she answered, "is the kind we use". I am sure it must have been this disappointment that has made me sceptical of print and almost completely resistant to the claims of advertisers.

All this summer when the Chisholm family and Mary's were having their private griefs, the war situation was not improving. In early June came news of the sinking of *HMS Hampshire* with Kitchener on board. Kitchener was a legend and regarded as a potential saviour. In December my mother recounted 'one of the many war myths that crop up now and again...to the effect that Kitchener is still alive and a prisoner in Germany'. This tale came in my mother's instance from my grandmother via goodness knows how many intermediaries between her and the wife of an officer of the *Hampshire* reputedly sharing a POW existence with the hero. Soon after his loss came rumours of a great naval defeat for Britain. Though knowing nothing of the reason for them, I remember days of unexplained gloom in the house and in the streets where complete strangers stopped each other to ask if there was any fresh news.

'It has been a very trying week for Britain. Only last Wednesday was fought the most important Naval Battle of the War so far, off the coast of Jutland, when both sides suffered heavy losses. It was not put in the papers until Friday night and then was put in such a way as to read almost like a British defeat. It was a very gloomy weekend while Berlin celebrated it with flag-flappings and jubilation. But gradually as the details filtered out it turns out to have been a British victory tho' attended with heavy losses.'

176

I remember a solemn emotional service in church which I take to
have been on that black weekend.

I remember too another service affecting me personally with
another form of emotion when one Sunday morning in July I was
publicly, albeit unintentionally, humiliated by my Aunt Edith. She
had been fortuitously visiting us when 'domestic affairs were so
disturbing'. This remark had reference neither to marital disputes nor
to dramatic involvements such as the Thurber family had with drunk,
mad or naked cooks but meant merely that Mary was called home
to nurse her mother.

'Edith helped me a great deal, she has such a good way with children.'

I was proud to escort her to church on Sunday. She was in deep
mourning and we sat near the back but neither of these facts
rendered her as invisible as I could have wished. After the
Benediction my aunt sat down and began to search for her purse and
gloves. Seemingly the Baptist Church in Dublin Street was less
ostentatiously patriotic than the UF Church in Hawick—or had the
priorities of God and Caesar more correctly assessed. Most Scottish
Churches did I think at this time conclude morning service with the
National Anthem but when I, with the rest of the congregation,
snapped to attention Dedae was scrabbling under the pew for her
possessions. Unabashed and giggling a little she struggled to her feet
to join in the last few lines—but oh!—to a five-year-old, the shame
of having such an ignorant aunt!

CHAPTER TWENTY-FIVE

Land of the Mountain and the Flood

SUMMER OF 1917 saw us in Ballachulish on the shore of Loch Leven, a long sea-loch running between the mountains from Loch Linnhe to Kinlochleven, a township whose being mostly depended on the existence of the British Aluminium Company's factory. At this time there was also a POW camp high on the hill-side down which was being laid a pipe-line from the Blackwater Reservoir and Loch Elde Mhor to bring water for the generation of electricity. The work-force for this project consisted of a thousand German prisoners and five hundred British troops deemed 'unfit for active service'. My father had been an officer at this camp since December 1916.

We reached Ballachulish, my mother, Mary, Ian and myself in a manner one could not now, by train. We left the Edinburgh—Oban train at Connel Ferry to join one of the most enchanting of branch lines, closed alas in 1966, which ran from Connel to Ballachulish. For most of its twenty-eight miles it ran within sight of sea or sea-loch and of Lismore and other islands through the district made memorable by the Appin Murder and Stevenson's *Kidnapped*. More interesting to Ian and myself than the literary or historical associations was what resembled a miniature Forth Bridge over which the train crossed the rapids of the Falls of Lora.

We spent all June in 'rooms' in a pleasant stone villa some little way from the main road, belonging to a Mrs McColl who had a daughter called, peculiarly to my way of thinking, Ena. I confused her name with that of Eno, the lovely fizzy Fruit Salt. She was older than I was and went to school but did not mind playing with me. When she returned in the afternoons we clambered down the bank to the stream that ran past the garden and waded in the clear cold waters that whirled round great granite boulders nearly making us lose our footing. I puzzled off and on for years as to why my mother let me do this, she saw danger round so many corners. On a visit back I understood. My Torrent was no more than a Highland burn, its boulders mere stones.

Ballachulish was full of interest. It looked different from anywhere else we had known with sea and imposing mountains and houses set haphazardly here and there among great areas of heather as well as the more disciplined village ones. There were flooded slate quarries and piles of slates by the roadside and a narrow slate archway that the road went through. There was tall bracken by the beach that we could lose ourselves in and close to the water one of the delights of Highland sea-lochs, masses of yellow irises or flags. There were sheep-tracks among the heather along which we plodded to favourite picnic places carpeted with soft sphagnum moss and furnished with pink and white marble rocks to sit on or use as tables. The picnic places were often shared with the local bull, an inquisitive beast reputed to have none but the friendliest intentions. "...The children pat him on their way to school", said a villager reprovingly to my mother when she voiced apprehension. Despite this she was never quite happy about him and the picnic often shifted ground rather hurriedly, "...but don't irritate him by looking as if you were running away."

Though she felt strongly about bulls she never mentioned adders, perhaps they were not abundant locally. Years later when my youngest sister was small, I thought I saw one move among the heather above Blackfarland Bay on Bute. I called her to come away quickly. She did—quicker than I knew she could move. It turned out she knew nothing of adders but, having thought I said arrows, was expecting Red Indian braves.

When we passed groups of people round by the bakers we realised they were talking in some incomprehensible language which we were told was Gaelic. Soon we were able to converse to the extent of greetings, 'feasgar math', 'madainn mhath', 'oidche mhatch' and make, when in our oilskins, a passing comment on the state of the weather, 'tha fliuch'. The church, which my mother and I attended once or twice, not only employed the un-understandable language but added to our confusion by reversing the usual order of things and having us stand up to pray and sit down to sing. We looked across at, but never visited, the mysterious Eilann Munde where death-lights flickered. I recall the pillars at the head of the steps at the house gate where I used to perch to survey the life of the strath. Once the doctor passing in his car put his head out to tell me to mind and not fall or he would have to bandage me up. Sheep and cows were usually the only passers-by.

I remember two unfortunate occurrences during our stay. Though my second baby tooth was preserved as it came out safely in a bap, my first one vanished in the night and it was here that again I found reason to mistrust the written word. Somewhere, probably in *Home Chat*, I had read that inkstains could be removed with milk, so that when I upset a bottle of ink which I was not supposed to use, at a desk where I had no business to be, I filched some from a cream-jug and retired with it behind the bathroom door where I dabbed and rubbed ineffectively. It was deflating when Mary, who was not suffering from a guilty conscience so could go openly to the kitchen fetched more in a bowl and after stripping me of the dress finally after many libations succeeded in removing the stain.

Twice my mother and I made the journey to Kinlochleven to visit my father. On arrival she phoned him from the hotel and he, if free, would come down to have midday dinner with us. If there was time we walked up by the pipe-line to the camp, a rough walk, the gradient being a thousand feet in a mile, and were given tea in the Officers' Mess where I was made much of. There was an Officer's dog there who sang—that is when a record was put on the gramophone he threw back his head and howled.

To reach Kinlochleven we had to go by boat, at this time, apart from mountain tracks, its only link with the outer world. A new road from Glencoe was opened in 1922 the work I have always heard of

Italian and German prisoners. The boat could have been the *Mountaineer,* the *Comet* or *Scout* but the first time we went was 'the sturdy but unlovely *Lochness'.* I remember going on board in the rain (tha fluich) and being far too interested in the stir of the boatmen and their helpers, time-consuming as it was, to be irked as was my mother by some of the proceedings, particularly the slow loading of lorry-load after lorry-load of supplies and their stowing away in all the sheltered places so that passengers had the choice of standing in the rain or taking refuge in the cramped cabin below. We naturally, as befitted members of a family of yachtsmen, stayed above in the rain (I still find it almost impossible on any ship to seek craven shelter below) and were rewarded by the clouds clearing away to give us a sunny afternoon. I remember the raw unfinished look of Kinlochleven, row after row of new hutments set along unmade-up roads. Had I been taken oftener to silent films I would have recognised it for what it was, first cousin to gold-mining townships in the Wild West. Higher on the hillside were a few attractive houses for the employees of the British Aluminium Company. It was, I have read, because of objections to industry by some proprietors on the north side of the loch that the village had to be built on the south side, facing north. In winter it was almost without sun and in later years children were supplied with extra vitamins. I doubt if there was ever much of a village though Pennant mentions it in his tour of 1769—

'... Breakfast at the little village of Kinlochleven on most excellent minced stag, the only form I thought that animal good in.'

My mother has noted in her journal an incident whose significance had escaped me. Though she writes elsewhere in a quite different vein of the 'awful' war and needless slaughter, I daresay her reaction on this occasion was typical of current times and thoughts.

'Halfway up [the loch] we had to stop and deliver some packages to the CO Camp... A boat came out, manned I suppose by conscientious objectors, two at least looked the part, and drew alongside while things were handed down... It is disgusting to see good food being thrown away on those cowardly wretches. One of them in the stern never raised his eyes to the boat. They mostly affect longish hair and go hatless.'

181

Poor prisoners of conscience. Surely it would have been too much
to have been exiled to that dark glen and then to have had packages
of bad food thrown down at them.

In July we moved to the schoolhouse at Kinlochleven where we
stayed until the end of August. This was a modern house with a huge
vegetable garden but, my mother lamented, no grass for the children
to play on. Perversely we rather liked running up and down the
stony paths between the cabbages and beans. We did occasionally
play in the attached playground but there felt like trespassers. Of the
flower garden I remember masses of mignonette, interesting both for
its foreign-sounding name and its rusty green blooms. At intervals
since I have vainly tried to cultivate it and at last have it in Berkshire
not from my efforts but the green fingers of another. At Kinlochleven
its scent, mingling with the salt of the sea-loch, the honey smell of
sun-warmed heather and the astringency of bog-myrtle made a
unique bouquet.

The wives of the company officials dutifully called on my mother
and we were invited out to tea but I remember none of the children
we must have met. I do however remember one of the houses, a real
Ideal Homes' bungalow, all white-painted woodwork and very
bright floral chintzes further embellished with tropical birds, chosen
perhaps to offset the winter's gloom. As my mother noted, living in
Kinlochleven during the First World War was rather like being on a
small island miles from civilisation, although admittedly civilisation
had not much to offer between 1914 and 1918. Sometime after we
left there seems to have been only one daily boat leaving to connect
with the railhead at Ballachulish and that at 6 am. My mother was
not much able here to indulge in her passion for long walks, as almost
the only road going a short way down the opposite side of the loch
was the most midge- and cleg-ridden place I have ever experienced.
We went shopping most mornings which we enjoyed for there was
usually some activity at the pier and sometimes the passage of a
works' train sporting that rarity, a woman engine-driver. There were
builders engaged in more huts rumoured to be for the accommodation
of girl munition workers from the Potteries. My mother commented,

'It will be a drastic change for them' so I was glad to read recently in *A Short History of Kinlochleven* by Barbara Fairweather of the Glencoe Folk Museum that, 'the hostel accommodation was very comfortable. Each girl has a separate cubicle. There was a dining-room, a sitting-room and baths and a laundry'. There were musical evenings and dancing and some of the girls settled in Kinlochleven.

Ian, who had always been able to twist his mother round his little finger and who was still being described by her as 'such a dear sweet-natured wee soul that we can't help petting him' was now causing her to write of his budding boy-like characteristics. 'He has already told us what he wants for his birthday, trains and cars. He is a regular boy in that way... The boy in him is coming out. He was trying to push Elaine off the pavement coming home.' We have photographs of him at Kinlochleven, thick hair cut in a fringe, looking deceptively sweet as I, the recipient of pinches and nudges delivered while his countenance shone with angelic goodness, well knew. We both throve in the good Highland air and the boy in my little brother flourished. He made more frequent attempts to murder Charles but eventually over-reached himself and unexpected retribution fell. While shopping among the mazes of huts which made up the mini-metropolis he had some altercation with his mother and ran away and refused to come back. I was almost rigid with horror for being a less indulged criminal I knew that what with rudeness, disobedience and worse than all the making of a spectacle of himself and his mother he was heading for real trouble. None of this got through to him, regardless indeed of impending doom the potential little victim but ran faster. Finally my mother had to set off in pursuit of him. This struck me as very funny, I doubt if I had ever seen her really run before and I began to laugh, behaviour which did not endear me either. I can still see, on those rough stony roads, a defiant little figure pursued by a lady in large shady hat and the long-skirted pink and cream striped dress she often wore. Half turning to laugh at her he of course eventually tripped and grazed his knees. Yanked to his feet by an indignant mother in the early stages of pregnancy his cries of pain changed to howls of apprehension as he found his programme

183

going awry. No sympathy to be got here for sore knees. The budding scrap of manhood was dragged home where his mother attended first to correction then first aid.

Happier memories than of this unusual reversal of our childhood roles are of evening walks with Mary up a mountain path above the schoolhouse. It was high enough to be reasonably free of midges and, although there was no access to the hillside as deer fences enclosed it, outcrops of heather and bluebells grew on it. We searched as ever for white heather but the whitest we ever found was heath not the real lucky heather. We sang all the war-time songs, 'Tipperary', 'Keep the Home Fires Burning', 'Pack up your Troubles' and 'There's a Long, Long Trail A-winding'. Next year I was to master the right hand of this nostalgic melody and it and 'There is a City Bright' were my show-pieces for weeks. Mary had hard work explaining to us the whereabouts of Blighty, 'Carry me Back to Blighty' being one of her favourites. I daresay she found Argyll a far cry from her Midlothian village of Gorebridge.

At the end of August we travelled back to Edinburgh—boat to Ballachulish, train to Connel Ferry and there a night in an hotel. Supper and breakfast in the hotel seemed meals quite other than their everyday equivalents at home. In the morning we had a walk to the shore to stand nearer the baby Forth Bridge before our father put us into the train for Edinburgh. We shared a compartment with two ladies who had a flask of chicken-broth. Enraptured by Ian's innocent looks they offered him some. My mother was hastening politely to refuse as chicken-broth was one of his pet hates and he was apt to show his distaste rather forcibly. However he must have been equally charmed by the ladies because to our great relief he smiled aimably and graciously accepted a bowlful which he drank to the dregs.

We then, clutching our belongings, probably tumbled out of the train to 'change at Larbert'—we always seemed in those days to be changing at Larbert, not a station with otherwise great potential—before reaching Edinburgh, a cab, 39 Inverleith Gardens and for me, on Monday 15th October, my first taste of school.

CHAPTER TWENTY-SIX

School Take-aways

MY FIRST BRUSH with organised education proved almost completely baffling. It took place at a Kindergarten two minutes walk from home. The teacher may have been clever, even advanced in her views, possibly feminist. I feel this on the slender grounds that her niece, who lived with her, was very clever or so we were told and she herself had a mannish hair-style, the first I had even seen. Her cleverness however availed me little as she rarely taught me and she had little credibility in my mind as I confused her with the Gryphon in *Alice in Wonderland*, her surname being faintly similar. On my first day I arrived a week, or perhaps only an hour, late, so all the other children knew what they were doing—or I thought they did, which was as bad. On arrival I was taken up two flights of stairs in the small terraced house—more confusion as the place seemed more like a home than what I had been given to understand a school would be—to a landing where I hung my coat. This was not a proper cloakroom and there was no lavatory. The school day was short so fortunately I never needed to 'go' for I never discovered where I would have gone. I had with me my new school-bag with slate and slate pencil. Some children also carried small tins with little pieces of damp sponge in them. The slate reminded me of Ballachulish, of the quarries and of the thin slivers of slate on the shore which with varying success we skimmed over the water. I liked the sensuous feel of the slate pencils, smooth and cool, if not always very efficient while the unexpected squeak of them on slate could set my teeth on edge. Another happy memory of school-bags is of the smell that came later, an accumulation of leather, cedar pencil shavings and digestive biscuit crumbs!

I was put to sit at a long desk with some other girls. To my left was a wall with window which I knew would yield the same view as that of my bedroom—Arthur's Seat, Castle and Pentlands. I never got close enough to see it but the knowledge of its presence provided a measure of reality in an otherwise mad world. Of my school-mates I remember Harold who like me was an untidy writer so we briefly fraternised over re-copying lines in our copy-books, 'All that glisters is not gold' 'Time and Tide wait for no man'. Then there was the wavy-haired Frieda with a sailor collar which and whom I admired hugely. Kathleen was older and spoke kindly to me. Delicate and often absent, she had what I suppose was a curvature of the spine, but her nature made nonsense of her deformity. There was Dennis and his sister Muriel from New Zealand (or Australia—all one to me) and a girl whose parents either had—or had not—gone down in the *Lusitania*. At the interval—what for?—no milk, no play, no leaving our seats, no lavatory—we could only talk and the two bad boys threw paper darts. Our teacher vanished. Perhaps she had a cup of tea—or knew the way to the lavatory.

Lessons were a mystery to me. Children leapt up and down, frantically waving their arms. This seemed approved behaviour but I had no clue as to why. I once drew 'oohs' and 'ohs' of horror as I innocently made to leave my seat to show some completed work to the teacher. Occasionally some of us were shepherded downstairs to what in a normal house would have been the drawing-room to sit around one table while the teacher sat at another. One day, lost in work—or dreaming—I thought I heard her say,

"Elaine, come to the table," and rushed up and stood rigid before her. She regarded me with surprise. What she had said was, "Eileen! Your tables." As I crept back there was Eileen with her squad resignedly waiting to begin their chant. Small wonder I have to this day preserved a numerical block which permits me to do calculations only by flashes of insight. I do remember originally enjoying

186

'borrowing subtraction' so much more grown-up than mere addition. Nothing was explained about tens or units or any such high-falutin fancies, we simply blissfully just 'took away'.

"Eight from seven you can't borrow one eight from seventeen," and under the desk with your fingers. This manoeuvre changed the top-line figure of the next column to one less but not to worry, we simply 'took away' from that. This procedure served me well until I went to my next school where, despite getting the right answers, I was told I could not get them that way and was introduced to a farrago of mathematical nonsense as to the morality of borrowing and paying back. Rather illogically I was encouraged to be fair and after borrowing from the top line to distribute my favours and pay back to the lower. This seemed an unearned bonus for the lower line and an undeserved slap in the face for the kindly upper one. Whichever way one looked at it the moral seemed to be that no more than life was subtraction fair. Unfortunately I then found myself at the mercy of a less moralistic teacher who said outrightly that we were all wrong and that the only way to subtract was to take away from an imaginary ten and then add. This was too much for my limited mathematical abilities and I very sensibly reverted to my first proven 'take away and fingers' method which (with the additional check of when in doubt add the two bottom lines) I have employed ever since. Fortunately it is but rarely that real life confronts one with long lines of subtraction. At this time I also enjoyed Long Division, an equally unexplained but pleasant and alas, dying out art. I especially enjoyed the zig-zag working and the neat double lines drawn with ruler at the end when the sum came out exactly.

All the minor confusions however, were as nothing to that caused by the sudden cry of the teacher in the upper room.

"The Modulator!"

Bags, books, pencils, slates were swept away. One acolyte unrolled a yellowed scroll of cracked parchment and hung it on the easel. A second presented the teacher with her pointer and we were away. Dohs, res, mes, fahs, sohs, resounded all around, apparently at random. As suddenly as it started it was all over—the racket subsided, the scroll was rolled up, the class relaxed and books and slates reappeared. Never at any time did I connect this class-room aberration with music... In late January chicken-pox wrought a merciful release—though it ruined my birthday—and aside from a few weeks before we re-took to our camp-follower life I was able to escape my Kindergarten, little enhanced by the experience apart from the acquisition of some smudged pastel drawings on dark paper of old men in gowns, God, Joseph, Moses and the like and an extended study of the peculiarities of life.

My second and only other school was St Oran's School for Girls (small boys admitted) in Drummond Place. It had originally been known as 'Mrs Henderson's' and I think, but am not sure, that my aunt Edith had taken some classes at it. More notably it was the latter day descendent of a small school that Mrs Henderson's husband, Mr Thomas Syme Henderson, had run in India Street which Robert Louis Stevenson had attended.

My cousin Kathleen and an out-of-school friend Verna and myself all entered St Oran's the same morning in October 1918. K was as nervous as any of us but her shyness made her show off and as we waited for the mistress in our first class-room I remember her sitting on the lid of her desk, asking these strange classmates to spell difficult words. When they failed as she knew they would—she could spell anything—she triumphantly spelt them out herself. At this time with day girls and a few full-term and weekly boarders there were around a hundred pupils in the school. The Principal was a severe-looking, rather old-fashionedly-styled lady who dressed well in muted colours and wore her hair on top of her head like a cottage bun. She wore pince-nez which, when fixing us with admonitory stares, she took off between finger and thumb, at the same time drawing in her breath in an intimidating reverse hiss. We wildly over-exaggerated her age and because of it and a reputedly tart tongue held her in some considerable awe—possibly her intent.

Number 25 Drummond Place was at the middle of the north side of a spacious terraced Georgian square with cobbles and a garden in the centre. Place in this instance is the equivalent of the French

188

'place', one of Scotland's many linguistic links with the 'Auld Alliance'. Picardy Place, the only remnant of the Huguenot weavers' village, perhaps once a square, is not far distant. The entrance to No 25 was like that to all the other houses, up a step or two and over the area on a stone bridge to the front door. Like a few others it was a four, rather than three, storey house. There was a basement to the front and at the back where the ground fell away to a small garden, a double basement. A well-proportioned dining-room with a finely carved chimney-piece opened off the hall which itself had rows of pegs and pigeon-holes for shoes for the youngest pupils. More coats hung in the room which in a private house would have been the parlour. When the school expanded this turned into a school-room, 'the morning-room' or Room 1, and coats were banished to the less public basement.

Upstairs was a large L-shaped drawing-room used for singing and drill, dancing, eurythmics and prayers. Hymns frequently sung in the morning were the stirring 'Onward Christian Soldiers' usually heralding a new term, 'Courage, Brothers, do not Stumble' and the image-ridden 'Holy, Holy, Holy, Lord God Almighty' with the saints casting down their golden crowns (why?) and the further unexplained and disorderly scene of cherubim and seraphim falling down around a glassy sea. A lovely hymn. I also liked 'Star of Peace, to Wanderers Weary' which brought pictures of Newhaven with its harbour of fishing boats. The euphoric 'Summer Suns are Glowing' was a third term favourite, though often the glory of the morning having occasioned its choice, a glance at the window could show the promise dimmed and the singing an act of faith. We sang the Paraphrases, 'O God of Bethel' and the Scottish Metrical Psalms, 'The Lord's my Shepherd' and 'I to the Hills will lift Mine Eyes' but my almost top favourite (to the proper tune in the Scottish Church Hymnal) was 'All Things Bright and Beautiful' with the purple-headed mountains and river running by,

'The tall trees in the greenwood,
The meadows where we play,
The rushes, by the water,
We gather every day.'

No controversial rich man with poor man at his gate, spoilt this doxology of things of good report. Armistice Day was always 'For all the Saints' every verse of it, and on the last day of the session, a hymn with the lachrymose first verse,

'Childhood's years are passing o'er us,
Soon our school-days will be done.
Tears and sorrows lie before us,
Hidden dangers, snares unknown.'

This we sang, completely unconcernedly, to a very jaunty tune.

Through double doors from the drawing-room was the Principal's bedroom later to become her sitting-room to which we used to see Janet, a gaunt-faced factotum, surprisingly possessed of an unsuspected sense of humour, bear in trays of luscious teas for visitors. Next was a small music and class-room. I have many memories of it for when in our last year only four of us stayed on to do University 'Prelims' and Bursary work it made a convenient class-room. It was there earlier that our most prosaic member took almost perpetual issue with Shakespeare and other imaginative souls if they made a blossom bloom out of season. I recall too her snort of disgust as she came on

'Ah! yet does beauty, like a dial-hand,
Steal from his figure…'

and her cry, "It's the shadow that moves!" It was there too that a visiting specialist, a family friend of one of our members, asked her what her father thought of the Baltic situation. Even if we had not been non-political to a girl—we knew loads of history but no current politics—this was an opening we would never have given her for she was only too ready at any time to expound on Dad's views. She leant back, balancing her chair on two legs as she gave his and her reading of the position while all around her captive mates shot darts of pure hate at her. Then there was the day much earlier when there must have been some crisis of seating for we were all seated on the cold linoleum floor, on our best behaviour, listening to our Headmistress reading an interminable poem—ten long verses, well-nigh interminable—called 'The Pipes at Lucknow' and I was too scared to

190

stretch when my foot most painfully went to sleep.

Upstairs again, banisters and floor covering getting progressively less grand, was the front class-room, scene of Kay's spelling-bee, with next to it the Kindergarten which no matter what class was being taught there, smelt always of plasticine and clay. On Saturday mornings a dancing-class was held there which my little brother briefly attended completely contrary to his wishes. His attendance ceased the morning he refused to dance, even when the teacher herself came over the room and holding out her hand tried to cajole him. As he refused again she tossed her head back in annoyance. He tossed his too, but unfortunately, as he was sitting on a bench against the wall, hit it a sharp crack. She did not say 'Serve you right' but she looked it and his shamed mother decided enough was enough.

At this same age he embarrassed me even more deeply. A friend's father occasionally called for her at the close of morning school in his chauffeur-driven limousine and for three-quarters of my way home I shared in her treat. One day Ian had to wait to go home with me. As we started to enter the car, not having kept it standing for a minute, her father, a cossetted-husband type, frowned and asked who was the little boy? He had known me for years but no doubt had never taken in the fact that I had a brother. However his daughter, who treated him and all his pronouncements very reverentially, patiently explained the situation and we were all three permitted to seat ourselves. Dad was a kindly man enough, though unpredictable in his temper and he had no way with children. Like many such he believed he had. When we went to afternoon tea in his house we were set down to a magnificent meal in the diningroom but at least two of his guests dreaded his appearance. I was one, for he always asked me the brain-teaser, "If a herring and a half cost a penny and a half how many can you buy for a shilling?" I never knew and even after having had it explained to me still felt I had some half herring lying about unaccounted for.

Kay was the other victim and suffered even more intensely than I did. She was rather a favourite of his and for all she tried to make

191

herself inconspicuous he would spot her and burst into a music-hall song which as I remember went,

'K...K...K... Katy,
K...K...K... Katy,
She's the only girl that I adore...'

What a hazard to childhood are self-styled funny-men feeding their own egos.

When going home in the car his daughter and I used to listen deferentially to Dad's remarks—often what we secretly felt to be rather lèse-majesté jokes about the mistress who became joint Principal and her sister whom he had known in his youth and referred to by their Christian names—but on this occasion he turned his attention to the little boy beneficiary of his largesse and asked him some question. It was just unfortunate that at this time Ian was going through one of those 'passing phases' common to little boys and passing all too slowly, when they think they are amusing and have absolutely no discretion as to whom they exercise their wit on. He therefore answered, if not rudely, at least in a manner seen by his benefactor to be impudent.

"Andrews! Stop the car! This rude little boy must get out."

My friend and I were nearly in tears and I made to get out too.

"You don't need to go. Just this rude little boy. I don't have rude little boys in my car."

Patiently his poor daughter explained the situation again and how Ian was not allowed to walk home alone and finally among rumbles her father relented, the door was closed, my rather scared little brother almost smirked and Andrews proceeded on his stately way down Inverleith Row.

Back in school, behind the Kindergarten was the Back Room where I became the humiliated owner of a horrible red Arithmetic Book. Owing to some mix-up the copy issued to me was a teachers' one with answers to all the problems at the end. This though destroying one's faith in the infallibility of teachers was of no use in my hands. I had assumed that all the copies were alike and was anyway too ignorant to have been able to doctor my solutions with its help and too innocent to have thought of trying. In spite of which when some weeks later the answers were discovered it was taken from my hands and the extra pages torn out before my eyes and the eyes of the class leaving me with a mutilated copy and the feeling I had been branded as a cheat. Rather high-handed action it was too—our parents paid for our books.

Up again were the two rooms where the few boarders slept, but the room at the back, the Top Room, with Edinburgh's magnificent northern prospect, was another class-room. It held what one of the Staff, no doubt ironically, dignified by the name of Staffroom—a deep cupboard where they hung their coats and left their umbrellas. Beside the Top Room was a music room separated from it by a lavatory, the same lay-out as on the floor below. The more than inadequate sanitary arrangements of this and similar schools of the first quarter of the twentieth century seemed to have aroused no critical comment from children, staff or parents. There was in the basement another lavatory (three for the whole school) almost lost in an enormous bathroom. We were not meant to know about it until the cloakrooms moved downstairs and then, despite its vast space, were supposed to enter one at a time. Perhaps this was just for 'niceness'. If the authorities had thought they were thereby preventing some nameless vice they were wasting their time for none of us, despite being steeped in *Eric, or Little by Little* and *David Blaize* among other Public School stories, would have recognised one. The one-at-a-time rule was an insult to the possibilities of this giant bathroom which was ideal for practising dances or acting out dramas or indeed just gossiping so that it speedily became one of our regular howffs. Another was the top-storey music-room to which we sloped off to enjoy our packed lunches as soon as the gong had sounded and the pupils who 'took' school dinners had filed into the dining-room, followed by the hawk-eyed Principal, to where starched white cloths had been laid over the green baize table-cover. Before inauguration of the basement cloakroom had legitimised traffic up and down the dark curving stairs, return from the bathroom was hazardous as it involved passing the high-up very old-fashioned looking black phone. Of course all telephones of that period look old-fashioned now but that one looked old-fashioned then—and our Headmistress spent an inordinate amount of time at it. Creeping furtively up we were sometimes surprised by a brisk, "Come along girls! What are you doing down there?" as she followed the removal of her pince-nez with her nerve-freezing hiss. Once were we abashed and that was when we came giggling up to be confronted by her milder partner who only commented as she fixed my cousin with a look, "And such a quiet little mouse too!" This perceptive remark shook us. In the face of authority Kay was a quiet little mouse, but among her peers quite other.

CHAPTER TWENTY-SEVEN

The Road to Learning

ST ORAN'S, despite early limitations of space, was a good school. As young children we had well chosen 'reading books' which opened avenues of interest in literature, history and mythology. Our garden sunflowers were enhanced by the story of Clytie. Robert the Bruce, Alexander the Great, King Alfred and more jostled together in a thin little red book of story enshrining fact. We had of course Hume Brown's *Scottish History* but as balance *England and the English* which made us realise a world lay beyond the Tweed. The book which really stirred me was the first of a series of World History. This blue volume, *On the Shores of the Great Sea* was of germinal value for me even though I was not to set eye on Athens or any other of the Mediterranean places it mentioned for nearly another fifty years.

We were coached in swimming, hockey, tennis and for a brief spell cricket, and had a flourishing Girl Guide Company. Music, drama and art were in specialist hands although credit for many excellent productions must go to Miss Dougall and her friend, Mrs Jack Scott who designed settings and costume. There was a memorable *Midsummer Night's Dream* which captured the especial magic of the wood near Athens better than any I have seen, bar an equally rewarding experimental one on television, perhaps because the actors apart from the court characters were all juniors.

Soon after I arrived at the school I starred as Minna in *Jan of Windmill Land*. I was no actress but could speak clearly and dance—and Minna had a solo clog dance. Jan was excellent. He was

195

played by a child who knew not shyness. We did not care for each other—a pity for young lovers—but seemed to perform adequately. It was my first and only experience of treading the boards. My chief memories of the night are of the excitement of performing on a real stage, that of Lauriston Hall, of the extreme cold and being up really late and travelling to and fro in a taxi. Also the surprise of being told when we reached home that a near neighbour had spent the evening acquiring a baby daughter. My mother no doubt was less surprised. There was a material bonus for us from this play. The Dutch costume, stitched by my mother, of full brightly striped skirt and starched buckram headdress (with brass curtain rings sewn on for earrings) became ours and adapted with different scarves and necklaces and headgear saw me through a succession of Fancy Dress parties as Gypsy, Norwegian or Italian or—a real flash of inspiration here—Roumanian peasant. The red beaded bodice was an authentic Norwegian one from Hardanger brought back for my mother from one of Uncle John's trips abroad. My mother said I was really too dark for a Norwegian.

Some years after I went to the school Miss Dougall became joint principal with Miss Blackstock and it was possibly then that the adjoining house, Number 24, was acquired. A door was knocked through in the kitchen quarters and another between the two parlours and the Kindergarten and dormitories vanished into Number 24. The parlour in 25 shed its rows of pegs and became an interesting classroom, intensely unpopular I have no doubt with the staff but full of possibilities for their scholars in whose hands it became the setting for a perpetually recurring pantomime whenever one or other of the principals passed through to retrieve possessions left in the other house. They did this frequently. The door would open, unheralded by the knock an errand-sped pupil would give, and we would scramble to our feet, chanting, "Goodmorning Miss Blackstock! Goodmorning Miss Dougall!" as the case might be. As here we sat at table and chairs the commotion was much worse than it would have been with stable desks. One girl would leap to close one door, another trip over bags and cases to open the second. Miss Dougall wafted through graciously. Miss Blackstock was brisker and apologising to the mistress would draw in her breath, "Goodmorning girls sit down you don't need to stand". The lesson being resumed, we then sat, ears cocked, for the re-entry of the intruder and a repeat performance. Eventually a rule was established that a class in this room was excused from rising to its feet—but there still remained the ticklish question of The Door. Enquiring grimaces were directed at the mistress in charge as to the propriety or not of rising to help. Miss Dougall was little trouble but with Miss Blackstock it depended on the mood. Sometimes she coped with her own opening and shutting; at another time while we, heads down, industriously studied, she would fetch up before a closed door "Come along girls! The Door!"

Despite these setbacks to the flow of education we must have been well taught in that room for my other memory of it is as the stage for our triumphant rout of one of His Majesty's Inspectors who was completely unable to fault us in our knowledge of Chaucer's *Prologue to The Canterbury Tales*.

With the expansion of the school we now 'did' science, the Back Room having been converted to a laboratory with bunsen burners down a central table and balances down a side wall. It was more fun than maths, though in its own way more frightening, and I cannot blame the two science teachers I knew for failing for me to lift a veil from it. My mother had no scientific genes to pass on; if my father had, they went astray. My partner, who was also my best friend, seemed to be similarly disadvantaged. As we came up with yet another peculiar result we surprised sometimes a reluctant look almost of admiration on our teacher's face.

The rooms had lost their friendly names and succumbed to the bureaucracy of number. The Drawingroom, now Room 2, fulfilled the same function as before, being the venue for Prayers, singing and in alternate years prizegivings, but no longer did the senior classes do drill there. Instead we went to a Swedish Gymnasium where a spare lady harried us up and over a horse and up and down rib-stalls and ropes. She had us cast off our tunics and perform in our navy blue knickers. Whether in the Drawingroom, Room 2 or a hired hall

197

in Queen Street or George Street, for prizegivings we all wore white dresses with white stockings. The strangeness of our apparel made us feel unreal and we worked ourselves up into panics as we awaited our turns to go forward on to a real stage to recite our pieces or play our solos—or worse, duets.

"What will I do if my music falls off the stand?"

"I can't remember a word!"

"I'm going to sneeze."

A normally good-tempered teacher was provoked into a near paroxysm of rage and a line of girls into hysterical giggles at the inane, "Suppose my hands drop off!" They couldn't—they wouldn't?—but what a picture if they did. Better to concentrate on the prettier picture made by an attractive girl who blushed when the lime-light was on her. From pink she would advance to a rosy bloom never more appropriately than when she played Edward McDowell's 'To a Wild-Rose'.

The Church of Scotland minister whose church the boarders attended was often invited to present the prizes and make the obligatory speech. Famed for his active ministry and dramatic pulpit style, he embarrassed us by his habit of illustrating his remarks with references to his children, two of whom at one time or another attended the school and must have been even more embarrassed. Embarrassing their young was not a thing that worried the parents of my childhood. Generally speaking they appeared to give little thought to their children's feelings nor entertain the idea that their scathing judgements might do permanent damage to their offsprings' confidence or emotional or mental security. There was some fearful theory about the benefit of being told the Truth (by those who loved you best) 'for your own good'. I recall when shopping with my mother meeting a school friend with her mother. On parting I was jeered at for something 'stupid' I had said. Next time we met, we both kept mum (had she been upbraided too?) and I was mocked for having nothing to say. Life is definitely not fair!

Worse was the time I was derided for 'making terrible faces'—my tentative smiling overtures to a baby in a pram but I must admit my mother's tactlessness was far outpaced by the cruelty of another, who when my mother commented (it was only rude if a child made a personal remark) on how the other's daughter had grown said unconcernedly, "Oh, she's just a lump—far too dumpy". The lump, a sweet-natured child, just smiled but it struck me even then, as being not only a cruel but peculiar judgement as the mother was almost square. I wondered what vision she had of herself in her mind or saw reflected in the glass.

When I first went to this second school I walked there in charge of Alice, an older girl who had also her younger sister Dorothy in tow. When I in turn had my younger sister Marjorie in my care we rarely walked as it was almost impossible to hurry her so despite parental disapproval at our missing a healthy fresh air trot—in reality a frenetic tear-stained rush—we were often forced to travel by luxury of (tram) car. Dashing into the bedroom where my mother was peacefully breakfasting in bed to break the dire news I was grudgingly told to take the fare from the mantelpiece where my father had placed the loose money from his pockets the night before. If there were not enough coppers then I had to take a piece of silver (but bring back the change). Alice and Dorothy and I were often joined by another pair of sisters, a serious Betty and a casual Dorothy whom however I admired as she could spell words of nine letters, like sometimes. None of them paid much attention to me which I did not resent as they were all older and, I felt, much wiser. At Goldenacre Eileen joined us, also older, but she did not despise me being one of the nicest and least affected of people I have ever met. Her sister and another really big girl also met us there and then Alice felt free to forge ahead with Betty and Car and Peggy leaving the rest of us in convoy to make what pace we could along the long stretch of Inverleith Row. It was a mercy my mother had accustomed me to walking but even so I remember how my shins ached! They did so even worse a year or so later when I walked with my friend Maisie and her father. He set the pace, a smart one to suit himself and would never have listened to our moans had we dared to complain. Whether Edinburgh people walked because they were hardy or because the cable-cars were slow I do not know but Inverleith Row and the steep streets of the New Town were full not only with school-children but with businessmen every morning before nine o'clock. My father regularly walked from Trinity to Princes Street.

My parents' intention was that when I reached Canonmills I should turn right up Brandon Terrace past our old-style tiled dairy and so by Fettes Row and Dundonald Street to Drummond Place, not however going along Cumberland Street, reputed in those days to be 'not such a nice street'. It is now a rather prestigious address. The others were respectable streets of small shops and tenements but the way was longer and less interesting than our preferred route up Canon Street with what in my memory was an ice factory dripping on one side and rather poor property equating in parental minds with germs, on the other. Across Eyre Place we entered the old railway yards near the Scotland Street Tunnel. Probably only bold or unimaginative children were happy venturing this way alone for to those brought up in suburban streets the yards were large and alien feeling, but traversed in company they gave in their wild-flowered wastes a sense of space and adventure. Off Scotland Street ran Bellevue Lane whose surface for some reason made the best slides in a cold winter. I am reminded of this walk every time I go now for free-range eggs for in the front yard of the Berkshire farm is a lamp standard inscribed 'Scotland Street' which I must have passed almost daily for years. Where Scotland Street joined Drummond Place we had to pull ourselves together. Standing there was an inconvenient pillar-box to which Miss Blackstock often made an early morning sortie, her eagle glance as keen then despite the hour as at any other time.

"Where are your gloves, girls? Put them on and pull your hats straight," and this with only a few yards to the school steps. Not only was Miss Blackstock a stickler for correct behaviour in the streets, but she appeared to possess hordes of like-minded friends with nothing better to do than travel the car-lines and roads of Edinburgh—though not apparently the Scotland Street Tunnel yards—with no end other than to report on the sartorial and other shortcomings of St Oran's girls. How often had we heard, "A friend of Miss Blackstock…in a Granton/Corstorphine car last week was shocked to see a St Oran's Girl … without her hat/gloves … eating sweets … dashing about from seat to seat," or in some way acting as less than a lady and bringing discredit on her school.

Miss Dougall's friends were afoot too but she herself was apt to notice lapses from good behaviour in school. "Would you do that in your mother's drawingroom?" was a favourite question, immortalised for us in a one time variant, "Would you throw a banana-skin at your mother's drawingroom wall?"

The slip in decorum calling forth that rebuke must have been caused by skirmishing at break which in winter was taken in whichever room a class's previous lesson had been, except for the sacrosanct dining-room. An exception was made for the senior forms who all congregated in Room 2 where a musical pupil often enlivened the time by playing the more acceptable of popular song and dance tunes, her choice governed by the knowledge that the two Principals were enjoying their tea and biscuits within earshot through communicating doors. In the summer we crocodiled over the cobbles to the gardens to which all householders in the Place held keys. We were given to understand this was a dearly wrung concession and well drilled as to how we had to behave. No dashing through flower-beds or climbing trees or casting down paper bags, apple cores (or banana skins) though surprisingly we were allowed racquets and balls for Rounders or French Cricket. French Cricket was a passion with us. It is possibly the ideal sport. Any number of players can take part, there are no teams so no-one can take umbrage at not being picked and all play for themselves alone. We played it at school, we played it at picnics, we played it on the beaches and we played it in our gardens in the evenings. The gardener seemed to manage to ignore the irruption of some seventy girls into his very pleasant territory of which I remember especially a magnificent laburnum and the more mysterious and shady parts with foxglove and wild hyacinth.

CHAPTER TWENTY-EIGHT

Peter Rabbit and the Bard

BESIDES MY horrid red arithmetic book illegally augmented with answers, two of my English books, which mattered more, also gave me trouble. Why was I the one misfortune lit on? There were too few of Nelson's pocket Hans Andersens so I was given the class copy which had inscribed in it the forbidding initials 'F.A.B' (Flora we-never-knew-what Blackstock). Perhaps I was meant to erase them and write my own name but never dared so never knew whose book it was. A worse case was that of an earlier really interesting reading book. The copy that landed on my desk had been wrongly bound and few of the stories about Freddie and the Flamingoes or Kinmount Willie or Pet Marjory read consecutively. When this was discovered the mistress gave me as was only right, the class, ie her, copy which on this occasion had 'Belle M Dougall' on it. I was allowed to take it home but in class had to pass it over to her so again did not know whose book it was. At the end of the year I managed to get left with the faulty copy which was most irritating for not only was it a book I would then have re-read for pleasure but it had a bearing on the future. The various stories were supposedly told to two children. The brother may have been John, his sister was certainly Penelope… 'there are four bites to this cherry'. I had never met the name before but fell in love with it there and then in the back-row of the big south-facing classroom in 25 Drummond Place adding it to my roster of favourite names for my family, from which in the fullness of time it was indeed transferred to a daughter. Fortunately her father had some other reason for liking what was not then a very usual choice.

Our youngest daughter, besides bearing a family name, that of her father's mother, grandmother, and great-grandmother back I do not know how many grands, shares it not only with them and my Uncle Willie's wife and the much loved mother of a school-friend but as importantly to me with Kate Green, heroine from an earlier reading-book. In a school bulb-growing competition Kate Green sold her carefully tended pot of daffodils, thereby giving up her hope of the glory of winning First Prize, so as to be able to buy a bunch of grapes for her ailing little brother. The National Health Service is blamed for much but not often surely for being the occasion of preventing saintly actions by the young! I am glad to be able to recount that the charitable lady judging the competition did in some now forgotten way recompense Kate's unselfish gesture. It was, incidentally, not the saintly action but the name, Kate, that appealed to me.

From our art classes we produced attractive pottery but apart from one wearable blouse made when I was about fifteen the stream of products from years of needlework consisted of what a dazed Brownie daughter labouring for badges would later term 'useless articles'. There were the white nightdress cases with blue stamped transfers waiting to be embroidered with white silks. Kay and I were initially rather enamoured of them, she choosing the daffodil pattern as a compliment to her half-English ancestry and I the thistles for my true-blue Scottish blood. Long before we had chain-stitched and hem-stitched and puckered them up and they had turned the nasty shade of grey to which we eventually reduced all needle-work, we were heartily sick of them. The white knitted socks for babies were another trial. They were worked (and so easy at the beginning of a period to pick them up and go round the wrong way) on four thin, thin steel needles with thin, thin, white wool. On three-quarter completion, as far as we got, no baby or Teddy Bear in the land could have been forced into their tight yellowing bands. One girl definitely had the edge on the two of us for mangled needlecraft but with the excuse of having lived most of her fifteen years with four brothers in some wild spot in Kenya. She treated the whole business of being

203

moulded into a semblance of a middle-class town miss with considerable derision.

It may well have been that our sewing-mistress was herself a skilled sempstress but she had not moved into the world of the Twenties schoolgirl. Admittedly in the winter we did sometimes still wear 'long-combs' though more often vests (even if we did call them semmits) and our breeks, beginning to be more genteelly referred to as knickers—never yet as pants or briefs—were elastic-waisted and elastic-legged. No longer did we keep them up as when I was small by button-holes and buttons on a bodice. (Elastic round the waist was considered to impede circulation. For this same reason our socks tended to fall down—garters were also bad.) Our slips and petticoats by now were often factory-produced celenese. We wore Liberty Bodices until the day when our reluctant mothers realised we were growing up and away and out of them and shepherded their shame-faced daughters into Corsetry Departments to be equipped with corselettes. In the main, what we were taught in our sewing classes took no cognisance of the evolution in girls' clothing. We made undergarments of beautiful delicate white lawn with broderie anglaise borders. Sometimes we further embellished them with lace. On petticoats and knickers we worked seams with running stitch and minute backstitching and overcasting with fine needles but principally it seemed we stroked gathers. This, for those who have never been forced into doing so, is a very time-wasting operation. On the fine lingerie we were attempting to turn out, the gathers had to be of equal size and fairly tightly drawn together. While doing this the thread quite often snapped. Likewise when we had finished off with three little stitches on top of each other, and triumphantly reached the desired stage of stroking between the gathers, it was all too easy in our exuberance to break the slender needle. I duly learnt to perform those seemingly required womanly skills but at what expense of time and material—and I doubt if I have stroked a gather since. One year, we all of us scorned to wear the French knickers we had taken a session to achieve, nor for reasons of decency would our mothers have let us—two girls, though hobbled could have worn a pair between them. Next year the more modest garments that emerged were so tight we could not sit down in them.

The very different strengths of our two Principals made them a good team. Miss Blackstock was I suspect the more intellectual and the better administrator. She was not as easy to know as Miss Dougall but no way as stern as our awed respect for her made us imagine. Miss Dougall tended to be sentimental but was genuinely interested in us as individuals. Some of our parents thought she had 'odd' ideas. If by that they meant she had the kind of ideas that made other people think, they were right. She it was who dropped into our sceptical little minds seeds of now accepted truths; as for example the power of thought, the influences of music and of the differing individual awarenesses of colour. She it was too who had us learn a poem I have never since found which began,

'Did you hear the sheep go by
Upon a Monday morning?
Oh, did you hear the sheep go by
Without a word of warning…?'

It was a compassionate indictment of man's inhumanity to animals. I had never enjoyed meat—(keeping chewed up bits in my mouth all through the pudding course until I could flush them down the lavatory)—neither the taste of it nor the thought of Peter Rabbit on my plate nor the sight of the pitiful victims of the gun hanging outside butchers' shops, but I am sure this lost poem set me on my first steps towards rational vegetarianism. Predictably our elders thought it a queer poem, not very poetical, which it probably was not,—and with a nasty subject.

Miss Dougall's own favourite colour was blue, the blue of a stained glass Virgin's robe or the deep blue of Hebridean seas for she was much influenced by the current Celtic Revival and cult of Iona, popularly and emotionally purveyed through the researches of Margery and Patuffa Kennedy Fraser and Margaret Kennedy. Their concerts of song and clarsach brought a new dimension of Scottish culture to public attention. I feel Miss Dougall's must have been the inspiration for the school's name for although most Edinburgh girls' schools were called after saints I find it difficult to credit Miss Blackstock alone with the flight of fancy they drew from his legend. Oran was a monk of Iona who offered himself as a living sacrifice to be buried under the foundations of a chapel, all previous attempts to build having been frustrated by evil spirits who threw down the walls as soon as half erected. Once Oran had gone singing to his fate the spirits were appeased and the building prospered. Privately I thought it stupid of Oran and dastardly of the other monks and could not understand how they could continue to live and pray above him and yet be considered holy. Miss Dougall however wrenched inspiration from this tale—I am sure Miss Blackstock was far too sensible—and saw it as an encouragement to St Oran's girls to be ready to help others and like the Guides to laugh and sing under all difficulties.

I was in no position to be critical for I wrenched advantage from St Oran winning a blue fitted writing case for the best attempt at writing a school song. Indeed I think I may have been the only entrant. Certainly it was never sung. Rather cunningly I managed to work in the school colours of blue and green.

> "Blue was the sky above them,
> And green the earth around,
> When through Iona's island
> A sad procession wound."

Jesting apart, we were made aware of the needs of others and contributed to the Edinburgh Childrens' Shelters and to deprived people further afield not forgetting the Young Trawlers' Union. This was possibly the junior branch of the Mission to Deep Sea Fishermen which provided canteens and hostels for fishermen ashore. Once a year the tall thin lady secretary visited us accompanied by an intrepid and often bearded skipper who addressed us as we sat in rows before him on chairs and the floor in the erstwhile drawingroom. For two years my cousin was school secretary for the union and after the talk the two officials took her out to lunch. Kay was so unnerved that no matter how enticing the menu she always felt politeness demand she order fish!

One area of Number 25 that did not change with the addition of Number 24 was Miss Blackstock's teaching territory, the dining-room. With the green baize-covered table and mahogany and horse-hair chairs and the terrarium of ailing ferns, it was a trauma-ridden place. In our early years she gave us general knowledge classes here and we became experts on such varied points as the number of spokes of an umbrella, the colours of the rainbow and whether when it arose after ruminating was it the front or back end of a cow which rose first. Later her field was largely Shakespeare and it says much for her teaching that we survived without becoming allergic to his works despite, or perhaps because, her classes were frequently disrupted by phone calls or visiting parents.

"Read on, girls," she exhorted as she rose and left the room. We never did. We were a pusillanimous lot and found the archaic speech embarrassing. Of us all there was only one who bothered to throw herself, and that with over-exaggeration, into the drama. A friend, normally liked—she of the Baltic question—at sessions in the diningroom we despised her. As shipwrecked mariners we put down our heads and dispiritedly muttered, "Yare yare."

"Come along, girls," Miss Blackstock spoke briskly, "Put some life into it."

"Yare yare," we would repeat, glaring at our prize orator who would be leaning sideways with a nautical lurch, waving her hand and firmly enunciating the yare-yarery of the first scene of *The Tempest*. What sailors said yare anyway? It was never heard on Uncle Harry's yachts or MacBrayne steamers.

Worse than any of the dramatic interludes, we might be forced into in the diningroom, skipping off to put a girdle round the earth or impersonating a love-sick swain (Do not scorn me, Phebe), were the extramural performances we might be called upon to execute, such as, on a darkening winter's afternoon, the Lighting of the Gas. As anyone who has ever lit a gas-mantle knows there are limitless ways of making a botch of it. And how many more when the mantle is the property of your critical headmistress. After matches had been found and struck, perhaps a taper lit, the volume of gas had to be

207

adjusted and the light applied at just the correct distance above or below the fragile mantle—there were two conflicting schools of thought on this point—without poking a hole in the incandescent film. The terrors of the Gas, even with its sudden explosive 'pop' were as nothing however to the horror of being bidden to summon Janet by Speaking Tube. Boarders could take the Speaking Tube in their stride but it was a severe strain on less-practised day-girls. The appalled victim had to stand tip-toe, semi-petrified with fright and incipient hysteria at an aperture to the left-hand side of the door and blow to awaken a whistle in the lower regions. She then had to retail Miss Blackstock's message into the invisible Janet's ear presumably pressed to the other end of this infernal device. Worst was the knowledge that one was also relaying it into the critical ear of Miss Blackstock and the ears of one's grinning friends cravenly rejoicing that on this occasion someone else was making a fool of herself. Often too there was another pair of ears attached to a more or less inert lump under a rug on the horse-hair sofa which was by way of being a sick-bay and to which anyone feeling too unwell to argue was led to recline.

CHAPTER TWENTY-NINE

Party Time

BEFORE THE First World War, after whose advent young wives and mothers deflected much of their energy to organisations such as the Red Cross where they studied First Aid, rolled bandages, picked over sphagnum moss for dressings and made and despatched comforts for the troops, the giving of and attending at tea-parties seems to have taken up a good deal of their time. There were the regular At Home days but my mother chronicles more cosy occasions, the various babies' tea-parties. The first I attended, at which also I was hostess it being my own first birthday, I was the youngest present but before I was two I enjoyed quite a season, becoming bolder and bolder as socialising went to my head, kindly dragging in my mother to join the dancing and collecting pink tissue paper decorations for her. On one occasion I regret to say I annexed all a young host's toys. In later life he was known world-wide as an ornithologist but at this time, being two months younger than I, he was unable to resist the harrying of his nest. These exploits, according to my mother, caused much amusement. She records only mine but as no doubt all the other party babies were behaving in much the same way I expect these cradle gatherings were riotous.

For family birthdays we always had small celebrations—except sometimes for mine which coincided with the worst period for childish ailments so I often celebrated in bed with coughs or spots or the less easily defined 'sickening for something'. After the Armistice parties became more ambitious. Ours, though fun, were a little difficult to arrange to everyone's satisfaction on account of Ian and his friends. My friends and my little sisters when old enough to join in, were perfectly happy to be dressed in our best, taffeta or net dresses with white stockings and dancing sandals of gold or silver or dyed to match our frocks. These were usually pastel shades with the occasional flame but one winter we were surprised by a young hostess in black taffeta with bright geometric shapes appliqued on. I thought it beautiful but there was whispering among less avant garde mothers as to how it was not quite suitable—black was too *old* a colour for a child. That was bad. During my childhood most parents saw the ideal child as one in a state of arrested development, their aim being to keep children children as long as possible with small regard as to whether the end result was innocence or ignorance. We were also perfectly happy playing the traditional games and oddly we never tired of hearing each other do our special party recitations, with or without expression, or playing our special party pieces.

> 'Dark brown is the river,
> Golden is the sand,
> It flows along for ever
> With trees on either hand.'

This is the first verse of the poem from Stevenson's *Child's Garden of Verses* that my friends regularly expected from me. In her journal my mother says she had coached me to say it with expression— probably a fruitless task. She herself had been told by a holiday acquaintance that she possessed a 'beautiful speaking voice' and had indeed been one of the star pupils of a well known elocutionist who taught at the Misses Carters' school for Young Ladies in Dennistoun.

A friend of mine dealt rather in faery, her poems were never resolved.

> 'Someone is always waiting there,
> In the little green orchard …'

> '"Is there any body there?" said the traveller,
> Knocking on the moonlit door…'

But our star was Eileen, she who recited in the forces' canteen in

Granton Square. She really knew how to use expression and after scaring us with 'Little Orphan Annie' ('the goblins'll get you if you don't watch out!') she seared our emotions with Charles Murray's tale of 'The Wee Herd'.

> 'He cut a sappy sucker from the muckle rodden tree,
> He trimmed it, an' he wet it, an' he thumped it on his knee;
> He never heard the teuchat when the harrow broke her eggs,
> He missed the craggit heron nabbin' puddocks in the seggs,
> He forgot to hound the collie at the cattle when they strayed,
> But you should have seen the whistle that the wee herd made!
> ....
> But the snaw it stopped the herdin' an' the winter brocht him dool,
> When in spite of hacks and chilblains he was shod again for school;
> ....
> But he afen played the truant—'twas the only thing he played,
> For the maister brunt the whistle that the wee herd made!'

Sometimes during the war I offered one of two popular songs, either 'Let the Great Big World Keep Turning…' or another favourite for which my father had sent me the music—no need then to define it as 'sheet music'—'If I were the Only Girl in the World, (and you were the Only Boy)'. I remember two ladies in a drawingroom in Granton Road, asking where I had come across it, dear? I expect my telling them it was a present from my father did not help any. Without saying more they managed to convey the tut-tutting impression that it was not quite suitable for a child—too old I expect—and of all subjects, about love. Myself I thought Eden sounded rather boring— who would want their only companion to be a *boy*?

> 'A Garden of Eden,
> Just made for two,
> With nothing to mar our joy,
> I would say such wonderful things to you.
> There would be such wonderful things to do,
> If I were the Only Girl in the World,
> And you were the Only Boy.'

Strict protocol was observed at these entertainments. Much less then than now, indeed scarcely at all, did parents heed the counsel of their children as to who would be acceptable guests so it could

211

happen that an unfortunate stranger child, a cousin from another school perhaps or invited "because I know her mother" would unwittingly steal another guest's speciality. Though inadvertent, this was poorly thought of but the worst party hazards were indubitably our younger brothers and their mates. Left to ourselves we would never have included them—though it did seem unkind to deny them all that unusually exciting food. Their mothers, in the way of mothers, probably thought there was something about them rather sweet. There was, however, no doubt about it that whereas putting us into our best clothes put us also into our best tempers and at least a show of good behaviour, forcing them into the de rigeur sailor suits or kilt had the opposite effect, provoking them into what the kindlier adults described as boyish high spirits. Sometimes our brother had a couple of friends to keep him in countenance but more usually a gang. No matter what number the result was inevitably the same— general disruption of our more orderly amusements; after which they would be directed, more or less tactfully, if they had not already swarmed there, to the large attic floor nursery from whence—it was immediately above the drawingroom—came thuds and bangs and crashes as our male guests happily fought with each other, doing no good at all to their party attire until their parents arrived to separate and take them home.

There were final (verbal) exchanges at the door.

"Huh! Don't think you beat me!"

"I'll get you at school, MacGregor!"

"So you think!·… oh yes thanks for having me… lovely party… you wait!"

In the Junior classes our school-day ended at one o'clock so most of our parties took place on weekday afternoons. I remember the excitement of rushing home to a changed house which felt and looked and smelt different. It felt different because it was warmer. A huge coal-fire, which for safety would be left to die down as the party assembled, was heating up the drawingroom and in the diningroom, transformed with coloured paper shades around the lights and decorations on the white starched table-cloth, the electric heater was full on. Normally one bar was switched on with our entry for meals. All the leaves in the diningroom table were in use and there were extra tables from a firm near by which also hired out red covered forms and for the drawingroom a slithery cover to protect the carpet. We could slide on it as we did on the polished wooden floors in the halls.

I can recall exactly the feel of those party afternoons. The unwonted tidiness of the house, in all but kitchen and pantry, almost made us tiptoe round the diningroom where we admired the plates of sandwiches, egg and paste and date, banana and tomato, the bowls of trifle and fruit salad and red and green jellies and jugs of home-made lemonade and final touch of sophistication, syphons of Soda and Kola and other garishly coloured drinks. Frail meringues and cakes were in silver baskets and heated-up Crawford's rissoles were added at the last moment in silver entrée dishes. For a birthday party, the diningroom had an extra dimension of smell from the plain but sweetish sponge under the Royal icing always ordered from a local confectioner. I could swear I was able to smell in anticipation the unique and delightful smell of the burnt blown-out ends of the wax candles. Before we had time to test any of the delicacies we would be called away to conceal our coats and school-bags (in the mouse-cupboard) and to make a snack meal in the kitchen of left-overs and cosmetically-failed sandwiches before going upstairs to wash and change.

Again it comes back to me—the shivering as I came out of my warm green Viyella blouse, gym tunic and thick navy woollen jumper banded with blue and green in the cold bathroom. We did not make many concessions to fashion, teeth and hair were well brushed and our dresses always pretty but underneath were our Liberty bodices and long combs. These last were apt to show at sleeves and neckline and had often to be stitched back.

Once ready, it was into the drawingroom where the furniture had been pushed back and the ornaments removed and we slid about enjoying the extra space, making sallies to windows which overlooked the front gate or hanging over the banisters when the doorbell rang.

213

Before now we had probably been joined by our cousin Kay and aunt, Dedae, who was good at playing the piano and had the reputation of being 'good with children'. She was also strong-minded enough not to be bullied by twenty or so excited pre-adolescents but to follow through the programme on the wall as drawn up and also decorated by my mother with designs of balloons and harlequins, with few deviations or disagreements until the last (and last again) tempestuous Haymakers.

We played the traditional party games—Here's a Poor Widow, The Galley Galley Ship, Nuts in May, The Farmer's in his Den, Musical Chairs and Musical Bumps, Spin the Trencher, Blind Man's Buff, Dree a Dree I Dropped it, See the Robbers Passing by, In and Out the Dusky Bluebells, Water Water Wallflowers and many another. For welcome rest we had Hunt the Thimble, Pass the Parcel and Pinning the Tail on the Donkey. Occasionally there would be a paper game with questions round the walls and a prize for the winner. That, with perhaps a balloon and any spoil from crackers, would be all guests took home from a party and no-one brought presents to the hosts. If you had been unable to eat your slice of birthday cake or had a sister or brother at home you would be given a slice to take away with you in a pink tissue bag with drawstring. Only one family among our school-friends had a different party life-style and from their's my brother came home with good, not to say expensive, gifts. The boys appreciated them—but their parents professed to be unimpressed.

I have a press photograph of a group of what are described as 'DAINTY DANCERS AT EDINBURGH COSTUME FROLIC' and further as 'A happy group of young revellers at the Monks of St Giles Ball, held in the Assembly Rooms, Edinburgh, on Saturday evening. The dresses were remarkably pretty and original in design.' This particular ball was held on Saturday the 10th of March 1923 and the young revellers in the picture at the Bairns' Frolic were the guests of one of the Monks and his wife. As I had no idea who or what the Monks of St Giles were I applied to a daughter of our host who wrote back, 'The Monks of St Giles were really members of a society who met for fun, I think. They had various meetings throughout the year when they had to read a poem or essay or some such offering and, all being professional or business people, they took a Latin name pertaining to their work. My father was Father Papyrus.' [He had a large Stationery business.] 'They were very sensible. They had these fantastic parties once every three years. The younger ones were up to about ten I think,' [at this one I was twelve and had my little sister in charge] 'then over eighteen at night. No teenagers! Every June or July they had a Strawberry Feast with whisky—for themselves!' Predictably I attended as a peasant—a so-called Italian peasant with beribboned tambourine belonging to Marjorie, authentic Norwegian bodice (and Dutch headpiece).

It occurs to me that neither my mother nor myself was over fond of dressing-up—no fonder perhaps than the boy in the Monks' Ball photo standing fair and square, in a no-nonsense way in his Boy Scout uniform—for my mother was artistic and enjoyed sewing and did indeed make fancy dresses for my little sisters yet at Melrose I was always a peasant and she the same crinolined lady. Even when it was Fancy Head Dress Night we went as fancy dress cousins of peasants—gypsies—with coloured handkerchiefs.

In 1925 when I was fourteen we did give a rather fine party. I could not better my mother's account.

'We are giving a large party in the Wardie Masonic Hall on December 23rd. At least it should be fairly large if all who have accepted turn up. Marjorie is to have her small friends from 5 to 8, then Ian's and Elaine's friends arrive from 7 to 10. For them I have engaged a violinist and pianist as they seemingly want to dance all evening (at least Elaine's friends do.) Marjorie's I expect will play games. Ian's friends are at a rather bad age and will probably make rather a nuisance of themselves. Ian was twelve last month. Moira was four the day after.

I have got Elaine a rather pretty lemon coloured crepe de chine for party wear. Marjorie will have the pink I made a year or two ago and I am making Moira a pale lemon georgette with plenty of frills.

December 31st
Our party was quite a success and everybody seemed to enjoy it. Scott-Lyon did the catering very well and sent such nice waitresses, like very superior maids of the old life as no doubt they were. We had also a very good pianist (Miss Fairbairn) and violinist (Mrs Dick) who played

215

well for the dances. I quite enjoyed it and was really sorry when it
finished though the night before I did not expect to be able to go as I
had a feverish chill and was in bed with a temperature and similar
symptoms of the flu which I had last year. I dosed myself with Aspirin
and also indulged in a little Coué-ism to the effect that I would be at the
party next day. Thanks either to the aspirin or Coué or both I felt better
in the morning (though not very comfortable) and I got better as the day
went on. I think probably the excitement and knowing that I had to be
there kept me going.

The children and I went down in the morning to see what we could do
about decorating the hall, rather an ugly place normally ornamented by
portraits of various Masons of the district, each as large as life and twice
as ugly. I should have liked to have taken them all down but all we
could do was to drape some coloured paper scrolls and strings of tinsel
here and there and hope for the best. I had painted three programmes
of the dances which we fixed to the walls and with a rug or two in the
dressing-rooms etc we could do no more.

Fortunately it was a dry day though the snow was lying thickly in the
streets and it was bitterly cold.

We went down early (about four) and found the caterers people busy
with the tables. Marjorie's friends had tea on arrival and supper before
leaving, the bigger ones having a running buffet, to which the boys at
least did full justice. I had Miss Fraser [a neighbour], Miss Fairlie and Mrs
McGregor [one of the mistresses at St Oran's and Marjorie's music
mistress] to help me with the little ones. Miss Fairlie, especially was
such a help and is awfully good with the children. She stayed on to the
later party and got some dancing. She is a nice girl and rather pretty...'

Lest anyone should wonder had Dedae fallen out of favour, no, she
would be in London with her mother, staying with 'the Gibbs'—Aunt
Lena and her family (before there was some temporary rift) having
taken Kay south to spend Christmas with her parents.

'I got them all, '[the younger children]' herded into supper while the
older lot were arriving. The latter included a host of Ian's rather
boisterous classmates as well as several girls of eighteen or so, so we
had rather a mixed lot. They danced all the rest of the evening at least
all Elaine's friends did and I think most of Ian's danced fairly well—
when they weren't ragging about with balloons and paper streamers,
varied by very frequent raids on the supper-room. Boys of that age,
(round about twelve) consider the 'eats' as the Americans say, the most
important part of a party. Ten o'clock came all too soon and after we
had seen them off we had to collect our various belongings, decorations
etc and get home. The taxi we ordered did not turn up but fortunately

we had not far to go and it was a fine frosty night as we trudged over
the snow with bags and rugs and a fire-guard!'

It was a bitter winter that, when not only the ponds were bearing but
the Union Canal froze over and in some places the Tweed and shores
of Loch Lomond. I enjoyed the fresh walk over the ridges of snow
as they sparkled under the street-lamps and crackled beneath our
home-going feet, compensation in its beauty I hope for my mother's
day of fever and aspirin and stress.

The Wardie Masonic Hall, popular with families in our
neighbourhood for parties, was also the venue for dancing classes
where we, and in the evenings our parents and their friends, learned
the latest ball-room steps. Our classes were a mixture of ball-room,
ballet, country and what I can only describe as imaginative dances.
I can remember among the welter of Mazurkas, waltzes, foxtrots, and
Petronellas, a Russian Dance with much stamping of the feet and to
Edward German music, a Shepherd's Dance. There was a rather
dashing Torch Dance in which we ran at speed diagonally across the
floor shading our eyes from our (imaginary) torches and as suddenly
in the opposite direction and we learnt, of course, the correct way
to dance an Eightsome Reel and all the figures of the Lancers.

Our family parties, though not tightly controlled, were reasonably
organised functions which—apart from young male voices off—
never got out of hand. I remember a much more relaxed one in a
neighbour's house which, after the initial solo piano playing and
recitations developed into a sing-song participated in, indeed to my
great surprise actively led by, the mother of the family, a cheerful
reddish-haired lady who sat by the fire beating time as she
encouraged us through the popular songs of the day, 'Felix Kept on
Walking', 'Barney Google, with his Goo-Goo-Googly eyes' and one
hitherto unknown to me 'What a Hullabaloo'. It was too and one
which she obviously enjoyed as much as any of us. She seemed to
me to exhibit the most admirable uninhibited behaviour in a parent.

At another house there was also a hullabaloo, though not a musical
one. We had grown to thirteen, fourteen perhaps, because during
supper there was a certain amount of 'sitting-out' on the stairs which

217

no one seemed to object to. As I remember it we thought it very adult behaviour and the stairs were absolutely packed. This was a party at which I might have suffered as an outsider because although most of us were related in some degree of cousinship even unto the third and fourth degree removed, I had never come much in contact with many of them. However a kind, almost grown-up girl (probably fifteen) called Hester took me into her charge which predisposed me favourably towards the name Hester for ever afterwards. After the gastronomic rather than erotic surfeits of sitting-out, the party felt the need to relax and embarked on a mad orgy of hide-and-seek all over the house—and taffeta and net dresses and dyed pumps and best kilts notwithstanding—through the dark and wintry garden. This hostess too seemed unperturbed—she could have been simply overwhelmed.

For years Dedae gave us the best Hallowe'en parties ever with all the trappings of 'dooking' for apples, biting into treacly scones swinging from pulleys, turnip lanterns, fortune-telling, witches and terror. A party of my very early school-days which made a tremendous impression on me was one at which the guests, or at least this guest, did not yell only because she was too nearly petrified with fright. We had been ushered up and into a darkened attic and set on chairs and benches to see a picture show. We had all seen magic lantern shows, still pictures often upside-down, but this was a new invention—moving pictures. The film involved a motor chase and I can recall our fear as we cringed back in our seats when the cars, growing bigger and bigger, appeared to be about to leap out at us from the screen although comonsense told us there could be no life-size cars concealed in Eileen's mother's attic.

There never of course were any but invitation functions—the casual day of the disco was far ahead. As I grew older the parties became more sophisticated, what in her journal my mother called 'really young ladies' dances'. She does not in her diary record resenting this as much as in real life she appeared to do. She never did like the thought of any of us growing up. The real bone of contention in the party season was the hour at which they ended. A quite usual span was eight to midnight. ("Ridiculous! Your father will come for you at eleven.") Sometimes a shared taxi avoided a confrontation but as she, and malgré lui, our father, were early bedders the pother arising when an invitation arrived from avant garde friends in control of their parents, desiring the pleasure of my company till 2 am (once even the wicked hour of 2.30 am) can—perhaps not—be imagined. She did however take great trouble shopping with me for dance dresses which I think she often bought with her own money. The peak of my early party-going was when I was invited to a Hogmanay Dinner Dance in the Ballroom of the Caledonian Hotel, Princes Street as partner for another sixteen-year-old met at Melrose whose father and elder brother with their partners made up the party. It was my first experience of really grown-up life and as I was a good dancer and had a good appetite, if not an educated palate (I eschewed the quails), I enjoyed myself hugely. On this occasion I fancy my hosts delivered me home at their discretion.

CHAPTER THIRTY

Kaleidoscope

IN 39 INVERLEITH Gardens one of my favourite pieces of nursery equipment was a kaleidoscope. Turn it slightly and up came different patterns as do now haphazardly memories of the past, some as bright as the Alice in Wonderland paper jig-saws, some as black as the messy pictures I assembled with stencils and carbon pads, some as indeterminate at the edges as the butterflies achieved from another art set by painting one half of a sheet of paper and then folding over and pressing it. So at the same table, one thinks of milk puddings, miserable tapioca and sago, marginally less objectionable rice (if there were sultanas in it) and all too frequent Farola, redeemed only by the Golden Syrup scrolls we dripped all over it from our spoons which barely camouflaged the rather usual smell indicating that the milk had 'caught' again. A happier memory is that of summer pudding, the cold version of delicious bread and butter pudding whose top layer of bread was always slightly browned. Summer pudding was a layer of bread, a layer of raspberries, a layer of bread, a layer of red currants, repeated as often as would a large mixing bowl hold. A plate on top was weighed down by a flat-iron and the bowl set aside for several hours or even over night. The result was as beautifully marbled as tipsy cake.

From that table to one in Dunbar, in the sitting-room of an old servant of my grandmother's. She and an aunt, Annie I think, had taken Kay and me by train for a visit. First we had a walk by the harbour and then the adults were settled with their cups of tea. Our hostess turned to the two of us with the tea-pot in her hand, "Long tea or short tea?" How could we know? It turned out to be a joke, relic of kitchen or nursery lore, the one poured from close to the cup the other from perilously high. Kay and I were enchanted, making as they say 'a good tea' that afternoon—of the long variety—to wash down the many slices of thick home-made shortbread.

Back from that table to the Crescent and a ceremonial Christmas, Boxing Day, or New Year meal. It had just been discovered that I was short-sighted and condemned to glasses, for continuous wear. I found them a nuisance in many ways but was quite enjoying them for the sake of the new face the world was showing to me—among other surprises stars had turned out to be not the amorphous blurs I had previously perceived—but I was still very self-conscious about wearing them. The festive atmosphere was rapidly dispersed when Dido (Great-Aunt Alice) called down the table to my mother, "Annie! What has that child done to her appearance?" My mother I regret to say, cravenly replied, "She insists on wearing them."

Away from that starched table to the one in *Eyes and No Eyes*, a nature book with coloured pictures and diagrams which led us from the tree with nuts, acorns, flowers, insects, and squirrels, and stumps with age rings to the carpenter with plane and the everyday (pre-plastic) artefacts of daily life. *Pictures from Nature* was a less deliberatively educational book of the fields and woodlands with idyllic illustrations in the style of Birket Foster. There was, in a way, more Nature about in those days. How many of today's children know of Jack Frost and get out of bed in the morning to stand entranced (if cold) before his delicate tracery on their windows?

Books, books and more books. An early *Scouting for Boys,* opened up a mine of miscellaneous information useful for survival in the wild (a slightly frayed twig makes an excellent toothbrush) and in suburbia, where armed with chalk we laid trails for each other. There were frequent gifts from Uncle John of copies of Arthur Mee's beautifully produced *My Magazine* and we also read his *Children's Newspaper.* We had Beatrix Potter from an early age, I remember some convalescence with invalid smells of camphor and eucalyptus

221

being cheered for me by the outdoor pictures in *Squirrel Nutkin*, and a book I loved and had read to me and read myself repeatedly, was *Four Little Brothers* by Ellinor F. Barrington-Kennett. In a brown cover with a surround of heartsease violets, it was illustrated by Gordon Browne, R. I. and told the story of Rex, Godfrey, Lionel and Humphrey, sons of a Victorian well-to-do country-not-quite-county family and 'happy nursery days with Daddy and Mother, and their dear Nana, at Melsonby Hall'. Other stories were woven in, Mother told them of Joseph and of the Ugly Duckling. It must have been biographical, for the domestic details and the boys' reactions are so natural. I feel our elders must have been tougher, it was read to us repeatedly with no shows of emotion but I can remember it was only with difficulty and barely suppressed gulps that I was able to do the same. Today I cannot read it even to myself without tears! But then I know the 'Many Years After'—but so did my mother and various nurses. Dated 1916 it reads,

> 'Since this story was written the great war has come, and first "Baby Humphrey," then "Rex," and then "Lionel" have all been called on to give their lives in action for King and Country and the cause of Honour and Truth. Godfrey is still on active service, fighting with a sad heart for the dear brothers who are gone...'

I think perhaps 'Mother' wrote the book for the afterword ends by telling of how she looks forward to meeting them in the land 'where there shall be no more death, neither sorrow nor crying', and where 'God shall wipe away all tears from their eyes'.

There were no restrictions on what we read or played on a Sunday, some families were forbidden cards even for such harmless games as Pelmanism or Racing Demon or, carried to extremes, dice for games like Ludo or Snakes and Ladders. With us, Sunday was a little different—there were special cakes for tea—but mainly because there was no school and our father was at home and read to us in the evening. He took us through several books of the Bible, as well as *Pilgrim's Progress, Marmion* and *The Lady of the Lake* and more. I enjoyed two what I called 'Sunday Books' though I did read them at other times. They had belonged to my father, perhaps for Bible

Class purposes. The thick one in a brown cover, was each chapter based on a text and often about individual Biblical characters. It was interesting and readable. I believe it was called *Sunday Afternoon Talks*. The smaller blue book was possibly older and each chapter had a different project for Sunday afternoons—to fill what might have been empty hours. Sometimes it entailed no more than making lists of flowers, or trees found in the Old or New Testaments, or alphabets of scriptural names of men or women or places, tracking down texts dealing with a specific subject or making Bible acrostics. Whatever it asked, it involved 'searching the Scriptures' and was fun.

The Scriptures pursued us out of doors. The pleasure of a trip home at lunchtime on top of a cable, or later electric, car might be wiped out by the mischance of finding yourself on the same car as an elderly man who must have been strongly propelled by an unrelenting conscience for he moved down the aisles unsmilingly proffering to each traveller a tract, with the invariable worlds, "Will you have a tract or would you rather not?" Of course you would rather not but it seemed as impolite to refuse as spineless to accept.

Much more to my liking were the Sea-side Missions—still found today in the holiday season in some of the popular, and I suppose preferably sandy, resorts. The teams ran Sand Castle Building contests which covered the beach with the most elaborate sea-weed and shell-decorated edifices, held occasional short services with hymns and distributed competitions to do at home. There was one which consisted of colouring the picture of a large tree heavy with harvest and giving for as many fruit as possible a text reference for some specimen mentioned in the Bible. I won a book called *Loyal Hearts* by Reginald Callender, M. A. for this. Inscribed inside is

C.S.S.M. — Crail
1923.
Bible Tree Competition
1st Prize
Elaine Chisholm
P Wilkie, Leader

On which triumphant turn the kaleidoscope is laid aside for the present.

Chapter Thirty-One

Where Brook and River Meet

THE HOGMANAY Dinner Dance was an outcome of an acquaintanceship made at Melrose Hydropathic and pursued there every year during our regular Easter fortnight's break. Easter being in those days an off-season for American and English tourists in Princes Street, and so in Mackay and Chisholm, my father found it a convenient time to take his annual holiday. Melrose Hydro, set in spacious grounds running down to the river path alongside the Tweed, with its own four-hole golf course, tennis courts, parallel bars, swings, see-saws, rings and other pieces of gymnastic equipment and a Home Farm (and statue of Sir Walter Scott and bloodhound Maida on the lawn) was a pleasant friendly place for people of all ages. The same Scottish, mainly Edinburgh, and North Country English families came year after year.

We travelled by train from Waverley, watching with rising excitement for the first sight of Gala Water, an inconsiderable stream but promising greater things in the Tweed, then after Galashiels, Melrose itself with the triple Eildon Hills beyond. Our father looked for the familiar landmarks as eagerly as we did for his family had spent many summers there and he had known Melrose well. At the station a conveyance awaited arrivals, for the Hydro was in Darnick, a mile from the town. On our first visits this was a horse-drawn wagonette, later a more prosaic bus. The long seats were inward facing so we were able to survey our fellow guests. The luggage was loaded separately on to a cart.

On reaching the Hydro we were confronted by a very broad flight

WHERE BROOK AND RIVER MEET

of between twenty to thirty steps leading to a glass porch, more a sun room, and entrance doors at first floor level. I cannot remember any guests flagging on the ascent. The elderly *must* have been tougher in those days. We rarely penetrated to the ground floor which besides housing the kitchens and storerooms also contained the hydropathic parts of the establishment, massage and treatment rooms, medical but not swimming baths. On a rare foray below, a group of us were disconcerted by semi-naked Terry-towelled figures drifting about with expressions of disapproval. Our family was nearly always given the same rooms—two adjacent bedrooms, one for parents and youngest child and the other for two or three of us and nurse or mother's help. Cut off up a short staircase with bathroom beside them and only one other room on the landing, it was practically a private suite. On cold days a coal-fire was lit in my parents' room.

The Hydro catered successfully for most tastes. There was dancing in the Recreation Room every evening except Sundays with music from a resident band. During the day the same room rang with the echo of racquets and shuttles on the marked out badminton court where frequent tournaments were staged. Outside the diningroom was a large bagatelle table on which we perpetually struggled to best each others' records as we hungrily awaited the sounding of the gong. There was also a carefully guarded billiard table which we fancied to be for the sole use of gentlemen. Peculiarly it was sited through elaborate frosted glass doors bearing the words 'Gentlemens' Cloakroom and Toilets' which repelled the invasion of a mixed gang of children and rather inhibited even small gentlemen.

On a Sunday morning there was a service in the large second floor drawingroom which had wide views to the hills. I enjoyed the combination of beauty outside and blessedly undidactic hymns within— 'O Worship the Lord, All glorious above...' 'Immortal, invisible, God only wise...' and the metrical Psalms and Paraphrases. A holidaying minister among the guests would read the lessons and pray but there was no danger of his over-running his time as he knew that like himself many of his congregation intended to go into

225

Melrose to church. Prayers caused a great stir as those wishing to kneel had to rise and turn right round before burying their noses in the various soft furnishings. Sometimes the younger and less discriminating worshippers found themselves bored by the owner of a fine voice, usually soprano or contralto, rendering a religious solo.

The next hours of Sunday were characterised more and more by feelings of increasing emptiness, for lunch, more than ample when it arrived, being dinner (evening dinner on Sunday paid lip-service to the Fourth Commandment being a self-service cold buffet to not cause the manservants and maidservants to appear to labour) was not heralded by the gong until two o'clock to give the church-goers time to return. We took the edge off our appetites by consuming supplies of fruit and Digestive or Rich Tea biscuits laid in by our parents in their bedroom. We could not even beguile the hungry hours with our usual diversion of badminton or bagatelle for the racquets, cues, shuttles and balls had all been locked away for the better keeping of the Sabbath (and I hope the billiard balls had been too). There was, of course, no dancing or whist in the evening but there was an entertainment in the drawingroom.

This was a concert run by the guests. Old and young attended this. I cannot remember any young persons taking part—or being invited to, we all knew our places in those days—but as audience we were actively involved. The room held a multiplicity of sofas, chairs, chesterfields, settees and chaises longues of which the most sought after, so far as we were concerned, were the Victorian love-seats. In these some happy occupants had their backs turned to the performers so should anything move us to mirth—and so much did—at least we could safely give way to laughter while more exposed friends had to struggle for self control. One regular guest always treated us to 'Devon, Glorious Devon', 'The Floral Dance' and other such riotous songs which we applauded wildly. The acclaim accorded however to the stout lady who year after year unrequitedly pled for the wings of a dove was muted to avoid risk of encore. As our eagle eyes early spotted incipient romances among the young adults the very hint of a love song from any of them was sufficient to have us lying back writhing in agonising mirth. The Hydropathic was popular with family men as it had no licence for alcohol but even without Bacchus all might not run smoothly. Eros could be enough.

One year a long-standing and seemingly suitable understanding (the parents were friends) disintegrated before us, casting a gloom over the dancing couples with the man left visibly disconsolate and the girl vanishing for days only eventually to reappear at mealtimes with swollen eyes. More mysterious was the disgrace, never apprehended by us, which befell a popular young man who spent some days in semi-retirement in the Manager's office. Nobody appeared to be able to tell us why, other than he had been in a girl's room. So what? We brushed the matter aside and continued with the badminton, the dancing, the bagatelle and the hide-and-seek.

We knew all the backstairs and accesses to tower and battlements and indulged in exciting games which involved racing along the long corridors and up and down the connecting stairways. Occasionally, of an evening, one or two of us would slip away from the dancing in the recreation room to turn off the switches foolishly placed in the wall outside the drawingroom so plunging the whist players into darkness. We would lurk in the corridor listening to the sounds of disarray among the tables then dash back to foxtrot innocently round the floor before an incensed player had found a switch. All in all I would have thought we must have been a considerable irritation to staider guests but I can remember no complaints.

My father was mildly interested in following Rugby so our holiday often coincided with the Melrose Sevens at Greenyards. They gave a great fillip to the social life of the Hydropathic, players and Rugby enthusiasts booking in for the week-end. Their excess energy spilled over on to us abetting our hide-and-seek and promoting mass games of Touch Rugger, all comers welcome with no discrimination for age or sex. I remember the pride of dodging a member of a team to score a try and the thrill when the luck of a Paul Jones threw one momentarily into the arms of one of those heroes to circle round and round the dance floor. At a more accessible level were the boys of St Mary's Preparatory School which started its summer term shortly after the Sevens. Many of the pupils were brought by their parents to spend the last few days of their holidays in Melrose. They knew all the ins and outs of the countryside, the Rhymer's Glen, the Faery Dean and the Eildon slopes and could make a morning's walk, dodging through hedges, taking short cuts, avoiding keepers, (or so they said) a very different thing from the still pleasurable, but admittedly tamer, outings under the auspices of a father—even one who had spent boyhood holidays in Melrose and who could still lead us to the tree in the Faery Dean on which he had reprehensibly carved out his initials.

My earliest romances—apart from the spiked paling one with Cecil—budded at Melrose. There was Norman who squired me to the dinner dance and the 'pictures', but first when we were nine was Wilfred who when accused by his elder brother of loving me more than any of his family staunchly avowed that it was so. Then there was the faithful and determined but, to me alas, uncharismatic swain who climbed with me to the top of the topmost Eildon, stone in pocket, there to lay it on the cairn after we had inscribed it with our initials inside a scratched-out heart. My heart was with a less reliable and more flamboyant type down below who had not summoned the energy to climb the hill. He had what it takes to attract young females—and all the other boys hated him.

Melrose has many memories. There was a long-pursued friendship with a girl of my own age from another part of Scotland picked up off and on through succeeding years, always welcomed when it briefly surfaced. There were walks by the Tweed to the weir with its attendant heron and often the first call of the cuckoo. There was the annual walk and visit to Abbotsford and runs in a hired car to Jedburgh, Dryburgh and Kelso. There was blossom on the slopes of Gattonside with above it fields of peeweets and the Pyrus Japonica in the gardens of Darnick. Of course there was the occasional fly in the ointment as when an otherwise pleasant car-owning Edinburgh jewellers' family invited my father for a run down the Tweed extending the invitation to include one of his family. My parents decided it was just the thing for my wretched little brother, solely on

228

the grounds that he was male and therefore the most suitable candidate for rides in motor cars (did being eldest count for nothing?). To make matters worse, it was an open car. He departed well wrapped-up, looking smug. An added barb was that the expedition passed innumerable places renowned in history and ballad which I had for long really wished to see and about which he neither knew nor cared.

Every year we made a pilgrimage to Melrose Abbey to gaze at the resting-place of the heart of the Bruce. On a warm day the approach to the Abbey was scented by wallflower growing above us on the walls. After wandering down to the built-up bank and path above the Tweed, we would leave and go to what I think was called the Abbey Book Shop where my mother and I immediately became immersed in books. The Hydropathic had an excellent treasure trove of a library where I spent a considerable amount of time but we always marked our Easter visit by buying each a book here. Over the years I acquired among others *The Abbot* and *The Monastery* and an anthology which I read and re-read, *A Book of Border Verse,* edited by George Burnett. On this or some other day we made a regular, courtesy shop call, this time for my father's benefit, to an ironmonger for he had known the family in his youth. He nearly always added to his stock of tools. While he was choosing, I prowled about savouring the real ironmonger smell. I am glad I did although I was not to know then that with the advent of the cellophane wrapped store it was to become one of all too many pleasures to live on almost exclusively in memories of the past. Our last annual call was again for my mother's benefit but I enjoyed it too. It may, for all I know, like that to the ironmongers, have been rooted in past friendship for this was to an antique shop, and as antiques were one of my grandfather's loves he perhaps had known it in those summer weeks when he brought his family to Melrose. My mother usually added to her collection of oriental plates. Years later, out of sentiment, on a brief visit I bought there a Crown Staffordshire floral decorated box, perhaps a patch box, with a mirror set inside and on the lid the legend, 'Inside you see what pleases me.'

229

CHAPTER THIRTY-TWO

A Mist of Memories

SAD THOUGH it was to wave our Easter holiday away there was hope to this farewell. Time is forever when we are young. Next year would come, the same friends reassemble, the same heady atmosphere of Border lore wrap us round, Tweed still flow past as it had for centuries before. In the gardens of neighbouring Darnick, round the peel tower, typifying at once the grimness and beauty of this Border land, the rough and spiky branches of Pyrus Japonica would break again into masses of flame and scarlet flower. I long ago read, in my *Border Anthology*, and laid to mind, a poem by Andrew Lang

'Three crests against a saffron sky,
Beyond the purple plain,
The kind remembered melody
Of Tweed once more again.

Wan water from the Border hills,
Dear voice from the old years,
Thy distant music lulls and stills,
And moves to quiet tears.
. . . .

A mist of memory broods and floats.
The Border waters flow;
The air is full of ballad notes,
Borne out of long ago.'

There are people born with no feeling for place. I am thankful I am not amongst them for at any time thoughts and memories of otherwhere can come swimming up, unasked, out of the mist of the

230

past to enrich me. I have memories of many more places than I have written of here. They are but the ones which most influenced me as a child, Edinburgh naturally most of all and for more than family occasions. We were fortunate in living there at a time when there were good concerts and theatre productions—and I in having a mother who enjoyed them and a father less interested—so that I was often her companion. She subscribed every year to the Max Mossel series of celebrity concerts on Saturday afternoons in the Usher Hall and there I heard Casals and Moiseivitch and Chaliaphine among others. I was transported back there quite recently from a dentist's waiting room in London when I dropped into conversation with a woman who, many, many years before, when a child of eight, had been coached by him for a solo part in a children's choir in Shanghai. Over the years she still recalled how sympathetic and kind he had been to a small and shy singer and how even at that early age she had found him inspiring. I remember him best in the rhythm and swell of the song of the Volga boatmen—as potent as the shell in Ardbeg in bringing before me a foreign land. I heard Dame Clara Butt fill the hall with her tremendous volume of voice not knowing that among the accompanying choir of schoolgirls was one who ten years later was to became a lifelong friend. There too, much later, I was to hear Paderewski but first I was to experience perhaps the most poignant artistic sensation of my life when I saw Pavlova, as the Swan, die, just there, in the right-hand forward corner of the Usher Hall stage.

Though as inhabitants of a capital city with a Royal palace we perforce became rather blasé at the sight of visiting royalties and notabilities, when young we quite welcomed the break in the school day when, on information received from kindly friend or parent, we were marched along to a nearby vantage-point, once in a puffing and peching crocodile up to Waterloo Place, to wave as a procession went by. In hindsight the most interesting occasion was on a Saturday afternoon in Ferry Road when unbeknown to us and indeed to them, our future King and Queen went by disguised as the Duke of York and Lady Elizabeth Bowes-Lyon.

231

Every year we were taken to the Theatre Royal, Broughton Street, next to the Cathedral Church of St Mary to see *Peter Pan* with Wendy, Tinkerbell, Tiger Lily, The Lost Boys, Smee, Starkey and Captain Hook and more especially Nana. At the intervals Nana, all one or two men of her, padded all round the wide balustrade of the Dress Circle, with excited infant paws poking and patting at her. Miraculously she never fell off.

Another dramatic performance I cherish from early days, this time in the King's Theatre, was of *Treasure Island* with Arthur Bourchier as Long John Silver. His true-to-print portrayal of the ruffianly sea-cook might have scared even his creator. I cannot now remember who played Pew but I can call back easily the absolute terror of those moments when we heard the tapping of his stick in the dark and froze to its menace as much as did Jim Hawkins and the poor old seaman in the Admiral Benbow.

In those far-off days it always seemed, and until recently has seemed, an uninteresting childhood enough. Nothing ever happened, no rich uncles died in Australia, but oddly, in the re-telling, it has become even to me more interesting. Trivial many of my memories may be. They are yet links with a past, local and universal so different from the lives of my children and even more, my grandchildren. In time to come, science may banish night-time in cities with perpetual daylight relayed from saucers in the sky and a new generation of grandmother will not be heeded when they talk of the minor magic of orange neon lights coming on one by one, both quite outshone by my anticipated and intimate participation in Leerie's not-very-pervasive dissipation of darkness in the street outside our home.

'My tea is nearly ready and the sun has left the sky;
It's time to take the window to see Leerie going by;
For every night at tea-time and before you take your seat,
With lantern and with ladder he comes posting up the street.'

Scientific marvels there are enough for us to wonder at today—kidney, heart and lung transplants, interspace satellites and cruise missiles—but even the transplants lack the intimacy and magic of our day-by-day superstitions. When you finished your fresh breakfast or

232

supper boiled egg you put your spoon through the shell lest a witch commandeer it as a boat in which to cross water, and no wise child walked under a ladder. Thirteen was a number to eschew but rowans at the gate were an insurance against those undesirable beings, witches. It was possibly because the powers of darkness so hovered around us that we found stability and serenity in the words of certain hymns and psalms although we were in no way a church-going family. My father had had a surfeit of church attendance in his youth and my mother had a questing mind. I remember as a teenager being faintly aggrieved that I could not, as did most of my friends, rebel against being forced to go to church because we never were. I never even crossed the threshold of Sunday School. Our parents were members of the nearest Church of Scotland which at this time operated a Free Will offering scheme. Every Sunday one's offering was sealed in an envelope and placed in the collection bag. Our pile of empty envelopes grew and grew on my father's marble-topped washhand stand until one Sunday it became too much for him and then having amassed a wealth of florins and halfcrowns he looked round and said, "Somebody has to take these things to church and get rid of them!"

Another sphere so different from today is that of food, less varied because more truly seasonal but more natural—no packaged quick meals with additives from freezers. During the First War there was much real deprivation although my brother and I were sheltered from that as far as possible, as I fancy were most children, by the sacrifices and ingenuities of their elders. Occasionally my mother or Mary experimented with cocoa and cocoa butter to make us chocolate, not as good as the products of Rowntree, Cadbury or Fry perhaps but nevertheless gratefully received. My mother chronicles many shortages in her Journal including that of matches which were unobtainable in local shops for at least six weeks. There was one main course dish, a standby of rationing which I enjoyed and, despite my tastes having changed, look back on with pleasure today, a mixture of butter beans and potatoes, flavoured with bacon. Like many delights of childhood I have never found since a butter bean to match them.

Tea 'uptown' was a frequent childhood treat. If it sounds uncharacteristically sybaritic it was besides being pleasurable almost a necessity to fuel us. We had probably walked most of, if not all the way mainly uphill from Trinity and after shopping were intending to walk back. Occasionally we found ourselves up the Bridges and then we sampled afternoon tea at Patrick Thomsons. PTs were 'good for' something—I remember buying navy gym-tunics there but mostly we chose from one of the many Princes Street Tea-rooms. If our father joined us, it would be Rentons where he and a group of business friends regularly lunched. Sometimes with him we went, even more conveniently, to the New Picture House cafe next door to Mackay and Chisholm. Crawfords, McVitties and Guest, Jenners, Mackies, and Maules all had their points. Jenners to me seemed overfull with large opulent ladies. It was however good for toasted tea-cakes.

Mackies was probably the one we went to most. It was airy and with a roof garden and one or two balconies offered more chances of a window table with view across to the Castle or even downward on to the traffic and heads of unsuspecting passers-by on the pavement. I liked it because it made my favourite cakes—I called them fish-cakes. Years later I ran them to earth in an Atholl Crescent Cookery Book masquerading under the name of Jap cakes. Round, they were sprinkled with grated nut in a commendable imitation of bread-crumbs. (As in the case of butter beans none I have sampled since have approached the standard of those early ones in Mackies.)

It is time for my mother to provide more authentic detail. In her journal for 1917 she writes under April 30th Monday…

'The ninth anniversary of our marriage. It seems an awful age. I hope we will be together when the next comes round. My only celebration was to take Elaine up to town and tea in Jenners. Jenners is now I think the most liberal of wartime tearooms. You are restricted to two oz of wheaten stuff, bread or scones, but you can have oat-cake and the waitress said all their other cakes were made of rice-flour which isn't in the rationing list so far. Of course I don't think people ought to take more than is absolutely necessary even of these things.

Aunt B, Elaine and I went to Mackies the first day of the restricted rationing. We were only allowed one cup of tea and either two scones, a cake and a scone or either of these with a slice of bread. One sugar bowl did duty for several tables and was removed by the waitress when the tea was sweetened. The worst of it was that both Aunt B and myself were frightfully thirsty and we couldn't even have another cup of tea. I was in Mackies again on Friday and there was a slight change for the better. You were allowed to have oat-cake in addition to the other things and they had gone back to having tea-pots and the sugar bowl had ceased to migrate. The waitress said that it had been a misunderstanding at first and that for two days or so there had scarcely been a soul in the place. I suppose the girls were beginning to tremble for their situations. If wheat is so scarce as they say it is, I think the sooner we adopt compulsory rationing' [this is in 1917, three years into the war!] 'the better.'

This spring, thoughts of food, or lack of it, filled much of people's minds. In January my mother reported

'Elaine is looking forward to her birthday. I told her it would have to be a cake without icing this time since it is illegal now to have iced cakes, sugar is so scarce.'

Then later

'Elaine is full of excitement over her birthday—on Friday. She is to get an iced cake after all. Seemingly the bakers can make iced cakes of the sugar they have in stock until the 1st of March after which date they must not make icing at all... It seems her birthday came just in the nick of time. Even the little apple charlottes we sometimes have instead of pudding for dinner are made without the sprinkling of sugar they used to have.'

'Fond Memory brings the light of other days around me.' Does it matter that Fond Memory can suffer from the all too-human disability of mis-remembering? I could have sworn that on Armistice Day, Monday, the eleventh of November 1918, my mother and I celebrated in our usual manner, up the beaten track to Mackies, to consume our two ounces of wheaten stuff, augmented with oat-cake and fish-cake, but no,—her Journal belies me. I do remember correctly the occasion of realising the War was over, the sirens and hooters which we heard walking along Inverleith Terrace where I was able to be on a normal school morning, school being closed for a week or two on account of an epidemic, probably influenza. (We had been sent home with special notebooks with a schedule of work to do at home.)

'Nov 11th...
Armistice signed with Germany today. The children and I were out this forenoon in the Park and coming home along Inverleith Terrace we heard the whistles and horns from the Public Works blowing and also the sirens from the boats in the Forth. I concluded from this that the Germans had agreed to the Armistice.

I felt very weepy.

We turned down Inverleith Row. One or two of the houses had put flags out already. Everywhere people were appearing at their doors and listening to the horns.

It was a gloriously bright Autumn day as if Nature itself was rejoicing. We met Mrs Scott on the way home in great trouble over the death from "Flu" of a great friend of hers.'

Oddly I remember this neighbour's distress at a time of rejoicing but not the reason for it.

'This epidemic is casting a gloom over everything. Nearly everybody has had it and there have been many deaths.

In the afternoon the children and I had been invited to tea at Mrs Malcolms in Stirling Road. Peggy M is at school with Elaine. Before going I took some photos of Baby and Elaine and Ian in the garden. Several houses on the way along had been decorated with flags since dinnertime. I bought four at Miss Charles little shop, one for each of the three and one for Peggy M. We had a splendid most unwarlike tea— mostly of Mrs Turnbull's making [Mrs M's Mother], shortbread, gingerbread etc almost a pre-war tea. And the children had crackers, which they always love... Tonight the ships on the Forth started off on another bout of whistling, horn-blowing etc. Mary and I from the drawingroom window watched the flashing of searchlights and several rockets. They are still going at it but not quite so strongly. I should like to see Princes Street tonight but I expect it will be impassable. Among all this siren-blowing and flag waving there must be many many sad hearts tonight. Many will come home but how many will not return. I told Elaine and Ian at bed-time that some day they would be telling their children about the last day of the Great War. Ian said he was going to have a hundred boys and girls so it will take some telling. Baby cut her third tooth yesterday...

236

And so the Kaiser's war ended with the sound of sirens, waving of flags and a splendid tea with crackers. Here too this account of part of a family background and one child's recollections of her life in Edinburgh during some of the early decades of the twentieth century also—for the time being—comes to an end. The one, despite the slaughter, grief and ongoing problems it occasioned, has found its place in history. I make no claim for the other than to hope it may merit kindly and forebearing eyes. From one of those eminently browsable books of the Old Testament so sustaining when a preacher is making heavy weather of a sermon I leave this thought from Zechariah—

'For who shall despise the day of small things?'

Family members who are married women are entered under their maiden names—

EMC is Elaine Mary Wilson, née Chisholm, the author.

Graham, David (son of David and Kate) 155
Graham, J. 123
Graham, John (Johnnie) 125–6, 129
Graham, Kate see Oswald, Kate
Green, Kate 203
guising 115

H
Haggart, Ella 36–7, 112
Haggart, Mary 2, 72, 112, 125, 180, 236
 at 'Strathearn' 34, 37–8, 49, 60, 233
  illness 50
  washday 41–4
 family 35–6
 in Hawick 172–3, 175
 in Kinlochleven 184
 mother's last illness 170, 177
 physical description 36
 during Zeppelin raid 165–8
hairstyle 9
Hallowe'en parties 173, 218
Harold (school friend) 186
'Hazelcliffe' see Bute, Isle
Henderson, Mrs, school 188
Henderson, Thomas Syme 188
Hester (party friend) 218
hill-climbing 171
Hislop, Agnes see Wilson, Agnes
Hislop, Marion Maclean (Cousin Minnie) 14, 120–1, 169
HMS Hampshire 176
Hogmanay Dinner Dance, Caledonian Hotel, Edinburgh 219, 224
holidays
 journey 143–4
 rail journey 20–2
 silver chest 142
 the valise 142–3
 see also Bute, Isle; Crail, Fife; North Berwick
Howie, Janet (m. J.T. Stewart) (Aunt Janet) 119, 133–6
Hoy, Mr (nurseryman) 91, 92, 93

hymns 189–90

I
illnesses 209
 chickenpox 46–8, 188
 colds and chills 49
 croup 48–9
 earache 48
 Spanish Influenza 50–2
 whooping cough 48–9
Institution (The Edinburgh Institution) 88, 122
Inverleith Gardens see Edinburgh, 'Strathearn'

J
Jan of Windmill Land play, (EMC as 'Minna') 195–6
Janet (factotum at St Oran's) 190, 208
John, Augustus (artist) 10

K
Kathleen (school friend) 186
Kennedies, (Inverleith Gardens neighbours) 16, 17, 169–70
'Kilunken', EMC's invisible friend 31, 85
Kindergarten 184, 185–8
Kinlochleven 180–4
Kirkcaldy 24, 65
Kitchener, Lord 176

L
Largs 157–8
late nights 218–19
Lauder, James Eckford 79–80, 94
Lauder, Robert Scott 64, 79, 94
Leith 67, 167
Linlithgow 162
Lizzie, cook 75
Loch Striven 156–7
Lochness (boat) 181
'Logie Aston' see Bridge of Allan
Lundin Links 12

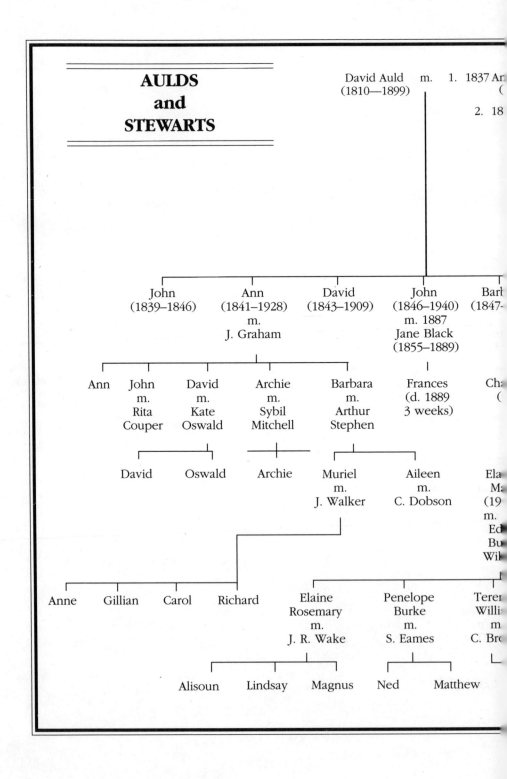

AULDS
and
STEWARTS

David Auld   m.   1. 1837 An
(1810—1899)   (

                               2. 18

John	Ann	David	John	Barl
(1839–1846)	(1841–1928)	(1843–1909)	(1846–1940)	(1847-
	m.		m. 1887	
	J. Graham		Jane Black	
			(1855–1889)	

Ann	John	David	Archie	Barbara	Frances	Ch:
	m.	m.	m.	m.	(d. 1889	(
	Rita	Kate	Sybil	Arthur	3 weeks)	
	Couper	Oswald	Mitchell	Stephen		

David	Oswald	Archie	Muriel	Aileen	Ela
			m.	m.	M:
			J. Walker	C. Dobson	(19
					m.
					Ed
					Bu
					Wil

Anne	Gillian	Carol	Richard	Elaine	Penelope	Terer
				Rosemary	Burke	Willi:
				m.	m.	m
				J. R. Wake	S. Eames	C. Br(

Alisoun	Lindsay	Magnus	Ned	Matthew